Managerial Issues in International Business

THE ACADEMY OF INTERNATIONAL BUSINESS

Published in association with the UK Chapter of the Academy of International Business

Titles already published in the series:

Managerial Issues in International Business

Edited by

Felicia M. Fai

and

Eleanor J. Morgan
School of Management, University of Bath, UK

First published 2006 by
PALGRAVE MACMILLAN
Houndmills, Basingstoke, Hampshire RG21 6XS and
175 Fifth Avenue, New York, N.Y. 10010
Companies and representatives throughout the world

PALGRAVE MACMILLAN is the global academic imprint of the Palgrave
Macmillan division of St. Martin's Press, LLC and of Palgrave Macmillan Ltd.
Macmillan® is a registered trademark in the United States, United Kingdom
and other countries. Palgrave is a registered trademark in the European
Union and other countries.

ISBN-13: 978–0–230–00193–0 hardback
ISBN-10: 0–230–00193–9 hardback

This book is printed on paper suitable for recycling and made from fully
managed and sustained forest sources.

A catalogue record for this book is available from the British Library.

Library of Congress Cataloging-in-Publication Data
Academy of International Business. UK Chapter. Conference (32nd : 2005 : University
    of Bath, School of Management)
    Managerial issues in international business / edited by Felicia M. Fai &
    Eleanor J. Morgan.
        p.   cm. — (Academy of International Business)
    Selection of papers from the 32nd Annual Conference of the UK Chapter of the
    Academy of International Business, held April 8–9, 2005 at University of Bath,
    School of Management.
    Includes bibliographical references and index.
    ISBN 0–230–00193–9
    1. International business enterprises—Management—Congresses.   I. Fai,
    Felicia M., 1971–   II. Morgan, Eleanor J.   III. Title.   IV. Academy of
    International Business (Series) (Palgrave Macmillan (Firm))
    HD62.4.A223 2005
    658′.049—dc22   2005057504

10   9   8   7   6   5   4   3   2   1
15   14   13   12   11   10   09   08   07   06

Printed and bound in Great Britain by
Antony Rowe Ltd, Chippenham and Eastbourne

Contents

List of Tables

List of Figures

Foreword

This is the thirteenth volume to be published by Palgrave Macmillan in the series of selected papers from the annual conference of the Academy of International Business (AIB), United Kingdom Chapter. The 32nd Annual Conference, on which this volume is based, was held at the School of Management, University of Bath on Friday 8 and Saturday 9 April 2005, organized by the joint conference chairs, Eleanor Morgan and Felicia Fai. The conference achieved a new record in terms of the number of submissions and in terms of the overall quality of papers presented: 79 papers were accepted for the conference sessions and 24 students presented their research to panels of experts at the doctoral colloquium.

The study of international business in the UK has, rather fittingly, become increasingly international in recent years. This was clearly evident at the Bath conference, where there were over 170 participants, of which 58 delegates (staff and research students) came from academic institutions in 21 countries outside the UK; indeed the challenges faced by those involved in international business, whether as academics or as practitioners, are universal. John Dunning, in a powerful contribution at the conference, highlighted ways in which international business links to the major economic and welfare challenges faced in the world. In drawing this volume together, the editors have focused on managerial issues; each of the chapters connects to these challenges in some way, while addressing issues that affect management in the process of wealth creation.

Research in the field of international business is conducted on a number of levels, from the micro to the macro. As international business comes to occupy a progressively greater role in the creation of wealth, so its impacts and potential impacts on social and welfare issues necessarily become greater. Thus, cultural difference matters within multinational firms as well as between countries, for business as well as economic performance and development. The internationalization of industries that customarily have been domestically focused, notably the service industries, is important for growth. The quality of entrepreneurship and management is critical for the performance of these firms and the countries that they unite through their activities. Issues such as these, and many more, are investigated in this stimulating volume arising from an outstanding conference. A further selection of the best papers from the conference will be published in a special issue of *Management International*

Review, edited by Eleanor Morgan and Felicia Fai. All of this serves to underline the vibrant state of research in international business in the United Kingdom and its international calibre.

Jeremy Clegg
Chair, Academy of International Business
United Kingdom Chapter

Notes on the Contributors

Vidar Askeland recently graduated from the BI Norwegian School of Management, Oslo, with an MSc in International Business. He previously graduated from BI with a Master in Business and Economics, and EDHEC, France with a Master's in European Business. His research and theses have primarily been aimed at theories of internationalization, and particularly on entry modes. He is currently working in the telecommunications sector.

Dev K. Boojihawon is a Lecturer in Strategic Management at the Marketing and Strategy Research Unit, Business School, Open University, UK. He obtained his PhD from the University of Strathclyde, Glasgow, in international strategy in professional service firms. His current research interests lie in the area of international strategy process in multinational subsidiaries, international entrepreneurship, and international strategy of firms in developing countries. Dev has made various contributions to academic conferences in international business and strategic management and has ongoing interests in developing further research in these areas.

Peter Buckley is Professor of International Business and Director of the Centre for International Business, University of Leeds (CIBUL), UK, visiting Professor at the universities of Groningen (The Netherlands) and Reading (UK) and Honorary Professor at the University of International Business and Economics, Beijing, China. He has published 22 books and over 120 articles in highly respected international journals. The Social Science Citation Index lists over 1100 citations to his work. He is a Fellow of the British Academy of Management and a Fellow of the Royal Society of Arts (RSA). He was elected a Fellow of the Academy of International Business in 1985 for 'outstanding achievements in international business' and was its Vice-President in 1991–92 and President from 2002 to 2004.

Chris Carr MA (Cantab), D.Phil (Warwick), DMS, ACMA, CEng, MIMechE is Professor in Corporate Strategy at University of Edinburgh, UK. Previously a senior lecturer at Manchester Business School, following lectureships at Buckingham, Warwick and Bath universities, he has spent 25 years researching strategic approaches to globalization, comparing some 20 countries worldwide through extensive field research particularly in the vehicle components industry. Prior to this he worked in industry for over ten years with British Aerospace and then GKN. He has published two books, *Britain's Competitiveness*

(Routledge, 1990) and *Strategic Investment Decisions* (Avebury, 1994) and extensively in academic journals, including the *Journal of Management Studies* and the *Strategic Management Journal*.

Simon Collinson is Senior Lecturer in International Business at Warwick Business School, University of Warwick (UK) and a Ghoshal Fellow in the UK ESRC's Advanced Institute of Management Research (AIM). He was previously Assistant Director at the JETS Institute, Edinburgh University, and has held visiting positions at NISTEP in Tokyo under a Royal Society Fellowship, at the AGSM in Sydney and at the Kelley School of Business, Indiana University. He has published in the areas of comparative organization studies; the constraints on corporate internationalization; the global organization of R&D, innovation, knowledge and technology management; international entrepreneurship and business infrastructures and management practices in Japan and China.

Gary Cook is Senior Lecturer in Applied Economics at the University of Liverpool Management School, UK and Visiting Fellow in Economics at Manchester Business School, UK. He obtained his PhD from Manchester Business School in the area of vertical integration strategies and contractual relationships. His current research interests lie in the areas of industrial clustering, with particular emphasis on the broadcasting and financial services industries, and corporate insolvency, particularly the rescue of financially distressed small and medium-sized enterprises. Gary has published widely and made numerous conference contributions in both areas.

Alison Dean is Lecturer in Strategic Management at Kent Business School, University of Kent, UK. She obtained her PhD from the University of Massachusetts, Amherst, in industrial organization and economic history, considering post-war change in the UK brewing industry. Her current research interests lie in the impact of change on firms' behaviour and strategy, in the contexts of professional service firms and the management of innovation. She has contributed to academic conferences in strategy and organization studies on such topics as managing change in the wake of privatization, using an options approach to encourage innovation, and the globalization of legal service firms. Her articles have appeared in such journals as the *Review of Industrial Organization, British Journal of Management* and *Creativity and Innovation Management*.

Dimitra Dimitropoulou is a PhD student at the University of Reading Business School completing her thesis on FDI and European Union countries.

Jing Lin Duanmu is a PhD student at the School of Management, University of Bath, UK. Her thesis is a qualitative analysis of inward invested multinational subsidiaries in China and the development of their relationship with indigenous Chinese suppliers in the electrical/electronic industry in Wuxi. She has won two awards for her work including the 32nd AIB UK Chapter doctoral prize. She also has research interests relating to the controversies and debates between different schools of heterodox economic approaches.

John Dunning is Emeritus Professor of International Business at the University of Reading, UK, and State of New Jersey Emeritus Professor of International Business at Rutgers University, USA. He is also Senior Economic Adviser to the Director of the Division on Investment, Technology and Enterprise Development of UNCTAD and serves on several journal editorial and advisory boards. He has authored, co-authored or edited 42 books on the economics of international direct investment and the multinational enterprise, and also on industrial and regional economics. His latest publications are *Theories and Paradigms of International Business Activity* and *Global Capitalism, FDI and Competitiveness*, a two-volume compendium of his most influential contributions over the past 30 years (Edward Elgar, 2002), and an edited monograph on *Making Globalization Good* (Oxford University Press, 2003).

Felicia M. Fai is Lecturer in International Business at the School of Management, University of Bath, UK, and was a Visiting Research Fellow at Rutgers Business School, New Jersey, USA. She obtained her PhD from Reading University which was published in 2003 as *Corporate Technological Competence and the Evolution of Technological Diversification* by Edward Elgar. Her current research interests lie in the role of intellectual property rights as economic indicators and strategic tools, knowledge transfers and foreign direct investment behaviour. She has made various contributions to conferences and academic journals in technology, innovation and international business on the subjects of corporate technological diversification, the role of language in the transfer of knowledge in cross-border alliances, and evidence of rising technological competencies in China.

Manuel Portugal Ferreira is Assistant Professor at the Escola Superior de Tecnologia e Gestão, Instituto Politécnico de Leiria, Portugal. Manuel obtained his PhD at the University of Utah in strategy and international management. His research interests involve examining entrepreneurial and strategic issues in industry clusters, as well as the inter-firm competitive dynamics and knowledge flows among clustered firms. Manuel's research has been focusing also on capabilities-based strategies of MNCs, cross-border acquisitions, and network effects in transition economies. In addition to several presentations at the Academy of International Business and Academy of Management among others, Manuel has published in Portuguese and international journals.

Pervez Ghauri is Professor of International Business at Manchester School of Business, the University of Manchester in the UK. He earned his PhD from Uppsala University in Sweden, where he also taught for several years. He has held positions at the Norwegian School of Management, Norway, the University of Groningen, Netherlands and Michigan State University, USA. He has published more than 15 books and numerous articles on international business and international marketing topics. He is Editor-in-Chief of *International Business Review*, the official journal of European International Business Academy (EIBA) and editor of the International Business and Management Series published by Elsevier Science.

Simon Harris is Reader at Strathclyde International Business Unit (SIBU), University of Strathclyde, UK, and is an elected committee member of the UK Chapter of the Academy of International Business. From an international marketing and finance business background, he has researched similarities and differences in strategic management behaviour in different contexts. His PhD thesis was a cross-national study examining the strategy formation–national values relationship, from the University of Leeds and won the 2003 Gunnar Hedlund prize for research in international business. His focus now is the formation of cross-border business relationships within firms, teams, alliances and projects for strategic ends.

William Hesterly is the Zeke Dumke Professor of Management at the David Eccles School of Business, University of Utah. His research on organizational economics, vertical integration, organizational forms and entrepreneurial networks has appeared in top journals including the *Academy of Management Review, Organization Science, Strategic Management Journal, Journal of Management, Journal of Economic Behavior* and *Organization and Business History*. He is the author (with Jay Barney) of *Strategic Management and Competitive Advantage*. Currently, he is studying the sources of value creation in firms and also what determines who captures the value from a firm's competitive advantage. Professor Hesterly serves on the editorial board of *Strategic Organization* and has previously served on the boards of *Organization Science* and the *Journal of Management*. He was also a consultant to various Fortune 500 firms in the electronic, office equipment, paper, telecommunications, energy, aerospace and medical equipment industries, and to smaller firms in several other industries.

Susan McGrath-Champ (PhD) is Senior Lecturer in human resource management and industrial relations at the School of Business, University of Sydney, Australia. Her research areas include the spatial aspects of industrial relations, expatriate training and performance management, and employment relations in the coal and construction industries. She has previously worked in industry and consulting in Australia and Canada. Susan has published widely in employment relations and social science journals. She is guest editor of a special edition of *Economic and Industrial Democracy* (August 2005) and *Labour and Industry* (December 2002, with B. Ellem).

Eleanor J. Morgan is Senior Lecturer in Business Economics, School of Management, University of Bath, UK, where she leads the Business Economics and Strategy Group. Her current research has two main strands – developments in competition policy, particularly the impact of EU merger policy on firms' restructuring decisions, and the innovation capacity of smaller European firms especially in peripheral regions. Her work has been published extensively in leading journals and she has published several books; *New Developments in UK and EU Competition Policy*, co-edited with Roger Clarke, is due to be published in 2006 as is *The New European Rurality: Strategies for Small Firms*. She was Founder Editor of the *International Journal of the Economics of Business* in 1994 which she continues to edit. She has twice served as an elected member of the executive committee of the Academy of International Business (UK Chapter).

Ursula F. Ott is Lecturer in International Business at the Business School, Loughborough University. She obtained her PhD in Economics and Social Sciences at the University of Vienna. She was an Assistant Professor at the University of Vienna, Department of Business Studies and a Research Scholar at the London School of Economics. Her research focus has been the application of game theory to problems in international business such as international joint ventures and international negotiations. Ursula has published in refereed journals and has received grants for her work from the Austrian Science Fund and the British Academy. She has made contributions to academic conferences in international business (AIB and EIBA) and game theory (Game Theory World Congress) and was invited speaker at research seminars at the London School of Economics and University of Cambridge.

Naresh Pandit is Senior Lecturer in Economics at Manchester Business School, UK, where he also obtained his PhD. He has published articles, book chapters and reports on business clustering in the broadcasting and financial services industries (funded by two ESRC grants and one British Academy grant) and on corporate insolvency and turnaround among small and large firms (ICAEW funded). He holds visiting appointments at Loughborough University Banking Centre, GaWC (Globalization and World Cities Study Group and Network), Loughborough University and at the Institute of Business, University of the West Indies. He teaches economics, international business and strategy at both MBA and executive levels and was the recipient of the 2002–3 AT Kearney prize for teaching excellence.

Robert Pearce is Reader in International Business at Reading University Business School. His recent research has focused on the strategic development of MNEs through differentiated subsidiary roles and decentralization of R&D and innovation. His most recent books are *Multinationals, Technology and National Competitiveness* (with Marina Papanastassiou) and *Multinationals and Transition* (with Julia Manea). *Multinationals in the new Global Economy* will be published in 2006.

Susan Segal-Horn is Professor of International Strategy at the Open University Business School, where she is also Director of the Marketing and Strategy Research Unit. Her research focus is globalization, international service industries and service multinationals. Current research projects include the branding of services, and the globalization of professional service firms. Susan has published four books and more than 60 academic articles. Her articles have appeared in such journals as the *Journal of Marketing Management*, the *Service Industries Journal*, the *European Journal of Marketing*, the *Journal of Global Marketing*, the *European Management Journal*, the *European Business Journal* and *Strategy and Leadership*. She is a frequent speaker on globalization and internationalization of industries and firms. Susan is a member of the publications committee of the Strategic Planning Society and Programme Chair of the Global Strategy Interest Group for the Strategic Management Society (USA).

Carl Arthur Solberg is Associate Professor in International Marketing and Management at the BI Norwegian School of Management, Oslo. He obtained his PhD from Strathclyde University, Scotland, on strategy development of small and medium-sized firms in globalizing markets. His current research interests lie in global strategy development, exporter–intermediary relations, and offshoring of productive capacity. He has made a number of contributions at various conferences in international marketing and business, and published among others in *Journal of International Marketing, International Business Review, International Journal of Information Management* and is editor of a Special Issue of *Advances in International Marketing* (Elsevier). He is currently associate dean of MSc in International Marketing and Management at BI. Carl Solberg has held visiting professorships in France, Finland and the USA.

Ana Teresa Tavares is Assistant Professor of International Economics at the University of Porto (CEMPRE, Faculty of Economics). She is also a Visiting Research Fellow at the University of Reading and at the University of Strathclyde. Her areas of specialization include multinational enterprise subsidiaries' strategies and evolution, the impact of multinationals on their host economy, and policies vis-à-vis multinationals. She has published several articles on these topics in journals such as *International Business Review, Transnational Corporations,*

Journal of Industry, Competition and Trade, among others. She is also author of several book chapters and is preparing two books on multinational subsidiaries' strategic evolution, and on multinationals, clusters and innovation. She is Associate Editor of the *International Journal of Management Reviews.* She has been a consultant to various institutions on public policy towards FDI and regional development.

Xiaohua Yang is Senior Lecturer in International Business in the Faculty of Business, Queensland University of Technology, Australia. Xiaohua obtained her PhD from the University of Kansas in the United States. She has previously taught in the United States and China and lectured in many countries. Her main research areas include internationalization of firms, expatriate performance management and training, international R&D strategic alliances, corporate social responsibility and multinational strategies, global business strategies, WTO and FDI. She has published many articles in international refereed journals and book chapters, and presented papers at numerous international conferences.

George S. Yip is Professor of Strategic and International Management, London Business School, and Lead Senior Fellow of the UK's Advanced Institute of Management Research. He previously held faculty positions at Harvard, UCLA and Cambridge, and visiting positions at CEIBS (Shanghai), Georgetown, Oxford and Stanford. He has been an Associate Editor of the *Journal of International Business Studies.* His research on strategy and international business is widely cited. His most influential book, *Total Global Strategy,* has been published in ten languages. He was elected in 1999 as a Fellow of the Academy of International Business.

1
Managerial Issues in International Business: Introduction

Felicia M. Fai and Eleanor J. Morgan

This 13th volume of the Academy of International Business (AIB) series, based on selected papers presented at the AIB UK 32nd annual conference, is organized around the theme of the managerial challenges that may face businesses as they internationalize. Within this theme, the nature of the contributions included in the book is diverse in many ways, not only in terms of the managerial issues discussed but also in terms of the theoretical perspectives, methodological approaches, levels of analysis and the industrial settings adopted in the research. This diversity reflects the variety and complexity of the challenges facing managers in today's global economy and well as the breadth and richness of the academic field of international business (IB).

One of the major issues addressed in IB has been how to explain the internationalization behaviour of the firm. Although there are a number of well-established theoretical frameworks, including stages models of incremental internationalization, transactions costs and network theories (among others), there is still a significant debate about their applicability and relevance. The established theories are recontextualized in the opening contribution by Carl Solberg and Vidar Askeland in which they demonstrate how the explanatory power of the different theoretical approaches may depend on particular conditions within the firm and its broader environment. They propose that the applicability of each theory depends on the firm's location in a framework with two dimensions: the level of the firm's preparedness for internationalization and the degree of globality in the firm's industry. In a multi-local industry setting, incremental internationalization theories are more relevant for firms with limited preparedness, whereas foreign direct investment theories based on transaction cost economics seem more appropriate for firms which are well prepared for internationalization. Network theory is seen as best suited to understand the behaviour of firms which are trying to compete in global industries but need to access resources externally to increase their ability to face growing internal and external complexity. The possible explanations of behaviour of firms with extensive resources and experience and entrenched positions in global industries are reviewed and encapsulated in the term 'global management theory'. The authors' propositions about the relevance of different theories within the contingency framework are substantiated by empirical findings based on two highly internationalized firms, Norske Skog and ASK Proxima-Infocus. The case evidence suggests that these firms followed different trajectories through the framework and shows how the different streams of theory applied in different phases of their development. Although further empirical work is needed, the framework advanced in this chapter provides some indicators for managers evaluating strategic options at different phases in the firm's internationalization process.

In Chapter 3, Ursula Ott focuses on international joint ventures (IJVs) as a mode of internationalization. She highlights the problem of information asymmetries in this complex organizational form of market entry. Information asymmetries bring opportunities for hidden action by the participants after contracts have been signed and the extent to which managers are able to control 'cheating' may be an important determinant of the success or failure of an IJV. This chapter examines the possible types of cheating in this organiza-tional setting and considers the design of appropriate incentive schemes to discourage such behaviour based on an analysis drawing on both economics and on cultural perspectives. First, the chapter examines culturally implied moral hazard problems in IJVs based on a typology showing the likelihood of different types of cheating according to the nature of the workplace and country. This is categorized into four groups and embedded in Geert Hofstede's cultural dimensions of power distance, individualism and masculinity to show how cheating behaviour may be related to the extent of hierarchical structure and rules in an organization and differs by country. Second, a modelling approach is adopted to analyse the moral hazard problem in IJVs more formally and to identify the types of incentives that may be appropriate to limit cheating – whether through shirking, embezzlement or sabotage – in different contexts. The findings highlight the importance of managers taking the likelihood of cheating into account in designing incentive schemes within IJVs and the need to tailor these according to the cultural and institutional context which affects the type of cheating most likely to be encountered.

Like the preceding chapter, Simon Harris and Chris Carr are also interested in the contribution that a consideration of national cultural traits can shed on managerial issues in IB. Their chapter, 'Managerial Perspectives on Business Purpose: Values, National Values and Institutions', provides a critical evaluation of the impact of culture and context on managerial attitudes. They develop propositions concerning the fundamental purposes that managers in different countries might be expected to have for their firms and their perceptions of their stakeholders, their aims and their strategic time frames based on the 'national values' research of Geert Hofstede, Andre Laurent, Charles Hampden-Turner and Fons Trompenaars. These are explored through case studies of global firms in different countries in two contrasting institutional settings – large multinational firms (MNCs) and medium-sized, owner-managed international firms. The strategic aims of managers in different countries are as predicted by national values research in both institutional settings. In the large MNCs, they also find close congruence in the managers' perceptions of their stakeholders and the time frames adopted in decision-making, but the national values research (which was developed based on large public companies) gave misleading expectations as regards the owner managers of medium-sized firms. This work suggests that managers face significant dangers if they make assumptions about overseas firms based only on their nationality when trying to forge cross-border business relationships and it highlights the importance of taking ownership patterns into account.

In Chapter 5, Manuel Ferreira, William Hesterly and Ana Tavares provide a conceptual analysis of the parenting of spin-offs and their role in the creation of regional industrial clusters. At the heart of their work is the idea that a parent firm can create and develop its own cluster in which it becomes the hub through a process of 'mothering' entrepreneurial employees. Such employees exit parent firms to create their own business in the same geographic location but continue to be dependent on the parent to some extent because of the benefits they gain from maintaining social and business ties and leveraging the parent's existing network of relationships. Equally, the parent firm is likely to benefit through its progeny from enlarged technological, business and geographic reach, and enhanced reputation and visibility. The emergence and evolution of the cluster are thus bound by the family tree of parent and offspring firms. Embeddedness in the cluster is essential to a firm's ability to generate successful offspring so, while parent firms need not necessarily be multinationals, this is more likely if the MNE is already well established locally during the cluster's emergence, or if their presence in a specific region is the driving force behind the emergence of the local cluster. In the light of the potential benefits to the parent firm, the authors conclude that the promotion of clusters through a 'motherhood' model may, in time, become a deliberate managerial strategy.

While Ferreira et al. consider new motivations and methods for the formation of clusters, Naresh Pandit, Gary Cook and Pervez Ghauri present an industry case study which examines why firms might be attracted to established clusters – in this case the City of London financial services cluster, an agglomeration noted for its extraordinarily large MNE component. They examine the small but growing literature that suggests motives for MNEs locating in clusters and their evidence reveals multiple motives among firms for locating in the City of London cluster. These relate to the complex nature of the production of certain financial services and encompass both conventional motives, such as access to labour, and less conventional motives such as reputation and prestige conveyed by the possession of a particular address. Indeed, firms tend not to locate all aspects of their complex activities in the cluster at the same time, but continually assess and reassess which activities to locate there. Their decision-making in this respect is influenced by the forces of deregulation in this sector, globalization and advances in information and communication technologies which enable them to coordinate activities across dispersed locations. The authors' analysis suggests that insights from economic geography can aid managers in such decisions.

The terms 'clusters' and 'networks' tend to be used interchangeably in many literatures, but while the previous two chapters demonstrate that networks can be formed within clusters, Chapter 7 by Dev Boojihawon shows that networks can also be formed outside clusters and can be a particularly effective way for small and medium-sized service firms to internationalize. Boojihawon examines entrepreneurship strategy and network dynamics in the international development of small and medium-sized enterprises in the UK advertising sector. Drawing on extant work on internationalization, international entrepreneurship and the internationalization of services, he proposes an integrative framework to investigate the international entrepreneurial behaviour and strategy process of three small advertising agencies (SMAs). It emerges that these SMAs were not forced to internationalize due to their inability to expand further in their domestic market but, rather, their internationalization was deliberate and entrepreneurial and they accelerated the internationalization of their activities by actively leveraging their network relationships. Such networks acted as bridges to new international clients. His findings show that while the process of internationalization for each SMA was different, they shared common characteristics – network relationships were dynamic, evolved continuously, and were shaped by organizational as well as industry characteristics. The findings emphasize the need for careful change management in the internationalization of entrepreneurial SMAs.

In Chapter 8, Susan Segal-Horn and Alison Dean continue the focus on service firms of the previous two chapters by examining the managerial issues arising from competitive change and innovation in the legal services industry – changes which have resulted in the creation of large cross-border legal service organizations. A combination of competitive and client expectations means that building an international network has become a strategic priority for larger law firms with corporate client-based activities. From their study of very large UK 'City' law firms, Segal-Horn and Dean identify the management issues these professional service firms face in responding to the demands placed upon their existing organizational structures and internal processes by international expansion. These involve structural, cultural and organizational barriers to cross-border integration. They identify seven managerial challenges: a shift to a managed firm and a decline in professional autonomy; choice of appropriate acquisition targets and managing integration with acquired firms; HQ–subsidiary management issues; the identification of firm-wide value systems to underpin shared corporate culture; the creation of common technology platforms and systems practices; the adaptation of human resource management practices, and building professional trust and satisfactory cross-border intra-firm working relationships. Finally, Segal-Horn and Dean suggest that international law firms appear to be constructing old-fashioned centralized global hub operations rather than more flexible transnational structures that are the aim of the major global manufacturing companies. Their research adds to knowledge of the legal services industry, which is under-researched and further extends the global strategy literature into the services domain by exploring globalization in this context.

Chapter 9 by Susan McGrath-Champ and Xiaohua Yang also considers micromanagement issues, in particular those surrounding the performance management–training interface in Australian firms in China. This chapter resonates with the earlier chapter by Harris and Carr on cultures and values. Specifically, McGrath-Champ and Yang seek to understand how cross-cultural training and career development for expatriates are integrated into performance management in international Australian ventures. They suggest that while managers broadly appreciate that employee training and career development correlate with job satisfaction and performance, little attention is paid to whether, how and the extent to which training and career development in overseas assignments are integrated into performance management systems in foreign ventures. Through an exploratory qualitative study of four very different Australian firms operating in China, their chapter identifies deficiencies in the current literature and in contemporary business practices which overlook the importance of training and career development in the design of performance management systems. They found large variations in the presence and extent of performance management systems in these firms, ranging from formal, standardized performance management in more established and internationally experienced companies, to a complete lack of performance management systems in small, less globally experienced companies. However, none of the interviewees identified close linkages between performance management, assessment and training, even those in firms with relatively sophisticated performance management systems. A further surprising finding was that performance management did not appear to be strategically linked with compensation or remuneration. The evidence from this work highlights the need for improvements in global human resource management among international firms and the need to adopt a more integrative framework of performance management as well as the need for IB scholars to address the paucity of literature in this area.

Doing business with and in China is one of the main contemporary foci for international business managers and scholars. Although there has been much previous work on the spillover effects of FDI on the host country, our understanding of how these occur at micro level and the managerial implications is limited. Within this broad area, knowledge transfer is of particular interest to inward-investing MNEs and Chinese firms alike. On the one hand, MNEs are concerned about the potential loss of proprietary knowledge in a crucial market with a reputation for paying little respect to property rights; the Chinese firms, on the other hand, are eager to receive knowledge to enable them to catch up on the global commercial stage. Chapter 10, which is derived from Jing-Lin Duanmu's forthcoming PhD and prize-winning contribution to the conference doctoral colloquium, contributes to the literature by providing a micro-level analysis of the knowledge transfers from US, EU and Japanese firms to their Chinese suppliers based on in-depth interview data covering 16 pairs of MNE–Chinese supplier relationships. Having found that the types of knowledge being transferred by MNEs is of low proprietary importance (with much of it related to management practices rather than firm-specific knowledge assets), she considers the issue of country of origin effects on knowledge transfers from MNE subsidiaries to their local Chinese suppliers. It appears that Japanese MNEs differ from US MNEs in their attitude to, intensity of, and rate of transferring knowledge to their indigenous Chinese suppliers. Moreover, by looking at this issue over various phases of their relationship development and identifying the changing dynamics within the supplier relationships, she resolves anomalies in existing related literatures about national behavioural differences between Japanese and Western firms. As a result, Duanmu draws a number of implications for managers of Chinese supplier firms as well as the managers of inward-investing MNEs in China about how best to transfer knowledge to this emerging economic giant.

Country of origin differences are also the focus of Dimitra Dimitropoulou and Robert Pearce's chapter. They analyse foreign direct investment (FDI) flows into an integrating Europe in the latter part of the twentieth century in order to identify the different strategic motives for MNEs' location decisions in this period. Using time series data for 1981–2001, their chapter analyses inward FDI to 15 European countries from three sources (US, Japan, intra-Europe). Their aim is to detect the ways in which MNEs' emerging strategic diversity is reflected in the motivations determining patterns of FDI location. Independent variables are adopted to depict three types of strategic motivation: market-seeking (which may decline with European integration), efficiency-seeking (which may have scope to increase with freer trade) and knowledge-seeking (reflecting MNEs' increased use of diverse sources for innovation and R&D). They also use existing stocks of FDI in each country to detect responses to either potential agglomeration benefits or strategic inertia operating against the optimized pursuit of new locations. They find that it is the newer Japanese investments that show most signs of strategic heterogeneity with indications of both efficiency-seeking and knowledge-seeking behaviour. In contrast, although traditional market-seeking motives no longer seem to drive US or European FDI, there are fewer signals of the strong adoption of other motivations and it seems that strategic inertia may persist in US and intra-European FDI.

The final chapter presents a summary of the presentations at a plenary session on new directions for IB made by three outstanding scholars in the field: Peter Buckley, George Yip and John Dunning. This session, which was coordinated and reported by Simon Collinson, reflects on the content of IB and its evolution and then provides the participants' views on a number of critical areas regarding the development of IB scholarship in the next couple of decades. Peter Buckley maps out the complex domain of IB and emphasizes the importance of reaching a consensus regarding the 'theoretical rocks' of the subject. As part of this, he suggests the need to explore the relationships with other disciplines and functional areas and highlights the way in which IB can act as a bridge between disciplines. John Dunning stresses the need to adopt a 'responsible agenda' beyond a focus on wealth creation, in tune with the evolving perceptions and values of stakeholders as well as emerging political and economic trends, and he identifies a number of critical areas on which IB research should especially focus. The discussion is set against the dual challenge of rigour and relevance facing IB and other researchers. As part of the call for relevance, the potentially significant contribution that developments in the academic field of IB can play by identifying relevant trends or relationships and by providing insights into future patterns of change as an input to managerial decision-making is stressed, particularly by George Yip, for whom practising managers are the field's core constituency.

It is one thing to map out future directions for IB and another to stimulate its advance along these particular pathways. We were fortunate that our call for conference papers resulted in a significant number of submissions that develop the IB field through their contributions to contemporary issues and in emerging or under-researched areas. As is evident from the discussion above, the selection of work in this volume includes some that complements the more usual IB approaches by integrating insights from other disciplines. The different perspectives of stakeholders in different countries and the impact of this on managerial decision-making are among the themes to emerge in a number of chapters which stress the importance of the context in which managerial decisions are made. The title of the book reflects the emphasis on managerial issues within its covers and as well as shedding light on issues of interest to managers, we trust that the orientation of this volume will make a contribution to stimulating further work by IB scholars on the concerns of management and their decision-making dilemmas.

We are pleased to acknowledge the help of the contributing authors who kindly agreed to their work being included in this collection and who have worked hard to meet the tight deadlines involved in its publication. We wish to thank the referees who participated in the blind review of conference submissions and provided the contributors with comments. Finally, our thanks go to the team at Palgrave Macmillan and to Jacky Kippenberger, in particular, for all their help in bringing this 13th volume in the AIB UK series to fruition.

2

The Relevance of Internationalization Theories: a Contingency Framework

Carl Arthur Solberg and Vidar Askeland

Introduction

This chapter discusses different theoretical perspectives on the internationalization behaviour of firms and in particular, incremental internationalization/ stages theory, transaction cost economics (TCE) and the network approach. Although these three established theories are all concerned with entry modes in international markets, their core constructs and assumptions differ as well as their conclusions and findings, both descriptive and normative. A fourth approach to internationalization theory, called 'global management', is introduced. By building on existing literature, the chapter supports and explains this concept which is developed because the global competitive environment presents new and different requirements as regards both theory and practice (Hamel and Prahalad, 1985; Porter, 1986; Hill et al., 1990; Yip, 1992). Logically, all theories incorporate the interplay between internal and external forces, but their emphasis on these dimensions varies greatly. These differences seem to be the source of a substantial amount of criticism of the theories and, in particular, raise the question of the potential for generalization.

This chapter introduces a framework based on Solberg (1997) that seeks to define the circumstances under which different theories of internationalization may have the most explanatory power. After describing the framework and its dimensions, the theories are reviewed and discussed with reference to their suggested locations in this framework. Case studies of two Norwegian firms, Norse Skog and ASK-Proxima-InFocus,[1] were conducted and analysed using the theories suggested in the framework to provide an empirical assessment. Both firms have internationalized extensively but have followed very distinctive patterns. Their internationalization processes are analysed by locating the firms and their industries with regards to the dimensions of the framework and then applying suggested theories relevant to their respective settings. Finally, the conclusions briefly recapitulate the key issues regarding the congruence between the theoretical suggestions and the empirical findings.

The framework

The framework, based on Solberg (1997), suggests that different theoretical streams apply under different circumstances (see Figure 2.1). The vertical axis represents the internal dimension, preparedness for internationalization, denoting the firm's internal capabilities for carrying out international activities. The horizontal axis illustrates the external dimension, industry globality, which ranges from a pure multi-local to a global industry (Porter, 1986). These two dimensions will be treated in the next subsections.

Preparedness

A firm's preparedness for further internationalization at a particular time t can be derived from how internationalized the firm is at that time (Welch and Luostarinen, 1988; Madhok, 1997). Hence, indicators of the level of firm internationalization should also be seen as drivers for further internationalization, as suggested by scholars within the incremental schools of internationalization (Johanson and Vahlne, 1977, 1990; Young, 1987).

The degree of internationalization has been assessed in terms of several dimensions with varying degrees of measurability. For example, Welch and Luostarinen (1988) and Dörrenbächer (2000) suggest using measures such as

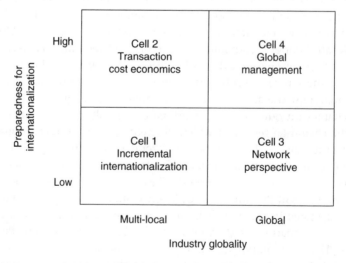

Figure 2.1   Framework for classifying internationalization theories

the percentage of sales abroad, the proportion of foreign employees and number of foreign countries in which the firm is established. These are mainly a result of a firm's quest for foreign markets and/or resources, and can be referred to as *operational* internationalization (Benito et al., 2002). However, although these factors provide a good snapshot of the level of firm internationalization, the concept of preparedness is more deeply embedded in the organization, and other indicators must be sought in order to understand the underlying elements assumed by various internationalization theories. *Strategic* internationalization (Benito et al., 2002) implies a deeper international commitment, where the firm decentralizes and internationalizes decision-making or value-adding activities. Such strategic internationalization demands, but also allows for, a deeper embeddedness of international commitment which implies a higher level of preparedness.

Welch and Luostarinen (1988) suggest a framework for assessing the degree of internationalization allowing for a more thorough understanding of how far a firm is internally organized for internationalization. They claim that it is not sufficient to look at operational internationalization but, in addition, the extent to which the choices are based on an overarching international strategy (strategic internationalization) and whether the organization is adapted to its international activities also need inclusion. Among other factors, strategic internationalization can be identified in terms of how the organization is structured through both formal and informal arrangements to support internationalization activities. Among the critical factors are the key personnel and their degree of commitment to the international venture (Aaby and Slater, 1989). In addition, financial strength is an increasingly important factor as internationalization often demands substantial investments.

A final key element of preparedness is the firm's market share in the reference market which can be approached in two different ways. It can be assessed in geographical terms, as emphasized by Leontiades (1984), but here needs measuring in an international context (Solberg, 1997). In a globalizing setting, it is increasingly important to look upon the reference market relative to a particular market segment or strategic group *across* national borders. A larger market share also indicates a presence in a wider range of geographical markets, giving the firm the opportunity to carry out moves and countermoves in multiple locations. Further, a strong position in a reference market can fund and support further internationalization both financially (Hamel and Prahalad, 1985) and through experience and competence, and is therefore a key strategic constituent in the firm's preparedness for internationalization.

Industry globality

Industry globality seeks to encapsulate the transition from a multi-local towards a global industry (Porter, 1986). Two key elements stand out as most important: the degree of homogeneity across markets and the degree of interconnectedness of the competition. In a multi-local industry, markets are heterogeneous, competition is locally oriented with a limited international ingredient, and fragmented – implying the possibility of entering a market 'unnoticed' by incumbents (Solberg, 1997). However, even industries with elements of international trade and MNEs may be classified as multi-local as long as they organize their subsidiaries as a portfolio of national businesses (Bartlett and Ghoshal, 1989).

A series of globalization drivers has contributed to an overall trend towards the integration of markets and competition. Globalization drivers can be divided into several dimensions which are obviously highly interconnected (Yip, 1989, 1992). External drivers include macroeconomic, social, physical, cultural and political or governmental aspects and can only be influenced by the firm to a limited extent. The political dimension has contributed strongly to internationalization through reduction of tariff and non-tariff trade barriers. Also, social and cultural convergence is taking place in terms of similarity in consumer behaviour and demand patterns (Held et al., 1999) which is a result of, and a motivating factor for, the global integration of business activities (Yip, 1989).

The most important aspect of industry globality for the purposes of this chapter is the competitive dimension, in terms of an integration of competition as the firms within an industry collectively pursue a global strategy (Yip, 1992). Competitive interconnectedness across markets implies that 'a firm's competitive position in one country is significantly affected by its position in other countries and vice versa' (Porter, 1986, p. 18). Companies facing this situation internationalize in their quest for scale, scope and learning economies (Benito et al., 2002). Such globalization drivers include global scale economies, steep experience curve effects, sourcing efficiencies, favourable logistics, differences in country costs and high product development costs (Yip, 1992). Hence, a global industry is typically characterized by a limited number of global players in addition to a segment of smaller, specialized companies (Solberg, 1997). Such oligopolistic competition is likely to be highly transparent, indicating the presence of interconnectedness. Also, these companies are in a favourable position for creating group-specific (Hunt, 1972; Caves and Porter, 1977) or more industry-specific entry barriers (Bain, 1956; Karakaya and Stahl, 1989).

Several indicators are suggested to measure industry globality. First, a greater number of MNEs and international strategic alliances within an industry signals a convergence of industry practices and behaviour. The increasing utilization of global alliances and cross-border mergers and acquisitions involves a cross-transfer of competences, further accelerating the convergence of strategic conduct and a concentration of international industry structure (Hagedoorn and Schakenraad, 1990; Nohria and Garcia-Pont, 1991). Secondly, global industries are characterized by a high level of intra-industry trade (Krugman, 1989). A third indicator is international price sensitivity, where a global industry shows a convergence of prices across countries, meaning that a price change in one country will affect the price level in another (Leontiades, 1984).

Cell 1: Incremental internationalization

A number of approaches and contributors to the incremental theories share a common emphasis on the importance of organizational growth, behaviour and learning theory (Coviello and McAuley, 1999). As asserted in the Scandinavian approach (Johanson and Wiedersheim-Paul, 1975; Johanson and Vahlne, 1977, 1990), internationalization can be seen as a cyclical and stepwise process, with each step allowing the firm to gain international experience at a market-specific level and also at a more general level which makes increased commitment in international markets possible. In the US approach (Bilkey and Tesar, 1977; Lee and Brasch, 1978; Cavusgil, 1980; Reid, 1981), building on Rogers (1962), internationalization is regarded as a stepwise, innovation-adoption process.

According to such theories, a firm lacking international experience is likely to prefer a low control mode such as exporting through an agent or distributor. As experience increases, the firm is better suited to move towards higher commitment, such as production units or greenfield operations, that accelerate the learning further. By building on resource-based theory (Penrose, 1959; Andersen and Kheam, 1996), these theories incorporate the concept of experiential knowledge as an internal competence. Such knowledge is also defined by Porter (1991) as a potential source for competitive advantage, which again can be seen as a determinant of the entry modes undertaken by MNEs (Kogut and Zander, 1993).

It is suggested that the incremental schools of internationalization apply in cell 1. From the perspective of firm and industry evolution, it seems likely that this cell (and these theories) in many cases represents the 'point of departure' for internationalization, with a firm with no international experience operating in a multi-local industry. Although not forced to do so by international competitors, the firm is likely to wish to expand internationally in its quest for scale, scope and learning economies (Benito et al., 2002) and to respond to external stimuli such as unsolicited orders (Welch and Wiedersheim-Paul, 1978). In this situation, the firm can be expected to exercise a slow and stepwise internationalization process, allowing a well-considered strengthening of internal capabilities, as suggested by the stage models.

It seems that the stage models have a higher applicability to the multi-local setting, where there is no minimum efficient scale enforced by large MNEs. In a global industry, the firm would probably not have the option of comfortably choosing to initially enter markets with the least psychological/cultural differences (markets implying low risk) or that are most appropriate in terms of the internal resources of the firm. Also, these contributions do not account for the complexity of interconnected global markets and the subsequent need for coordination of activities, but view each entry as an isolated action where firms face the trade-off between the need for growth and the risk implicated by each specific entry in a multi-local industry.

Several researchers have disputed the validity of stage models (for example Reid, 1983; Turnbull, 1987; Forsgren, 1989; Millington and Bayliss, 1990; Sullivan and Bauerschmidt, 1990; Andersen, 1993; Calof and Beamish, 1995), by questioning their applicability to different firms and environments. Much of the criticism disputes the deterministic nature of the stage models in assessing internationalization as a process through predetermined stages. Further, Turnbull (1987) and Rosson (1987) find that the mode of entry is a result of strategic choice, given the foreign market conditions, managerial philosophy and firm resources. In a redefinition of the Uppsala model, Johanson and Vahlne (1990) admit that a firm may 'leapfrog' stages if its resources are large, the market conditions are stable, and the managers have experience from similar markets.

In a multi-local industry structure, a firm with high preparedness is able to leapfrog the predetermined stages and can thus select markets and entry modes depending on its strategic motives, resources and external opportunities (Rosson, 1987; Turnbull, 1987; Welch and Luostarinen, 1988). The firm is then moving towards the second cell of the framework, where other theoretical explanations seem to apply. Another possible situation is that the industry globalizes before the firm manages to increase its preparedness. In this case, the internationalization behaviour of the firm will be explained by theories suggested in cell 3, as discussed later.

Cell 2: TCE theory

With increased preparedness in a multi-local industry, the firm is presented with a wider range of choices than in the preceding situation, both as regards *where* to enter and *how* to enter a foreign market. The firm is no longer bound by its lack of internal capabilities, but has sufficient financial resources and experienced, committed managers, and thus does not have to follow a stepwise pattern. Through formal and informal arrangements, the organization is better suited to cope with increasing complexity (Stopford and Wells, 1972; Hedlund, 1984; Bartlett, 1986; Welch and Luostarinen, 1988; O'Donnell, 2000; Kim et al., 2003) and is able to obtain and evaluate the necessary information about a market in order to make a rational choice in finding the optimal governance structure which is expected to minimize costs. It is suggested that the TCE approach is likely to be applicable in this setting.

A number of contributors (see particularly Williamson, 1975, 1979, 1981, 1985; Buckley and Casson, 1976, 1985; Dunning, 1980, 1981, 1988; Anderson and Gatignon, 1986) look upon the choice of entry mode as determined by the minimization of transaction costs following initial work by Ronald Coase (1937). Transactions costs arise due to the threat of opportunistic behaviour and small numbers bargaining given uncertainty and asset specificity, under the behavioural assumption of bounded rationality (Anderson and Gatignon, 1986). Hence, the entry mode decision depends on the trade-off between control, the benefit of integration, and resource commitment, which is the cost of integration (Malhotra et al., 2003).

TCE is criticized for being overly focused on the costs of the transaction versus the costs of internalization (Madhok, 1997). Although the approach appears to be especially effective in explaining vertical integration decisions (Erramilli and Rao, 1993), it neglects the concept of value creation. In the much broader eclectic theory, Dunning (1981, 1988) accounts for the internalization advantages of TCE in addition to the locational and ownership advantages (OLI), but this theory does not assess a subsidiary's contribution to the organization at large, instead stressing a top-down approach with a focus on HQ control.

Internalization demands high preparedness, as it presupposes extensive human and financial capital in the pre-entry, entry and post-entry phases, due to the need for information and the high resource commitment implied by this higher control mode. Further, TCE is appropriate within the multi-local setting because it incorporates a rather isolated approach to each entry, where the internalization decision is mostly determined by external, market-specific factors. This isolated view, with the specific transaction as the unit of analysis, is also a source of criticism of TCE; it is claimed that it fails to account for the strategic linkages between markets (Hill et al., 1990, for example). Critics of TCE claim that it is primarily used to explain a pattern of investment – extent, form and location (Johanson and Mattsson, 1987; Melin, 1992; Coviello and McAuley, 1999). It seems that the dynamics of the framework in Figure 2.1 can provide some support for this criticism. Even the smallest of firms will contribute through their internationalization as drivers towards industry globalization (Solberg, 1997). When one firm internationalizes, it should be expected that others in the same industry will do so as well, and, given bounded rationality, the firms will then react to the expected global competition, moving the situation 'automatically' from cell 2 towards cell 4. As the industry moves towards cell 4, TCE appears to be too short-sighted; rather than explaining 'a long-term process of international expansion' (Coviello and McAuley, 1999, p. 226), it only allows each entry decision to be considered in isolation.

Despite the suggested automatic drift towards the interconnected competitive situation of a global industry, the underlying logic of applying TCE in cell 2 seems valid. Given a multi-local industry, a firm with increased preparedness is able to abandon the incremental internationalization pattern of the stage models and faces a wider range of possibilities in deciding where and how to enter international markets, including through FDI. Hence, the framework appears to be useful in explaining the broadened range of possibilities as the firm increases its preparedness and moves from cell 1 to cell 2. In other words, the concept of preparedness is more evident in theories applicable to a firm with low preparedness (cell 1), whereas it is taken as an assumption by TCE. This implies that for a firm to be able to carry out a rational economic analysis, it must have a certain level of preparedness for internationalization. In addition, TCE appears to be too narrow to cope with the complexity of global competition (cell 4).

Cell 3: Network perspective

Theories suggested in cell 3 of the framework seem appropriate for a firm that operates in a global industry but lacks one or more of the dimensions of preparedness for internationalization, such as foreign market knowledge, committed and experienced managers and employees, market position or a solid financial base. This might be the case for latecomers in the internationalization process moving from cell 1 to 3 (Johanson and Mattsson, 1988) or for new firms that have entered a global industry instantaneously, the so-called 'born globals' (Oviatt and McDougall, 1994, 1997; Knight and Cavusgil, 1996, 2004; Sharma and Blomstermo, 2003). A firm in this cell does not have the option of stepwise internationalization towards a global market due to the threat of large established MNEs rapidly imitating their products. Such firms do not have the financial strength to compete head-on with larger firms and also lack key capabilities such as distribution channels and established customer networks. It is suggested that the network perspective is applicable in the setting of cell 3, due to the firm's urgent need to combine internal capabilities with resources outside the firm.

A growing body of literature regards markets and industries as a set of relationships structured in networks (Johanson and Mattsson, 1987, 1988; Håkansson, 1989; Axelsson and Easton, 1991). Firms have increasingly sought external resources in order to face growing internal and external complexity (Contractor and Lorange, 1988; Hagedoorn, 1995). The network perspective has emerged as a separate school of internationalization, displaying elements of incremental theory (Johanson and Vahlne, 1992).

Firms can access external resources through relationships (Holmlund and Kock, 1998) and in many cases these relationships are built over time. By drawing on theories of social exchange and resource dependency, the network perspective as a behavioural approach emphasizes how a firm may participate in interorganizational and interpersonal networks (Axelsson and Easton, 1991) involving stakeholder groups such as customers, suppliers, competitors, family and acquaintances. Such relationships may take many forms which vary in their degree of interdependence (Segal-Horn and Faulkner, 1999). Markets can be seen as the mode with least interdependence but the firms may engage in more formalized sets of cooperation by establishing supplier and distributor networks. Firms in industrial networks are coordinated through much more than merely price or hierarchical governance mechanisms (Håkansson and Ford, 2002).

The highest degree of interdependence takes place in strategic alliances, where either party can gain access to the other's resources. Although theories relating to strategic alliances differ from the network perspective as such, they share an important element, namely access to resources outside the firm's boundaries, thus making both applicable to the third cell of the framework. Firms' reasons for engaging in cooperative activities vary, and they have been approached using both an economics (Hennart, 1991; Buckley and Casson, 1996) and a behavioural logic (for example Rao and Schmidt, 1998; Doz, 1996; Arino and de la Torre, 1998). However, Granovetter (1985) suggests the network perspective is complementary to TCE due to the latter's lack of focus on the role and influence of social relationships. The network perspective also incorporates organizational capabilities and the resource-based view; lacking in-house capabilities, a firm can seek cooperative solutions to obtain these capabilities. This is especially valid in the increasingly complex business environment of global competition, where many industries face accelerating pressure for scale and/or scope.

Born globals, as mentioned above, may be found in this cell. By nature, such embryonic firms lack the internal resources for competing head-on with large MNEs, and thus suffer from the 'liability of newness' (Hannan and Freeman, 1984). However, these firms are able to build core competencies through knowledge sharing and development through personal networks, primarily through weak ties among key individuals. It is suggested that born globals internationalize through the development of such networks, enabling a stronger adaptation to foreign markets (Sharma and Blomstermo, 2003) which is actually facilitated by the absence of a leading company history or administrative heritage. The success of a firm's foreign entry relies on its relationships within a particular market rather than the cultural and market-specific characteristics (Johanson and Mattsson, 1988).

Cell 4: Global management

The interplay of globalization forces and competitive drivers eventually pushes the industry to become global (Yip, 1989). An increasing stream of literature discusses the complexity existing inside and outside an MNE operating in a global industry. The interaction between external and internal factors de-mands a more holistic approach to the coordination of the different units of the MNE in a diverse, but interconnected environment. The competitive environment is then affected not only by external factors such as relative prices, trade barriers, transportation costs and cultural differences, but also by behavioural factors relating to the firm. A global industry is often characterized by oligopolistic competition, with a high degree of transparency as regards the firms' capabilities and strategic actions. Hence, the strategic choices of a firm can be expected to have an impact on other companies in the industry, also in other markets (Porter, 1986). Firms located in this cell typically have a widespread global organization, extensive international experience embedded in the organization and its members, an entrenched position in key international markets and a strong financial base.

The stage models, TCE and the network approach differ in their main focus and, to some extent, they seem to be complementary. For example, the stage models see internationalization as a result of the internal capabilities of the firm, whereas TCE is mostly concerned with cost minimization in the light of market-specific factors. However, when approaching global competition, these theories fail to account for the complexity of both internal and external factors in global competition. This leads to the need for a more holistic view which incorporates elements from the various schools of internationalization. Although not a separate theoretical school, such theories are labelled the 'global management school' here. The multitude of factors involved makes it difficult to provide a sufficiently general theory while simultaneously capturing relevant elements at a more detailed level. A review of relevant literature in cell 4 is briefly given below.

The eclectic paradigm (Dunning, 1980, 1988) suggests three factors that influence a company's entry mode: ownership advantages, location advantages and internalization advantages (OLI). By combining the resource-based theory and the internal capabilities of the firm (ownership advantages) with external factors specific to a market (locational advantages), in addition to incorporating economic logic and rationality (internalization advantages), the eclectic framework provides a way of assessing the interplay between firm-specific and market-specific factors. However, the broadness and multiplicity of the eclectic framework make it also vulnerable to complexity and tautology, leading to difficulties in predicting causality. By introducing strategic variables, Hill et al. (1990) enrich the eclectic framework and TCE, thus making it more appropriate to cope with the MNE's need for overall coordination of its dispersed activities. Their framework builds on three main constructs, namely control, resource commitments and dissemination risk, which will influence the entry mode decision by firms wishing to achieve a global strategic objective. According to them, an entry must be evaluated by its role in the organization as a whole, and a higher control mode will be appropriate when facing a need for global consistency and coordination across subsidiaries.

Another approach to the MNE's adaptation to its internal and external complexity is to examine how each unit must adhere to its local environment to some degree while, at the same time, comply with the demands of the overall organization (Bartlett, 1986; Bartlett and Ghoshal, 1989). Rosenzweig and Singh (1991) discuss the pressure that a subsidiary faces for isomorphism with the local environment simultaneously with the pressure for consistency between the subunits of the MNE. Local responsiveness expresses the need for a certain degree of subsidiary autonomy, in order to respond to market-specific factors, and possibly allow subsidiary initiative (Birkinshaw, 2000), eventually enabling the subsidiary to develop a strategic role for the MNE at large, as a centre of excellence for example (Moore and Birkinshaw, 1998). This can be related to the 'heterarchic' model of Hedlund and Rolander (1990), which defines the MNE as a firm with several characteristics: many centres, in which traditional headquarters functions are geographically diffused; a strategic role for foreign subsidiaries; a wide range of governance modes from pure market to hierarchy, and a holographic organization, in the sense that all parts of the company have access to and share information and action programmes for market creation, for exploitation of comparative advantages, and for flexible global arbitrage.

Hence, local responsiveness must be balanced with the benefits of global integration to avoid organizational fragmentation. Such integration is commonly discussed from a top-down perspective, and involves mechanisms such as accounting-based changes (Shapiro, 1978), human resource management (Edström and Galbraith, 1977) or corporate culture (Jaeger, 1983). Ghoshal and Gratton (2002) suggest horizontal integration between subunits as an alternative to hierarchical governance. They identify four areas of action: operational integration, intellectual integration, social integration and emotional integration. In addition, global account management (GAM), the coordination of activities involved in serving one single customer in multiple countries, has emerged as both a result and a driver of globalization. According to Arnold et al. (2001), firms must carefully but proactively seek to exploit the advantages of GAM, but still balance such efforts with customer needs at a local level.

The preceding discussion reveals that the roles of, and linkages between, subsidiaries have changed drastically (Paterson and Brock, 2002) from a hierarchical to a heterarchical view of the firm, with a change in perspective from the MNC level to the subsidiary level (Birkinshaw, 2001). Choice of entry mode in this context cannot be seen in isolation, but is largely affected by its role for the organization at large (Buckley and Casson, 1996), and the post-entry elements of strategic coordination must be incorporated in the decision.

Analysis

The current section discusses the internationalization of two firms with reference to the underlying framework developed in Figure 2.1. The data were collected through several personal interviews with senior management in both firms.

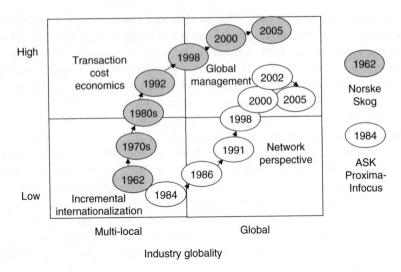

Figure 2.2 Trajectories of case firms within the framework

These interviews lasted between one and two hours and were followed up by personal phone calls to check on details. They were furthermore complemented by published and archival information. Each interviewee in the two companies received the story as it is reported in this chapter for verification.

The firms are located in this framework through their history of internationalization and different theories are applied in accordance with the suggestions of the framework. The trajectory of each firm in the framework is shown in Figure 2.2.

Norske Skog

Phase 1: Incremental internationalization

Norske Skog was established by Norwegian forest owners in 1962 to ensure a market for mid-Norway's forest resources and to give the raw material suppliers insights into the wood processing industry. The initial domestic production and sales were broadened to foreign sales through export, and later expanded to foreign production. The industry has internationalized intensively and there has been extensive consolidation at the same time. Today, Norske Skog is the second largest newsprint producer in the world with 24 mills in 15 countries and operating revenue of NOK 24 billion in 2003.[2]

The establishment of the firm was met with scepticism due to the founders' lack of industrial experience and limited financial resources. Nevertheless, the business was profitable and the company expanded and diversified both nationally and internationally. Although the home market accounted for almost 75 per cent of sales, foreign sales were recognized as important for future success from the outset. By initially setting up two mills instead of one, the company had excess capacity in the small domestic market and sought economies of scale at an international level early on in its development. However, as it lacked international experience, financial resources and an organizational structure to support foreign activities, exporting through independent agents appeared the best choice during the first decade. This allowed Norske Skog to increase sales substantially while, at the same time, extracting the necessary learning from each of its markets, in addition to gaining a more general understanding of international operations. The amount of foreign activities and their importance compared to domestic activities increased steadily and international experience was accumulated both at the personal and organizational level. Subsequently, the firm was able to carry out foreign sales in-house instead of through independent agents, and established a series of sales offices in European markets in the middle of the 1970s. Despite some interconnectedness across geographically close markets (for example Benelux), each market was treated separately with its own sales office.

The internationalization process of Norske Skog obviously complies with the incremental models. On the one hand, the entries were rather scattered in terms of both the psychic and geographic distance of the countries involved. On the other hand, there was a clear focus on entering the 'home continent' (Europe) before going into more distant continents and countries. More important was the lack of relevant international experience in this first period. This obviously impeded high commitment entries into foreign markets by this highly diversified company. However, as current international activities provided foreign knowledge, the firm faced a wider range of choices than suggested by the incremental schools. Some 'leapfrogging' of stages became evident as the firm increased its preparedness and the focus as regards entry modes shifted towards a strategic choice based on foreign market conditions, managerial philosophy and firm resources (Reid, 1983; Rosson, 1987; Turnbull, 1987). The question, then, is to assess what degree of divergence from the predetermined stages is acceptable in attributing a satisfactory predictability to the stage models. Although Norske Skog has largely followed the stage models, the explanation of entry mode choice shifted around 1980 from merely being based on the internal capabilities of the firm to also consider external factors such as market opportunities and impediments represented by a specific entry. This indicates a higher level of preparedness, and the firm can be located in the second cell of the framework, in which it is suggested that other theories are applicable.

Phase 2: Foreign production, market selection and TCE

During the 1980s, Norske Skog consolidated its operations in the Norwegian pulp and paper industry, with activities ranging from forestry, floorings and building materials to energy and paper production while, at the same time, emphasizing international growth. A regional sales office was established to improve the coordination of European operations. The first foreign production site was established in Golbey, France, in 1992, as a result of several beneficial factors such as financial support from the French government and access to skilled workers, a well-developed infrastructure and vast primary resources (natural forests and recycled fibre). Through discussions with company management, it seems clear that an economic approach is applicable to the French entry and later entries in less familiar European markets. However, despite still operating in a multi-local industry, each unit was aligned with the corporation as a whole. As other industry players also internationalized, the firm prepared for future global competition and went beyond rational economic analysis in deciding on each specific market entry.

The firm divested a series of non-core activities in 1994, which enabled managerial and financial resources to be centred on core activities, identified as production of newsprint and magazine paper. The few possibilities for differentiation in the industry, both between competitors and markets, created an intense focus on margins. Transportation and production costs were important cost drivers, implying a need for balancing the proximity to markets with scale in centralized production. Due to the need for and possibility of coordination among subunits, TCE appears too narrow, although the entry decisions obviously incorporated an economic rationale. The much broader OLI framework is more appropriate for capturing the overall picture of the organization at this time.

Phase 3: Global industry and global management

The intense internationalization activity made Norske Skog's transition from cell 2 to 4 rather swift. The relevance of a strong position in the reference market (Solberg, 1997) is apparent here. Its strong foothold in Europe can, in broad terms, be interpreted as serving as a 'cash cow' (Henderson, 1979) for the later investments in more distant markets. The industry had shown clear convergence with almost identical production processes among the players worldwide. The reference market can therefore be defined as the worldwide industry producing paper for publications, in which Norske Skog had a strong position, although best practice diffused quickly among competitors.

Norske Skog built a global organization with production units in five continents mostly through acquisitions. Through its acquisitions, the firm was able to capture market shares without increasing the total capacity of the industry. This was important in view of the considerable competition in the industry with intense pressure on margins. Further, there was a strong need for coordination among the dispersed units and activities to provide the optimal organizational structure. In seeking this, corporate management was divided into functional areas, namely production, sales and marketing, and supply and logistics, replacing the previous geographical division. This does not, however, imply that all decision-making was centralized at the HQ, but rather that corporate management was put in a position to coordinate the overall production and sales. In addition to operational responsibility, each functional division was responsible for identifying and exploiting global synergies. At the same time, each subsidiary was given autonomy with respect to how it achieved the set goals and, in many cases, local middle management and employees were employed in order to address market-specific conditions. Further, high transportation costs led to a certain regionalization of the industry. In response to this, and due to the need for strategic coordination over vast geographic distances, the regional headquarters in Australasia and South America remained.

The eclectic paradigm incorporates the preparedness dimension through the concept of ownership advantages. However, it does not directly address the issue of internal capabilities involved in choosing between the various entry modes, thus assuming a high preparedness, as proposed in the framework. Furthermore, these theoretical contributions clearly capture some of the broad internal and external factors (and the interplay between them) relevant for a firm and its entry modes in this setting. The firm is likely to align each entry with the organization as a whole, and hence each entry must be incorporated within the overall organization which is organized in line with the interplay between firm-specific, industry-specific and environmental forces. However, these theories are rather general, and do not seem to incorporate this dual pressure effectively, as well as the need for balancing global integration with local sensitivity. Also, the dichotomous approach to the choice of internalization seems to invariably favour high control modes as a prerequisite for global integration, without emphasizing the increasing role of the subsidiary. Moreover, although not entirely in accord with Hedlund's heterarchic model or Bartlett and Ghoshal's transnational company, Norske Skog in 2005 displays a number of their features, including local freedom, central coordination and the transfer of best practice between units.

ASK Proxima-InFocus

The internationalization of this company showed a very different pattern and pace from Norske Skog, largely due to the relatively strong external forces in the projector industry where it is based. There was rapid technological development and the industry structure changed quickly in the fast growing market. In the early years, from approximately 1985 to the early 1990s, various firms sought to provide a technological solution for projecting images and information in large formats and there was no established industry standard. Building on various core technologies, projectors were identified as a preferred future standard in the early 1990s. Like the computer industry, initial customers in the projector market were professional users such as companies and universities and later included home users, leading to the entry of a number of companies and subsequent intense pressure on margins. Today's projector industry includes large MNEs such as Sony, Toshiba and Compaq and can be seen as a global industry (with approximately 40 brands and 10 manufacturers worldwide). However, despite the convergence of product features, some segmentation exists; this ranges from low-end to high-end mostly sold through retailers and the AV reseller channel respectively. Markets tend to be served at a national level, especially in the sales and marketing function, to respond to country-specific requirements.

Phase 1: Start-up

ASK, founded in 1984, originally conducted R&D in LCD technology for the production of LCD screens but later turned its focus towards developing over-head panels for projecting images in larger formats. The Norwegian market was perceived as too small and the company had to act and think internationally. It defined its home market to be Europe but, as the firm suffered from unstable ownership and lack of financial support for marketing the innovations, it was unable to claim a position in the market. For example, the firm lost a contract for producing 10,000 LCD screens due to financial constraints, even though they had operational capacity. Facing this situation, it was difficult to fund R&D, and the firm initiated cooperation with Japanese developers to ensure access to leading core technologies. Cooperative solutions were also sought with German and later American developers to try to ensure that ASK was prepared for whichever would become the industry standard. The firm moved away from the difficulties associated with a pure R&D focus and through this type of vertical cooperation could assemble a final, marketable product.

Phase 2: Born global – international networking

By 1991, Tandberg Data, a world leader in data storage products, assumed ownership of the firm, and, although not implying any operational synergies, this gave the necessary security for banks, lending institutions, customers and suppliers. ASK soon entered an agreement with Polaroid, which marketed a line of overhead projectors in America under the label 'For Polaroid – By ASK'. With increasing competition, declining prices and continuously increasing minimum efficient scale, the company undertook an aggressive marketing campaign, building a network of distributors in countries all over Europe and some in Asia. With a strong product, they were able to choose their distributors and, through this, capture market shares in Europe. Key individuals were recruited from technology-intensive industries from 12 different nations providing both industry and also market knowledge. In 1996, ASK was spun off from Tandberg. This facilitated a more realistic valuation of the firm and ASK was listed on the Oslo Stock Exchange later that year.

Initially with no established industry standard, it can be argued that the firms in the first years operated somewhat locally (in cell 1) but, as industry standards emerged, large MNEs were able to market the products globally. ASK lacked international experience, distribution channels and financial strength, and was then located in cell 3 in the framework. The firm relinquished the focus on R&D and sought to assemble a product by combining its own components with elements developed externally. Informal, personal relationships were developed into contracts and agreements in some cases. For example, the successful partnerships with Japanese developers were partly due to a somewhat accidental meeting with a Japanese-American, who introduced ASK representatives to the Japanese business community. Still, at this point, the firm's approach to Japan (and other external suppliers and distributors) was deliberate and planned, not an ad hoc process of further developing personal networks. Although complying with the overall network logic of cell 3, ASK was gradually moving towards cell 4, as evidenced by its strong negotiation power primarily thanks to its R&D competencies. Tight linkages were established with suppliers, as the components were subject to a high degree of customization. Further, the firm did not have the option of choosing from a wide range of entry modes due to limited financial resources. Through intense negotiations and providing leading products, the firm was able to enter the markets at the large scale required in the industry. By building on such external resources, they could compete head-on with larger MNEs within the various segments of the projection market, instead of being a niche provider.

Phase 3: Global consolidation

Investors appreciated the company's strong presence in Europe and Asia and, by 1998, the decision was taken to acquire their American competitor, Proxima Corporation, which was somewhat unstructured at that period. The new company, ASK Proxima ASA, sought scale economies while providing both brands through the large distribution networks in all key markets. In 1999 (and implemented from 2000), the company was restructured into three business units: Products and Manufacturing, Americas and Europe/Asia (which was split in 2000) enabling a global and market-driven focus in product development, while retaining regional and local responsibility in the sales, marketing and service functions through regional business units and subsequently, the local representative offices.

The company changed its name to Proxima ASA in 2000, and as of 2005, the company was the second largest in the projector industry. A year later, the firm merged with the industry leader, InFocus, followed by further restructuring their global operations. This created an even stronger global foothold and allowed economies of scale to be exploited which was increasingly important in a growing market with only ten manufacturers. Decision-making was centralized in the American HQ, whereas regional HQ coordinated local sales offices. Production was outsourced to various low-cost Asian countries, and logistics was carried out by a global service firm. The former Norwegian HQ became an R&D unit with a global mandate alongside a technological unit in Oregon, USA. The new and larger organization could serve each market segment well; increasingly it sold through the PC reseller channel which substituted the traditional audiovisual channel in addition to the growing number of units sold through the web. Furthermore, the company assumed partial ownership in supplier firms, such as a lens manufacturer, still pursuing multiple technological standards, giving flexibility and reducing the risk from suppliers.

The extensive marketing network, together with the acquisition of Proxima, indicates a subsequent increase in preparedness, moving the firm from cell 3 to cell 4. Here, the firm continuously increased and restructured its organization, and combined the drives for global integration (especially in R&D and production) with local responsiveness (in sales, marketing and service) which it retained. The merger with InFocus further increased volumes, strengthened global presence and enabled a better approach to each market segment. Although the merger with InFocus can be seen as resulting in a loss of influence and decision power, it was a necessary consolidation to achieve the high volumes, global efficiency and coordination needed to face the intense competition. InFocus, traditionally servicing the professional market, has now lost shares in a dramatically increased market and yielded ground to firms like Sony and Toshiba.

Discussion

The two cases provide a number of insights and support the underlying framework presented in this chapter. A key issue is that the applicability of the various theories decreases when approaching the inner boundaries of the framework. The theories pertaining to cells 1 and 3 (that is, for firms with low preparedness for internationalization) seem to put a larger emphasis on the concept of preparedness itself. This is reasonable, as lack of internal capabilities becomes more relevant for such firms seeking to overcome this impediment through stepwise growth or external relations. For a firm with high preparedness (in cells 2 or 4), internal capabilities are emphasized less in the respective theories. Instead, the focus is on strategic opportunities and requirements either in a multi-local setting, with selective investments in preferred markets, or in a global industry with the focus on scale and scope.

The application of TCE in cell 2 has given particularly interesting insights. Theoretically, a firm in a multi-local context is likely to carry out an isolated analysis of each market in its rather patchy market selection process. This seemed to be the case of Norske Skog's entry into France in 1992. However, when an industry is likely to evolve towards becoming global, a firm with high preparedness in cell 2 must seek to develop capabilities to meet global strategic requirements in order to enter cell 4 rather than cell 3. In this case (when in cell 2, expecting a global industry in future), the firm will carry out actions to face the future global competitive drivers, something which itself drives the industry towards globality. This is evident in Norske Skog's emphasis on the future global newsprint industry; it also corresponds with the criticism of TCE which suggests that it is too isolated and fails to capture the alignment between subsidiaries and of the organization as a whole by excluding post-entry issues. In other words, cell 2 will, in many cases, be rather temporary and this chapter only provides theoretical support for the application of TCE in this cell, given that the industry remains multi-local.

Conclusion

The conflicting conclusions offered by different theoretical streams in international business have created different camps of academic theory. Although this research does not attempt to reconcile the different camps, the present framework offers bridges between them. After a brief review of the theory streams and their appropriate applications in this framework, it was used to analyse the internationalization experience of two firms. The underlying rationale for allocating the various theories to the suggested cells is substantiated by these case studies, revealing how key decision variables have changed with company and industry evolution. The framework has supported the application of relevant elements from a number of theories to the specific experience of the two firms studied. One the one hand, a key advantage of the framework is that it is dynamic as it incorporates changes in internal and external factors, thus revealing how the relevance of different theories alters with time and circumstances. On the other hand, although the framework suggests a logical range of applicability of the different theoretical streams, the theories should not be considered exclusively relevant in the respective quadrants of the framework. The contention of this chapter is that the suggested theoretical streams yield better and more consistent empirical results in each corner of the matrix than if applied without regard to the contingency dimensions used in the framework.

This chapter has enabled a strengthening and enrichment of the framework through theoretical and empirical discussions. In order to strengthen the arguments and investigate the potential for generalizing this framework, however, the empirical base must be broadened by studying a large number of firms from various countries. The framework may also be useful for managers, in that it makes it possible to capture the essence of a number of theories and hence reduce the gap between theory and empiricism. Managers are often driven by a certain paradigm and develop more or less well-founded theories of their own based on experience and different management gurus or consultants in fashion at any specific time. Sometimes this may result in less fortunate dispositions in international markets. Through locating the firm in the framework based on company and industry analyses, the process of applying relevant theory to practical issues becomes easier. We believe that this framework will enhance management's ability to evaluate the different strategic options in any given situation as expounded in the framework.

Acknowledgements

We would like to thank the management of Proxima ASA and Norske Skog for sharing their experiences: Ole J. Fredriksen (founder of ASK and former CEO of Proxima) and Svein J. Jacobsen (Board Member of InFocus), Torgeir Ose (Director Corporate Strategy) and Jan. A. Oksum (deputy CEO) of Norske Skog. Liv Karin Slåttebrekk, Birgitte Kristiansen, Christian Bjerke-Narud and Hans Martin Aulie contributed in the early phases of this work.

Notes

1. The company was originally called ASK LCD AS, before changing to ASK Proxima AS in 1998 and to Proxima ASA in 1999. In 2001, the firm merged with InFocus.
2. 1 NOK (2003) = $0.1412 and £0.1249.

References

Aaby, N.E. and S.F. Slater (1989) 'Management Influences on Export Performance: a Review of Empirical Literature 1978–1988', *International Marketing Review*, 6 (4), 7–27.
Andersen, O. (1993) 'On the Internationalization Process of Firms: a Critical Analysis', *Journal of International Business Studies*, 24 (2), 209–32.
Andersen, O. and L.A. Kheam (1996) 'Resource-based Theory and International Growth Strategies: an Explanatory Study', in J. Beracs, A. Bauer and J. Simon (eds), *Marketing for an Expanding Europe*, 25th EMAC Conference, Vol. 1, pp. 17–34.
Anderson, E. and H. Gatignon (1986) 'Modes of Foreign Entry: a Transaction Cost Analysis of Propositions', *Journal of International Business Studies*, 17 (3), 1–26.
Arino, A. and J. de la Torre (1998) 'Learning from Failure: towards an Evolutionary Model of Collaborative Ventures', *Organization Science*, 9 (3), 306–25.
Arnold, D., J. Birkinshaw and O. Toulan (2001) 'Can Selling be Globalized – the Pitfalls of Global Account Management', *California Management Review*, 44 (1), 8–20.
Axelsson, B. and G. Easton (1991) *Industrial Network: a New View of Reality* (London: Routledge).
Bain, J.S. (1956) *Barriers to New Competition: Their Character and Consequences in Manufacturing Industries* (Cambridge, Mass.: Harvard University Press).

Bartlett, C. A. (1986) 'Building and Managing the Transnational: the New Organizational Challenge', in M.E. Porter (ed.), *Competition in Global Industries* (Boston: Harvard Business School Press), pp. 367–401.

Bartlett, C.A. and S. Ghoshal (1989) *Managing across Borders: the Transnational Solution* (Boston, Mass.: Harvard Business School Press).

Benito, G.R.G., J. Larimo, R. Narula and T. Pedersen (2002) 'Multinational Enterprises from Small Economies: Internationalization Patterns of Large Companies from Denmark, Finland and Norway', *International Studies of Management and Organization*, 32 (1), 57–78.

Bilkey, W. and G. Tesar (1977) 'Export Behaviour of Smaller Sized Wisconsin Manufacturing Firms', *Journal of International Business Studies*, 8 (1), 93–8.

Birkinshaw, J. (2000) *Entrepreneurship in the Global Firm* (London: Sage).

Buckley, P.J. and M.C. Casson (1976) *The Future of the Multinational Enterprise* (London: Macmillan).

Buckley, P.J. and M.C. Casson (1985) *The Economic Theory of the Multinational Enterprise* (London: Macmillan).

Buckley, P.J. and M.C. Casson (1996) 'An Economic Model of International Joint Venture Strategy', *Journal of International Business Studies*, 27 (5), 849–78.

Calof, J.L. and P.W. Beamish (1995) 'Adapting to Foreign Markets: Explaining Internationalization', *International Business Review*, 4 (2), 115–31.

Caves, R.E. and M.E. Porter (1977) 'From Entry Barriers to Mobility Barriers: Conjectural Decisions and Contrived Deterrence to New Competition', *The Quarterly Journal of Economics*, 91 (2), 241–62.

Cavusgil, S.T. (1980) 'On the Internationalization Process of Firms', *European Research*, 8, 273–81.

Coase, R.H. (1937) 'The Nature of the Firm', *Economica* (NS), November, 386–405.

Contractor, F.J. and P. Lorange (1988) 'Why Should Firms Cooperate? The Strategy and Economic Basis for Cooperative Ventures', in F.J. Contractor and P. Lorange (eds), *Cooperative Strategies in International Business* (Lexington, Mass.: Lexington Books).

Coviello, N.E. and A. McAuley (1999) 'Internationalisation and the Smaller Firm: a Review of Contemporary Empirical Research', *Management International Review*, 39 (3), 223–56.

Dörrenbächer, C. (2000) 'Measuring Corporate Internationalisation – a Review of Measurement Concepts and Their Use', *Intereconomics*, 35 (3), 119–26.

Doz, Y. (1996) 'The Evolution of Cooperation in Strategic Alliances: Initial Conditions or Learning Processes?', *Strategic Management Journal*, 17 (7), 55–84.

Dunning, J.H. (1980) 'Toward an Eclectic Theory of International Production: Some Empirical Tests', *Journal of International Business Studies*, 11 (1), 9–32.

Dunning, J.H. (1981) *International Production and the Multinational Enterprise* (London: Allen and Unwin).

Dunning, J.H. (1988) 'The Eclectic Paradigm of International Production: a Restatement and Some Possible Extensions', *Journal of International Business Studies*, 19, 1–31.

Edström, A. and J. Galbraith (1977) 'Transfer of Managers as a Coordination and Control Strategy in Multinational Corporations', *Administrative Science Quarterly*, 22, 248–63.

Erramilli, M.K. and C.P. Rao (1993) 'Service Firms' International Entry Mode Choice: a Modified Transaction-cost Analysis Approach', *Journal of Marketing*, 57, 19–38.

Forsgren, M. (1989) *Managing the Internationalization Process. The Swedish Case* (London: Routledge).

Ghoshal, S. and L. Gratton (2002) 'Integrating the Enterprise', *Sloan Management Review*, 44 (1), 31–8.

Granovetter, M. (1985) 'Economic Action and Social Structure: the Problem of Embeddedness', *The American Journal of Sociology*, 91 (3), 481–510.

Hagedoorn, J. (1995) 'A Note on International Market Leaders and Networks of Strategic Technology Partnering', *Strategic Management Journal*, 16, 241–50.

Hagedoorn, J. and J. Schakenraad (1990) 'Inter-firm Partnerships and Cooperative Strategies in Core Technologies', in C. Freeman and L. Soete (eds), *New Explorations in the Economics of Technological Change* (London: Pinter Publishers), pp. 3–37.

Håkansson, H. (1989) *Corporate Technological Behavior: Cooperation and Networks* (London: Routledge).

Håkansson, H. and D. Ford (2002) 'How Should Companies Interact in Business Networks?', *Journal of Business Research*, 22, 133–9.

Hamel, G. and C.K. Prahalad (1985) 'Do You Really Have a Global Strategy?', *Harvard Business Review*, 4 (4), 139–48.

Hannan, M. and J. Freeman (1984) 'Structural Inertia and Organizational Change', *American Sociological Review*, 49, 149–64.

Hedlund, G. (1984) 'Organization in-between: the Evolution of the Mother–Daughter Structure of Managing Foreign Subsidiaries in Swedish MNCs', *Journal of International Business Studies*, 15 (2), 109–23.

Hedlund, G. and D. Rolander (1990) 'Action in Heterarchies – New Approaches to Managing MNCs', in D. Bartlett and G. Hedlund (eds), *Managing the Global Firm* (London: Routledge).

Held, D., A. McGrew, D. Goldblatt and J. Perraton (1999) *Global Transformations: Politics, Economics and Culture* (Oxford: Polity).

Henderson, B.D. (1979) *Henderson on Corporate Strategy* (Cambridge, Mass.: Abt Books).

Hennart, J-F. (1991) 'The Transaction Costs Theory of Joint Ventures: an Empirical Study of Japanese Subsidiaries in the United States', *Management Science*, 37 (4), 483–598.

Hill, C.W., P. Hwang and W. Kim (1990) 'An Eclectic Theory of the Choice on International Entry Mode', *Strategic Management Journal*, 11, 117–28.

Holmlund, M. and S. Kock (1998) 'Relationships and the Internationalisation of Finnish Small and Medium-sized Companies', *International Small Business Journal*, 16 (4), 46–63.

Hunt, M.S. (1972) 'Competition in the Major Home Appliance Industry 1960–1970', Unpublished PhD dissertation, Graduate School of Business Administration, Harvard University.

Jaeger, A.M. (1983) 'Transfer of Organizational Culture Overseas', *Journal of International Business Studies*, 42 (2), 91–114.

Johanson, J. and L.G. Mattsson (1987) 'Interorganizational Relations in Industrial Systems: a Network Approach Compared with the Transaction-cost Approach', *International Studies of Management and Organization*, XVII (1), 34–48.

Johanson, J. and L.G. Mattsson (1988) 'Internationalization in Industrial Systems – a Network Approach', in N. Hood and J.E. Vahlne (eds), *Strategies in Global Competition* (New York: Croom Helm), pp. 303–21.

Johanson, J. and J.E. Vahlne (1977) 'The Internationalization of the Firm – a Model of Knowledge Development and Increasing Foreign Market Commitments', *Journal of International Business Studies*, 8 (1), 23–32.

Johanson, J. and J.E. Vahlne (1990) 'The Mechanism of Internationalisation', *International Marketing Review*, 7 (4), 11–24.

Johanson, J. and J.E. Vahlne (1992) 'Management of Foreign Market Entry', *Scandinavian International Business Review*, 1 (3), 9–27.

Johanson, J. and F. Wiedersheim-Paul (1975) 'The Internationalization of the Firm – Four Swedish Cases', *Journal of Management Studies*, 12 (3), 11–24.

Karakaya, F. and M.J. Stahl (1989) 'Barriers to Entry and Market Entry Decisions in Consumer and Industrial Goods Market', *Journal of Marketing*, 53 (2), 80–91.

Kim, K., J-H. Park and J.E. Prescott (2003) 'The Global Integration of Business Functions: a Study of Multinational Businesses in Integrated Global Industries', *Journal of International Business Studies*, 34 (4), 327–44.

Knight, G.A. and S.T. Cavusgil (1996) 'The Born Global Firm: a Challenge to Traditional Internationalization Theory', *Advances in International Marketing*, 8, 11–26.

Knight, G.A. and S.T. Cavusgil (2004) 'Innovation, Organizational Capabilities, and the Born-global Firm', *Journal of International Business Studies*, 35, 124–41.

Kogut, B. and U. Zander (1993) 'Knowledge of the Firm and the Evolutionary Theory of the Multinational Corporation', *Journal of International Business Studies*, 24, 625–46.

Krugman, P.R. (1989) 'Industrial Organization and International Trade', in R. Schmalensee and R.D. Willig (eds), *Handbook of Industrial Organization* (Amsterdam: Elsevier Science Publishers NV), pp. 1181–223.

Lee, W.-Y. and J.J. Brasch (1978) 'The Adoption of Exports as an Innovative Strategy', *Journal of International Business Studies*, 9 (1), 85–93.

Leontiades, J. (1984) 'Market Share and Corporate Strategy in International Industries', *Journal of Business Strategy*, 5 (1), 30–8.

Madhok, A. (1997) 'Cost, Value and Foreign Market Entry Mode; the Transaction and the Firm', *Strategic Management Journal*, 18, 39–61.

Malhotra, N.K., J. Agarwal and F.M. Ulgado (2003) 'Internationalization and Entry Modes: a Multitheoretical Framework and Research Propositions', *Journal of International Marketing*, 11 (4), 1–31.

Melin, L. (1992) 'Internationalization as a Strategy Process', *Strategic Management Journal*, 13, 99–118.

Millington, A.I. and B.T. Bayliss (1990) 'The Process of Internationalisation: UK Companies in the EC', *Management International Review*, 30 (2), 151–61.

Moore, K. and J. Birkinshaw (1998) 'Managing Knowledge in Global Service Firms: Centers of Excellence', *Academy of Management Executive*, 12 (4), 81–93.

Nohria, N. and C. Garcia-Pont (1991) 'Global Strategic Linkages and Industry Structure', *Strategic Management Journal*, 12 (Special Issue: Global Strategy, Summer), 105–24.

O'Donnell, S.W. (2000) 'Managing Foreign Subsidiaries: Agents of Headquarters, or an Independent Network?', *Strategic Management Journal*, 21, 525–48.

Oviatt, B.M. and P.P. McDougall (1994) 'Toward a Theory of International New Ventures', *Journal of International Business Studies*, 25 (1), 45–64.

Oviatt, B.M. and P.P. McDougall (1997) 'Challenges for Internationalization Process Theory: the Case of International New Ventures', *Management International Review*, 37, Special Issue, 85–99.

Paterson, S.L. and D.M. Brock (2002) 'The Development of Subsidiary-management Research: Review and Theoretical Analysis', *International Business Review*, 11, 139–63.

Penrose, E.D. (1959) *The Theory of the Growth of the Firm* (Oxford: Blackwell).

Porter, M.E. (1986) *Competition in Global Industries* (Boston, Mass.: Harvard Business School Press).

Porter, M.E. (1991) 'Towards a Dynamic Theory of Strategy', *Strategic Management Journal*, 12 (8), 95–117.

Rao, A. and S.M. Schmidt (1998) 'A Behavioral Perspective on Negotiating International Alliances', *Journal of International Business Studies*, 29 (4), 665–94.

Reid, S.D. (1981) 'The Decision Maker and Export Entry and Expansion', *Journal of International Business Studies*, 12, 101–12.

Reid, S.D. (1983) 'Managerial and Firm Influences on Export Behavior', *Journal of Academy of Marketing Science*, 11 (3), 323–32.

Rogers, E.M. (1962) *Diffusion of Innovations* (New York: Free Press).

Rosson, P.J. (1987) 'The Overseas Distribution Method: Performance and Change in a Harsh Environment', in P. Rosson and S. Reid (eds), *Managing Export Entry and Expansion* (New York: Praeger).

Rozenzweig, P.M. and J.V. Singh (1991) 'Organizational Environments and the Multinational Enterprise', *Academy of Management Review*, 16 (2), 340–61.

Segal-Horn, S. and D. Faulkner (1999) *The Dynamics of International Strategy* (London: International Thomson Business Press).

Shapiro, A.C. (1978) 'Evaluation and Control of Foreign Operations', *International Journal of Accounting Education and Research*, 14, 83–104.

Sharma, D.D. and A. Blomstermo (2003) 'The Internationalization of Born Globals: a Network View', *International Business Review*, 12, 739–53.

Solberg, C.A. (1997) 'A Framework for Analysis of Strategy Development in Globalizing Markets', *Journal of International Marketing*, 5 (1), 9–30.

Stopford, J.M. and L.T. Wells (1972) *Managing the Multinational Enterprise* (New York: Basic Books).

Sullivan, D. and A. Bauerschmidt (1990) 'Incremental Internalization: a Test of Johanson and Vahlne's Thesis', *Management International Review*, 30 (1), 19–30.

Turnbull, P.W. (1987) 'A Challenge to the Stages Theory of the Internationalization Process', in P. Rosson and S. Reid (eds), *Managing Export Entry and Expansion* (New York: Praeger).

Welch, L.S. and R. Luostarinen (1988) 'Internationalization: the Evolution of a Concept', *Journal of General Management*, 14 (2), 34–56.

Welch, L.S. and F. Wiedersheim-Paul (1978) 'Initial Exports, a Marketing Failure?', *Journal of Management Studies*, 17 (4).

Williamson, O.E. (1975) *Markets and Hierarchies: Analysis and Antitrust Implications* (New York: The Free Press).

Williamson, O.E. (1979) 'Transaction Cost Economics: the Governance of Contractual Relations', *Journal of Law and Economics*, 22, 233–62.

Williamson, O.E. (1981) 'The Economics of Organization: the Transaction Cost Approach', *American Journal of Sociology*, 87 (3), 548–77.

Williamson, O.E. (1985) *The Economic Institutions of Capitalism* (New York: Free Press).

Yip, G.S. (1989) 'Global Strategy . . . in a World of Nations?' *Sloan Management Review*, 31 (1), 29–41.

Yip, G.S. (1992) *Total Global Strategy, Managing for Worldwide Competitive Advantage* (Englewood Cliffs, NJ: Prentice Hall).

Young, S. (1987) 'Business Strategy and the Internationalization of Business: Recent Approaches', *Managerial and Decision Economics*, 8 (1), 31–40.

3
Cheating and Incentive Schemes in International Joint Ventures

Ursula F. Ott

Introduction

This chapter deals with cheating in a cooperative enterprise in an international context. Since an international joint venture (IJV) is a complex organizational form of market entry, the information asymmetries between the parent firms and their cooperative venture may be an important determinant of the success or failure of the endeavour. The problem of cheating may exist between the players in an IJV because of the possibilities for hidden action by the participants. This chapter, therefore, aims to develop a typology to show the likelihood of cheating in this international context. It develops a theoretical model that should help managers to decide on appropriate incentive schemes within the remuneration structure for employees in IJVs, based on cultural and institutional differences, to reduce the likelihood of cheating.

The chapter is organized as follows. The next section deals with culturally implied moral hazard problems in IJVs based on a typology showing the likelihood of cheating according to country and organizational type (a sociological starting point). The third part of the chapter provides a theoretical model to reveal the problems of shirking, embezzling and sabotage (from an economics perspective) and the fourth section develops managerial implications for culturally sensitive incentive schemes. Conclusions are drawn in the final section.

Research on IJVs over the past three decades has largely focused on success factors, performance measures, stability and control issues based on qualitative and quantitative studies. The insights gained from these studies of IJVs showed their complexity and the possible tensions due to information asymmetries between the firms involved. These asymmetries can be derived from the players' geographical and cultural distance. This chapter develops a formal analysis of the information asymmetries of players in an IJV which should help managers to predict future behaviour in an IJV and to consider suitable options when negotiating contractual agreements to help to attain the desired performance.

IJVs represent an inherently problematic organizational form. Designed as a hybrid of two or more firms from different countries, the strategic configuration implies tension between the parent firms and the IJV itself, which is set up with managers from each of the founding parties. The strategic archetypes (Killing, 1982; Datta, 1988) therefore comprise the relationship between the managers of the parent firms, their representatives in an IJV and finally, the IJV itself. In a comparatively simple case, the IJV is founded as a business with three players – the foreign firm, the local firm and the IJV. In considering the tension between these firms, the focus lies on the managers involved and this complicated setting can be examined using a multiple-party approach (Osland and Cavusgil, 1998).

The multiple-party approach can be used to deal with the objectives and perceptions of all kinds of managers involved in the IJV business, such as the managers of the local and the foreign firm as well as the local representatives and the foreign expatriates in the IJV. Insights gained show that US parent company managers and Chinese parent company managers use different measures of performance; the US parent tends to be interested in the return on investment or internal rate of return, while the latter are more likely to focus on dividends or dividends plus taxes. Osland and Cavusgil found evidence of foreign parent companies not acting in the best interest of the IJV by selling components and materials to the IJV at high prices. It appeared that local parents were interested in increasing worker productivity so as to increase the dividends that they received from the IJV.

Although adding the human resource perspective to the analysis of IJVs can be seen as a complication of the underlying problem, it is necessary to point out the different reference groups within the organization of an IJV. Shenkar and Zeira (1987) emphasized in an earlier paper that there are three main groups of employees in an IJV: the foreign parent's expatriate managers in the IJV, the host parent transferees (employed by the local firm and transferred to the IJV) and host country nationals (directly hired by the IJV). Additionally, the literature considers third country expatriates of the foreign parent, the local parent and the IJV. Shenkar and Zeira also mention the impact of foreign headquarters' executives and the host headquarters' executives who play major roles in the parent company or as board members of the IJV.

Personnel matters in IJVs raise the issue of compensation, which is not only a problem related to national salary levels. In China, there is downward pressure on expatriate salaries generated by demands for pay parity between foreigners and locals. Another Chinese problem is the insistence on replacing expatriate personnel within a few years, resulting in much higher start-up costs. In IJVs all around the globe, both host and foreign representative managers who work for the IJV may have a conflict of loyalty between the venture and the parent companies even though the IJV's regulations sometimes require managers to cut ties with their parent companies. Chinese local managers remain, for instance, 'loyal to their parent company rather than to the venture, not necessarily out of identification with that company but rather because so much in one's life (e.g. housing social welfare) is contingent upon the work unit' (Shenkar, 1990, p. 87). Shenkar (1990) cited an example of an IJV in which a weak work ethic led to frequent thefts and lax working habits and nepotism permeated the staffing of the local workforce. For instance, when a Chinese–Australian IJV employee, the son of a senior official in the Water Department, was caught stealing, the water supply was cut off. The nature of an IJV not only generates benefits for both parties involved but also conflicts of interest, which could result in deception, fraud and low levels of effort.

Besides the specific IJV problems mentioned above, cheating must be considered as an issue of a general nature. Some authors have already focused on cheating as an issue in management and the workplace. Hennart (1993) showed shirking and cheating are possible whether transactions are handled through prices or through hierarchies. On one hand, such behaviour may occur among the self-employed when the reward is dependent on output and cheating is a means of benefiting within the market situation. On the other hand, the transactions which occur in a hierarchical structure influence shirking as this is the only way in which the employee has the freedom to benefit where there are fixed wages or salaries rather than incentive schemes. Mars (1994) has drawn from the fields of management, criminology and social science to explain workplace cheating. The author avoids psychological explanations of workplace behaviour and instead focuses on the pattern of regularities in kinds of cheating. He devised a conceptual framework to investigate cheating for four categories of jobs which he called the 'hawks' (entrepreneurial manager, salesman), 'donkeys' (supermarket cashier), 'wolves' (dock worker) and 'vultures' (driver deliverer). These four categories of jobs showed the scope for cheating resulting variously from individual freedom to group pressure at work and illustrated that both individual and group structures at work can lead to reduced effort. With regards to IJVs, these studies help to show that uncertainties in a culturally distant setting could contribute to the greater possibility of misunderstanding between players, to differences in terms of individual and group behaviour and to different incentives to work or to cheat. Table 3.1 gives some definitions of types of behaviour related to cheating as well as examples of such behaviour on an organizational level which have been found in IJVs.

This chapter aims to show that cheating (defined to include all the types of behaviour shown in Table 3.1) is not only a culturally implied option in an IJV but also needs to be considered when setting up incentive schemes. It deals with the special application of moral hazard problems to the organizational design of an IJV and to problems of culturally implied cheating based on a game-theoretical framework.

Table 3.1 Definitions of cheating, broadly defined, and examples

	Definition	Examples
Shirking	To have a lax working habit in order to benefit from fixed wages by putting in reduced effort; to evade an obligation; to avoid the performance of duty, as by running away	'1000 beds in Chinese factory', lax working habits and lack of effort, deception, sending 'dead wood' to IJV
Embezzling	To appropriate to one's own use fraudulently, as property entrusted to one's care; to apply to one's private uses by a breach of trust; as to embezzle money held in trust	Theft, fraud
Sabotage	Malicious waste or destruction of an employer's property or injury to his interests by workmen during labour troubles	Water supply cut off when son of a senior official in a Chinese Water Department was caught stealing
Paying bribes	To give a bribe to a person; to pervert the judgement or corrupt the action of a person in a position of trust, by some gift or promise	Seen as 'greasing the wheel' and smoothing the bargain, especially when haggling is considered as an art

Culturally implied moral hazard problems and incentive schemes

Given the different objectives of the reference groups mentioned above, we have to consider a moral hazard case for the managers. Suppose we have a three-player setting, in which the manager of the local firm, P_{Loc}, the manager of the foreign firm, P_{For}, and the manager of the IJV, A_{IJV}, are related to each other in a multi-person decision-making scenario. Thus, we have to consider three different utility functions dependent on their attitudes towards risk and their informational asymmetries. Difficulties arise because of information asymmetries due to different cultural programming. Barkema and Vermeulen (1997) related the differences in the cultural background of the IJV partners to Hofstede's (1983, 1985) cultural dimensions. In this study, the authors showed that differences in uncertainty avoidance and long-term orientation cause problems and have a negative impact on IJV survival. Whereas cultural differences in power distance, individualism and masculinity could be tackled by making explicit agreements, these differences are more difficult to resolve, since they affect the partners' perception and adaptability to opportunities and threats in their environment. These findings are interesting and led to the development of a special focus on personnel issues in IJVs.

Meschi (1997) explored the extent to which the longevity of an IJV affects the intensity of cultural differences experienced in a sample of 51 IJVs set up in

Hungary. At the centre of interest lies the cross-cultural issue of joint management. Chronic instability and a record level of failure can be related to the problems which trace back to cultural factors, such as mutually incompatible social or organizational models. Individual and collective frictions can arise between the local professionals and expatriates working in an IJV operating as an independent organization that federates the operations of two or more parents. The success of the IJV is dependent on the congruence between the different cultures involved. Meschi emphasized that the partners must develop a joint strategy of cultural integration. The cultural transformation required for culturally incompatible partners to become compatible is a time-consuming, incremental and evolutionary process and therefore dependent on time and learning.

Li et al. (2001) contributed to the literature on IJVs in China by an extensive study of parent firms from Western and Eastern countries and Chinese local firms in so-called East–West and East–East joint ventures. The data suggested that their oriental culture is valuable for East Asian firms in terms of enhancing efficiency and enabling rapid market entry. Joint ventures established by partners from East Asian cultures might find it easier than their East–West counterparts to manage human resources in China. This may partially explain why many East–East joint ventures showed significantly lower capital commitment, suggesting that they had more labour-intensive operations than the East–West joint ventures. The effects of societal culture, however, seem to be moderated by the technological resources of the investors. The authors found that IJVs established by firms from East Asian collectivistic cultures failed to achieve a better performance than those from individualistic cultures. Thus, a similar culture did not always lead to better performance. Especially in technology-intensive industries, IJVs established by Western individualistic cultures had their own competitive advantage. These East–West joint ventures showed lower sales but higher rates of return on assets than East–East joint ventures, which can be explained by the more advanced technology and well-established brand names of the former. The authors suggest that large cultural distances could be overcome by sending expatriate managers who understand both cultures well and this may improve communication with local partners as well as help in building strong networks.

Zhang and Rajagopalan (2002) examined credible threats between partners in IJVs by using an infinitely repeated prisoner's dilemma game. In their first case, the Japanese multinational corporation acting as the foreign parent in an IJV in China had a larger overseas market than the Chinese partner, which had only a limited local market. Because of its limited market, the Chinese partner usually did not have enough orders to fill its capacity and so the Japanese partner was able to make free use of the 30 per cent production capacity belonging to the local partner. Even when both the partners had orders, the expatriate managers would sequence the Japanese partner's orders ahead of those of the local partner. The IJV's ex-factory price was set at a very low level so the IJV showed no profit. The Chinese partner was threatening to end the IJV, according to the local manager, because it could not benefit from it. In the second case examined by Zhang and Rajagopalan, the Japanese partner cheated through its internal transfer pricing system. It bought the IJV's products at a low price but sold raw materials and components to the IJV at a price approximately 10 per cent higher than market. Since none of the local partners had expertise in the IJV's business, they could not counter with any credible threat of retaliation. The foreign partner (Japanese) could run the IJV independently, so the local partner had no possibility of punishing this behaviour. In contrast, the locals had a credible threat at the set-up phase since without their help the Japanese partner would have had difficulty in renting lands, registering the business and recruiting workers.

Husted (1999) and Habib and Zurawicki (2002) have shown that the cultural background, not just economic and political variables, influences a country's proneness to corruption in a country. Husted (1999) found that the cultural profile of a corrupt country can be described as one in which there is high uncertainty avoidance, high masculinity and high power distance. Furthermore, in the case of collectivistic and high power distance countries, masculinity is the single cultural variable that contributes to corruption. Habib and Zurawicki (2002) analysed the level of corruption in the host country of FDIs and examined the corruption level between the host and home country. In general, foreign investors chosen from Germany, Italy, Japan, Spain, UK and USA were found to avoid corruption because they considered it wrong and it was seen as leading to operational inefficiencies. The study found that foreign firms were unwilling to deal with the planning and operational pitfalls related to a host environment with a different corruption level from the home country. The discussion of cheating ('fiddling') should therefore consider the cultural implications of the moral hazard problem at a firm level rather than the institutional perspectives dealt with in the above-mentioned papers.

Indicators showing national differences in corruption (defined as the abuse of public office for private gain) and the propensity to pay bribes are produced by the Transparency International Organization and are given in Table 3.2 for 12 countries. The scale of the indices is from 0 (the most prone to corruption or bribery) to 10 (which indicates the least evidence of these types of behaviour).

It can be seen that countries like Sweden and the Netherlands, which have a high degree of consensus and group coherence, do not favour corruption and bribes whereas China has the lowest scores, showing the prevalence of corruption and bribery in this country. Since China is considered a collectivist country where relationships are important, corruption and bribe paying could be connected to the importance of group consensus and group benefit. This

Table 3.2 Corruption perception index (CPI) and bribe payer's index (BPI)

Country	CPI	BPI
USA	7.5	5.3
Britain	8.7	6.9
Germany	7.7	6.3
France	6.9	5.5
Italy	5.3	4.1
Spain	6.9	5.8
Sweden	9.3	8.4
Netherlands	8.9	7.8
Japan	7	5.3
Singapore	9.4	6.3
Malaysia	5.2	4.3
China	3.4	3.5

Source: Transparency International (2003).

leads to the research question: can we find explanations based on culturally implied cheating in this context?

Under the assumption that cheating could occur in all societies, we need to show the structure and the nature of the workplace which encourages this behaviour. We use Hofstede's power distance index (based on the importance of hierarchy) and relate this within a matrix to group behaviour based on a combined index based on the extent of individualism and of the degree of masculinity (score of individualism plus masculinity). This gives clusters of countries which have a similar hierarchical structure and group behaviour structure, as shown in Figure 3.1 which can be used to classify the likelihood of workplace cheating.

Nineteen of the 20 cases considered can be allocated clearly to one of the four quadrants in this matrix, with Italy alone proving difficult to classify. The resulting four groups can now be connected to the various forms of cheating,

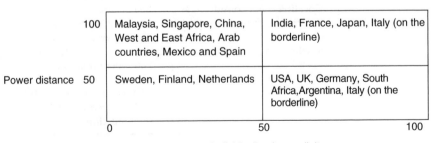

Figure 3.1 Power distance in relation to individualism and masculinity

from individual and isolated to group specific. Thus, cheating (as a general term including shirking, embezzling, sabotage and bribery) should not be used as a psychological or cultural stereotype; it can be found in all countries in different forms or with different explanations.

Table 3.3 shows a typology of fiddling using Hofstede's dimensions of power distance, masculinity and individualism which is based on Mars (1994). The terms 'strong' and 'weak' grid, as used by Mars, indicate the extent of hierarchical structure and rules in an organization and can be connected to power distance and, in a wider sense, to the degree of uncertainty avoidance.

'Tight work groups' occur in societies with a high power distance and a low combined individualism and masculinity index where the collectivistic

Table 3.3   Cheating at work in relation to Hofstede's dimensions

	Collective achievement, caring and nurturing (collectivism, femininity)	*Personal achievement, assertiveness (individualism, masculinity)*
Strong grid: high power distance (hierarchy)	*Tight work groups* Strong hierarchical structure and group consciousness. Cheating will be part of the group culture (embezzling, shirking) Malaysia, Singapore, China, West and East Africa, Arab countries, Mexico and Spain	*Isolated subordination* Hierarchical structure with high performance and achievement perception, fixed structure of time and work Cheating will be a pleasure (sabotage, shirking) India, France, Japan, Italy (on the borderline)
Weak grid: low power distance (equality)	*Loose work groups* Group dynamics and equality are important within the group, collectivism dominates individual achievement. Cheating is not considered as beneficial for the group (shirking) Sweden, Finland, Netherlands	*Individual entrepreneurialism* Individualistic behaviour and high performance as well as individual achievement expected, freedom from hierarchies. Cheating is used to gain higher rewards (sabotage as deliberate means to achieve better performance) USA, UK, Germany, South Africa, Argentina, Italy (on the borderline)

Source: Adapted from Mars (1994).

approach is combined with a structured workplace and the importance of rules. Asian, Arab and South American societies have this type of strong relationship-based approach with clear patriarchal structures.

As part of a group-based behaviour, the individual members of a group are encouraged to bend the rules. There is even special recognition to be gained by cheating in a group context. Additionally, the group could decide to put low effort into the venture and shirk or even embezzle for the benefit of the group or members of the society.

'Loose work groups' are found in societies with low power distance and a low combined individualism and masculinity index. The group members are autonomous and enjoy a consensus-based work ethic. The low hierarchical score and the focus on nurturing relationships (feminine society) indicate that importance is attached to sticking to the rules of the community. The workplace is considered to be a platform of equality and collective approaches in decision-making are practised. The incentive to circumvent the oppressive work environment by cheating is not seen as beneficial for the group and not considered as useful for the group consensus. Nevertheless, cheating could occur as part of a collective behaviour.

'Isolated subordination' occurs in societies with a high power distance and a high combination of individualism and masculinity where the members of a company work in a strictly determined scheme of rules and regulations as well having a sense of individual achievement. Sabotage is not infrequent since this is a means to create pleasure in a strict and tight work environment. Strong hierarchical structures can lead to shirking. This is consistent with Hennart's (1993) statement that in a fixed hierarchical structure shirking costs occur, since it is the only way to create benefits and pleasure.

'Individual entrepreneurialism' occurs in cultures with a low power distance and a high individualism/masculinity ranking where there is an individualistic approach towards workplace ethics. Freedom of decision-making and equality between the members determines the relationships. Sabotage is not infrequent. As mentioned earlier, when the reward is dependent on output, cheating is a means of benefiting within the market situation. This is based on the pricing system described by Hennart (1993).

Having examined the four classifications in Table 3.3 in turn, it appears that the presence of some types of cheating and shirking costs (as discussed in Hennart, 1993, in terms of markets and hierarchies) will be found in each of the situations and the previous examples of cheating can be related to these classifications. The typology is helpful in allowing distinctions to be drawn between shirking in a tight and hierarchical set-up, embezzling in a collective group (relationship/tribal) based environment with a strong hierarchy and sabotage in societies with an individualistic approach.

The model

A model examining appropriate incentive schemes to encourage truth-telling and to avoid culturally implied moral hazard in IJVs will be developed in this section. This links to earlier work on the development of creative incentive schemes in IJVs as a means of encouraging learning between the different cultures.

Cyr and Schneider (1996), for example, investigated human resource management policies and practices in IJVs in the Central East European context, including Polish, Hungarian and Czech firms with Western European partners (French, German and Swedish expatriates). Human resource management policies contributed to learning and innovation within the IJV by encouraging communication and through policies dealing with rewards, transfers and training. The authors found that the employees were in favour of a bonus system, and the implementation of such a system may have increased the motivation to perform at more competitive levels. Though monetary rewards are important to all workers, other forms of incentives should also be relevant in the Central East European context. Overall, the findings from this study of East–West European joint ventures showed the relevance of creative incentive schemes in encouraging learning between the different cultures.

The model developed below provides an analytical approach to the design of such incentive schemes. It uses Hofstede's indices of cultural dimensions, namely power distance, uncertainty avoidance, individualism, masculinity and long-term orientation.

Suppose now that there are two principals, P_{Loc} and P_{For}, and an agent A_{IJV}. Principal i, $i = P_{Loc}, P_{For}$ is interested in decision c_i and has utility U_i, a value function $V_i(c, t)$ dependent on the decision and the type and, furthermore, pays incentive I. Incentives could be offered by the local or the foreign parent and indexed according to the parents I_{Loc} and I_{For}. Let us now distinguish between incentives which are based on efforts (e) and those on costs (c^*). Thus, we can offer the following incentives:

$$I_{Loc} I_{Loc} (e_{Loc}), I_{Loc} (e_{For}), I_{Loc} (c^*)$$
$$I_{For} I_{For} (e_{For}), I_{For} (e_{Loc}), I_{For} (c^*)$$

Incentives can be given for the ability to cooperate on a cultural level; for example, depending on the cultural distance of the players, there could be incentives offered for the ability to bridge gaps between culturally distant employees. Hofstede's indices can be used to show the distance between the local and the foreign reference group and the related greater or lesser effort to bridge the gaps. Therefore, a greater effort is implied for much more distant cultures (American–Japanese) and lesser effort for close cultural groups

(German–Austrian). We can, therefore, relate the greater effort to higher costs of culture and argue that there is a need to provide incentive schemes to encourage cooperation where these costs are high.

Two types of incentive schemes can be distinguished, namely:

(a) incentives for the ability to cooperate (the capability of parent firms and their representatives for adverse selection *ex ante*), and
(b) incentives for the effort (learning or shirking) to bridge culturally distant employee groups.

To start with Hofstede's cultural dimensions, uncertainty avoidance can be linked to the risk attitude of the players; thus a risk-taker might be able to bridge a cultural gap between the American and Asian employees more easily than a risk avoider. Power distance can be linked to the hierarchical structure of the employee groups and the ability to cooperate top-down or bottom-up, respectively. The cultural fit of the hierarchies could be linked to the distance and closeness of groups and to greater or lesser effort to overcome difficulties based on a hierarchical structure. The degree of masculinity can be linked to the type of incentives offered, such as relationship or money-based reward schemes. Individualism can be linked to whether incentive schemes are based on individual or collective behaviour, either in terms of promotion as an incentive for individual achievements or for cooperative group behaviour. Thus a culturally sensitive approach can be used to predict the likelihood of difficulties with regards to cooperation within an IJV and to identify appropriate incentive schemes to tackle these difficulties.

Let us now show the relationship between the indices and the effort levels in terms of cultural cooperation. We can assume that we have either performance based on effort levels $q(e_{Loc}, e_{For})$ or a disutility of effort $v(e_{Loc}, e_{For})$ of the local and foreign players which are related to cultural dimensions shown in Hofstede's indices.

The effort levels associated with masculinity/femininity as a relationship dimension will be shown as $e_{CC}=(e_M, e_F)$ with the relationship $0 \leq e_F < e_M \leq 1$. This means that the feminine society already gives priority to a caring, relationship-based attitude, while the masculine society has to put more effort into cultural cooperation since it does not come naturally to this cultural type. The low effort in building relationships or lack of importance ascribed to such relationships in more masculine cultures might otherwise lead to failure in an IJV.

The individualism/collectivism index shows different attitudes towards individual and group achievement. The priority given to individual performance in cultures ranking high in individualism will lead to less effort being placed on cultural cooperation. This can be represented as $e_{CC}=(e_{Ind}, e_{Coll})$ and $0 \leq e_{Coll} < e_{Ind} \leq 1$.

The power distance index shows the extent of hierarchical structure and the extent to which power is unevenly spread in different cultures and can also be related to the different set of rules for relationships and appropriate behaviour. This leads to the following culturally implied cooperative efforts $e_{CC} = (e_{HPD}, e_{LPD})$ and $0 \leq e_{LPD} < e_{HPD} \leq 1$.

The uncertainty avoidance index shows the attitude towards risk and is not considered of major importance in this context, but rather as an underlying issue.

Incentive contracts to deal with shirking, embezzlement and sabotage are developed in this section. These draw on game theoretical applications found in information economics and contract theory (Holmstrom and Milgrom, 1991; Macho-Stadler and Perez-Castrillo, 1997). Hofstede's indices provide an ideal basis to correlate the discrete levels (high and low effort) with the extent of efforts to achieve cultural cooperation where e_{CC} depends on power distance, masculinity and individualism, as discussed above. The incentive schemes are for both players, foreign and local.

Shirking

Proposition.   If an IJV has employees of two national cultures, then the incentive schemes should take into consideration different effort levels as these are culturally sensitive.

Proof.   Let there be two efforts related to the management of an IJV – the effort level of the local representatives and the foreign expatriates. We can distinguish between $e_{Loc} = (e_{Loc}^{H}, e_{Loc}^{L})$ and $e_{For} = (e_{For}^{H}, e_{For}^{L})$ The outcome of the IJV q_i with $i \in \{1, 2 \ldots n\}$ can be written as $q_i(e_{Loc}, e_{For})$ and $q_i = e_{Loc} + e_{For}$. It is ordered from the lowest to the highest value $q_1 < q_2 < \ldots q_n$. Let $P_i^{L} = p_i$ $(e_{Loc}^{L}, e_{For}^{L})$ be the probability for cases in which the agent offers a low level of effort $P_i^{L} > 0$. The principal(s) prefer a high level of effort. If the principal demands high effort e^{H} (which will be the case when q_i is large for I), the problem becomes interesting since any fixed payment would only get the agent to choose e^{L}. The incentive payment $I(q_i)$ depends on the final result. Yet, the final result is a combination of both representatives' efforts.

The joint incentive scheme can be rewritten in the following way:

$$\max \sum_{i=1}^{n} p_i^{H} \left[\prod (q_i) - I(q_i(e_{Loc}, e_{For})) \right]$$

such that

$$\sum_{i=1}^{n} p_i^{H} \, u \, (I(q_i(e_{Loc}, e_{For}))) - v(e_{Loc}^{H}) \geq \underline{U}$$

$$\sum_{i=1}^{n} [p_i^H - p_i^L] u(I(q_i)) \geq v(e_{Loc}^H) - v(e_{Loc}^L)$$

$$\sum_{i=1}^{n} p_i^H u(I(q_i(e_{Loc}, e_{For}))) - v(e_{For}^H) \geq \underline{U}$$

$$\sum_{i=1}^{n} [p_i^H - p_i^L] u(I(q_i)) \geq v(e_{For}^H) - v(e_{For}^L)$$

Embezzlement

Proposition. If an IJV has employees of two national cultures, then the incentive schemes should consider the culturally implied embezzlement.

Proof. Let us consider that embezzling is the reason for both low effort levels. Thus, we can distinguish between embezzling by the foreign player and embezzling by the local representative. Under the assumption that embezzling is culturally implied, we can treat embezzling by the local player (in case of a feminine society or collectivist society) as relationship related. Embezzlement by a foreign expatriate could be related to the individualistic or masculine features of the home society. We, therefore, assume that embezzling can occur in various societies, though with different motives and explanations. Thus, it is important to develop incentives based on the different backgrounds and not only on the output level.

$$e_{Loc}^M = q_i - emb_M \rightarrow e_{Loc}^L, \qquad e_{Loc}^F = q_i - emb_{Rel} \rightarrow e_{Loc}^L$$

$$e_{Loc}^{Ind} = q_i - emb_{Ind} \rightarrow e_{Loc}^L, \qquad e_{Loc}^{Coll} = q_i - emb_{Coll} \rightarrow e_{Loc}^L$$

$$e_{For}^H = q_i - emb_M \rightarrow e_{For}^L, \qquad e_{For}^F = q_i - emb_{Rel} \rightarrow e_{For}^L$$

$$e_{For}^{Ind} = q_i - emb_{Ind} \rightarrow e_{For}^L, \qquad e_{For}^{Coll} = q_i - emb_{Coll} \rightarrow e_{For}^L$$

Furthermore, let us consider shirking as a culturally implied behaviour. We can, therefore, distinguish between cultures in which shirking is seen as acceptable behaviour and cultures in which it is unacceptable.

Therefore, in an IJV with at least two cultures, we have to consider incentive schemes to prevent embezzling and shirking.

$$I(q_i(e_{Loc}^M)) = F \pm r_M(e_{Loc})$$

$$I(q_i(e_{\text{Loc}}^{\text{F}})) = R \pm r_{\text{F}}(e_{\text{Loc}})$$

$$I(q_i(e_{\text{Loc}}^{\text{Ind}})) = \text{Promotion}$$

$$I(q_i(e_{\text{Loc}}^{\text{Coll}})) = \text{Holidays with the family and so on}$$

Sabotage

The joint outcome can induce either one or the other agent, or both, to put in a lot of effort. There is an option of sabotaging and another option of learning included in the choice of effort level.

Case 1:   The local representative intends to contribute local expertise, raw material, production knowledge and the foreign representative provides technological know-how and managerial skills – effort levels are verifiable when skills are complementary. Thus, both contribute a high level of effort q_i $(e_{\text{Loc}}^{\text{H}}, e_{\text{For}}^{\text{H}})$.

Case 2:   The local representative contributes a low effort to the IJV, whereas the foreign expatriate works hard and contributes a high effort level giving q_i $(e_{\text{Loc}}^{\text{L}}, e_{\text{For}}^{\text{H}})$.

Case 3:   The foreign expatriate wants to put in little effort and the local representative puts a high level of effort into the IJV. This is the case when the local's expertise is easily observed and the locals want the IJV to prosper. However, the foreign expatriate only wants production knowledge or market entry knowledge and provides little in terms of managerial or technological know-how (free-rider). This gives the following relationship: q_i $(e_{\text{Loc}}^{\text{H}}, e_{\text{For}}^{\text{L}})$.

Case 4:   Both representatives rely on the other's contribution and intend to provide a low effort. Thus, the joint outcome is q_i $(e_{\text{Loc}}^{\text{H}}, e_{\text{For}}^{\text{L}})$.

Proposition.   If an IJV has employees of two national cultures, then the contracts should consider sabotage and learning.

Proof.   Let us consider the case when the effort level for both parts of the management (local and foreign) can be divided into sabotage and learning in an IJV. Under the assumption that the local agent can use his effort for either sabotaging or learning, $e_{\text{Loc}}^{\text{Sab}} + e_{\text{Loc}}^{\text{Learn}} = 1$. The same is true for the foreign partner.

The IJV can have a management team which could have both foreign expatriate and local representative learning or sabotaging, or either party learning and the other one sabotaging. In Table 3.4, the effort required for learning has the value x and the effort for sabotage will be $100-x$. The payoffs in the matrix are given for the foreign firm first and the local firm second. The outcome is

Table 3.4   Sabotage and learning

		e_{Loc}	
		Sabotage	Learning
e_{For}	Sabotage	$(100-x; 100-x)$	$(100-x; x)$
	Learning	$(x; 100-x)$	$(x; x)$

dependent on the effort levels of both partners. We can show the following pairs of value $(100-x; 100-x)$, $(x; x)$, $(x; 100-x)$ and $(100-x; x)$. The success of the joint venture depends on the Nash equilibrium of both players learning in an IJV.

Incentive schemes are based on the output $I[q(e_{Loc}, e_{For})]$ and are therefore connected to the effort levels of local and foreign players. Since sabotage was related to jobs and cultures with high points of the grid as a response to hierarchical structures, it is important to consider incentives based on the cultural effort to bridge gaps or differences in power distance $e_{CC}=(e_{HPD}, e_{LPD})$. Ideally, IJV success is connected to learning instead of cheating which is related to cultures with a lower power distance score.

It is considered human to look for the best outcome within relationships, whether this means to adhere to a group consensus, to play fair, to look out for benefits in order to maximize individual profits or to enjoy the pleasure of manipulating hierarchical structures. The culturally implied moral hazard can be avoided by the appropriate incentive schemes. It is important to distinguish between the cultures which are prone to shirking, embezzling and sabotaging and to target incentive schemes according to the underlying cheating concepts.

Managerial implications

Although compensation schemes in multinational enterprises consider base salary, tax issues, allowances and benefits (such as social security, medical coverage and pension plans), incentive payments have not tended to consider cultural distance and its implications such as different effort levels, difficulties in cooperation across countries and cheating after signing contracts. This chapter has analysed culturally implied moral hazard problems and developed contracts based on the differences between culturally determined behaviours affecting performance in an IJV.

The compensation schemes in a culturally sensitive incentive plan could, for instance, take the base salary into account and relate to it a bonus system based on culturally determined effort levels and a parameter for the cultural distance between the players. The analysis of the effort levels according to Hofstede's cultural dimensions showed the perspective in terms of foreign expatriates and host country representatives. The incentive schemes should be targeted to the national cultures involved and the likelihood of culturally implied cheating after signing the contract. It is important to note that, in reality, this is not a one-shot game; contracts will have to be updated periodically in order to adjust them to actual behaviour and its impact on the success of the IJV. This kind of repeated moral hazard scenario merits further investigation.

Conclusion

This chapter aimed to show the tension associated with multi-person decision-making in an IJV setting. It considered information asymmetries based on the distance between the players in both geographic and cultural terms. The complexities of the IJV as an organizational form were analysed and related to the presence of a variety of groups in an IJV. This research suggests that the literature on IJVs needs to focus much more on solving complex strategic issues rather than concentrating as heavily on the motives for founding IJVs as it has in the past.

First, the problem was analysed and the link between the real life scenario and the theoretical framework was developed. Based on the moral hazard problem of cheating after signing the contract, it was shown that the behaviour of players in an IJV is related to culturally implied cheating behaviour. The corruption perception index and the bribe payers' index were considered as measures for the actual perception of the proneness to cheating of a selection of national cultures. This was conceptualized in four groups (tight work groups, loose work groups, isolated subordination and the individual entrepreneurialism) and embedded in Hofstede's cultural dimensions of power distance, individualism and masculinity to show the relevance of hierarchical structure and group behaviour for cheating.

Second, the chapter showed the importance of using an abstract approach to help understand the complexities of IJVs and, in particular, the culturally implied moral hazard problems. The tools applied in the chapter, based on economic theory, were introduced and the theoretical perspective on incentives was related to earlier literature.

Finally, drawing on the introductory sections, a variety of mechanisms were provided to apply to the various problems of moral hazard within an IJV. Hidden action and the problem of free-riding were linked to the type of player and incentive schemes were developed to discourage such behaviour. The analysis of optimal contracts showed the importance of incentives in which effort was linked to the above-mentioned culturally implied moral hazard problems. Further research could help in refining the choice of incentive schemes, but the results discussed here provide useful pointers to dealing with cheating in its various forms in IJVs.

References

Barkema, H.G. and F. Vermeulen (1997) 'What Differences in the Cultural Backgrounds of Partners are Detrimental for International Joint Ventures?', *Journal of International Business Studies*, 28 (4), 845–64.
Cyr, D. and S.C. Schneider (1996) 'Implications for Learning: Human Resource Management in East–West Joint Ventures', *Organization Studies*, 10 (2), 149–68.
Datta, D.K. (1988) 'International Joint Ventures: a Framework for Analysis', *Journal of General Management*, 14 (2), 78–91.
Habib, M. and L. Zurawicki (2002) 'Corruption and Foreign Direct Investment', *Journal of International Business Studies*, 33 (2), 291–307.
Hennart, J.-F. (1993) 'Explaining the Swollen Middle: Why Most Transactions Are a Mix of "Market" and "Hierarchy" ', *Organization Science*, 4 (4), 529–45.
Hofstede, G. (1983) 'The Cultural Relativity of Organizational Practices and Theories', *Journal of International Business Studies*, 14 (2), 75–90.
Hofstede, G. (1985) 'The Interaction between National and Organizational Value Systems', *Journal of Management Studies*, 22, 347–57.
Holmstrom, B. and P. Milgrom (1991) 'Multitask Principal–Agent Analyses: Incentive Contracts, Asset Ownership and Job Design', *Journal of Law, Economics and Organization*, 7, 24–52.
Husted, B.W. (1999) 'Wealth, Culture and Corruption', *Journal of International Business Studies*, 30 (2), 339–60.
Killing, J.P. (1982) 'How to Make a Global Joint Venture Work', *Harvard Business Review*, 61 (3), 120–7.
Li, J, K. Lam and G. Qian (2001) 'Does Culture Affect Behavior and Performance of Firms? The Case of Joint Ventures in China', *Journal of International Business Studies*, 32 (1), 115–31.
Macho-Stadler, I. and J.D. Perez-Castrillo (1997) *An Introduction to the Economics of Information – Incentives and Contracts* (Oxford: Oxford University Press).
Mars, G. (1994) *Cheats at Work – an Anthropology of Workplace Crime* (Aldershot: Dartmouth).
Meschi, P.X. (1997) 'Longevity and Cultural Differences of International Joint Ventures: toward Time-based Cultural Management', *Human Relations*, 50 (2), 211–27.
Osland, G.E. and S.T. Cavusgil (1998) 'The Use of Multiple-party Perspectives in International Joint Venture Research', *Management International Review*, 38, 191–202.
Shenkar, O. (1990) 'International Joint Ventures' Problems in China: Risks and Remedies', *Long Range Planning*, 23 (3), 82–90.
Shenkar, O. and Y. Zeira (1987) 'Human Resource Management in International Joint Ventures: Directions for Research', *Academy of Management Review*, 12 (3), 546–57.
Transparency International (2003) www.transparency.org/documents/cpi.
Zhang, Y. and N. Rajagopalan (2002) 'Inter-partner Credible Threat in International Joint Ventures: an Infinitely Repeated Prisoner's Dilemma Model', *Journal of International Business Studies*, 33 (3), 457–78.

4
Managerial Perspectives on Business Purpose: Values, National Values and Institutions

Simon Harris and Chris Carr

Introduction

Doing business internationally always involves developing business relationships with people in other nations. The cultural differences faced in forging cross-national links are well known but the development of satisfactory business relationships is a prerequisite for successful international mergers, alliances and joint ventures, or even for effective overseas distribution deals. This chapter explores whether the purposes ('strategic intents') of managers differ between nations and, if they do, whether these differences are in line with previously ascertained and popularly known cultural values. It explores the relevance of national values research in predicting the beliefs that managers in different countries hold about the purpose of their businesses. The specific aspects examined here are the *stakeholders* which managers recognize as important, the *aims* that are pursued for the benefit of these stakeholders, and the *time frames* within which the managers expect their strategic decisions to be realized. Institutional structure can have an important influence on these elements, so the empirical work in this study is based on data collected in two different types of firm, which allows the impact of the structural differences to be explored. The findings have implications for managers trying to develop business relationships abroad and suggest the possible dangers of making assumptions about the purposes of overseas firms based purely on nationality.

Management styles in different countries have been widely compared – for example, paired comparisons have been made between the US and Japan and between the UK and Germany. Typically, the outcomes are generalized statements concerning managerial approaches, which have sometimes been absorbed into conventional wisdom in the form of stereotypes (for example,

Pascale and Athos, 1981; Hickson, 1993; Lawrence and Edwards, 2000). For instance, it is suggested that business decisions in the US tend to be 'shorter term' than is typical in Japan and in some European countries (Jacobs, 1991). Managers in Germany and Japan are supposedly far more concerned with product attributes and quality in comparison to managers in the UK and US, where there is more focus on marketing aspects (Hayes and Abernathy, 1980; Hayes and Limprecht, 1982).

One of the few variables available to explore reasons why such differences exist is based on the notion of national values. Though national values are well researched, the possible causal linkages between such values and different management practices have received considerably less attention, except in the area of human resource management (Laurent, 1986; Schneider, 1988). There are strong grounds, nonetheless, for believing that national values, as usually studied under the umbrella of 'cultures research', may well influence the way that strategic decision makers think in different countries; these are examined in the next section. Another possibly more important explanation for differences in managerial practice, however, is institutional structure (Carr and Tomkins, 1998; Whitley, 1999). Ownership structures differ between countries for historical reasons (Pedersen and Thomsen, 1997), and these alter the owner-manager agency relationships and can influence behaviour (Pedersen and Thomsen, 2003). There is some empirical support for the view that ownership and governance structures influence management practice (for example, Schulze et al., 2003; Wright et al., 2002).

This study examines these explanations empirically through case studies carried out in two contrasting institutional contexts. One set of respondents were professional executives of multinational companies, subject to international capital markets, in the worldwide vehicle components industry in Germany, Japan, the United Kingdom and the US. The second set of respondents were owner managers of medium-sized, young electronics firms, who were also addressing global markets, but as they did not have agency relationships with outside shareholders, they were not directly subject to international capital markets.

National values and the purpose of business

'Artefacts and norms' (including rituals and practices) may respond to new environmental and organizational contexts, strategies and interventions, and may be learned at the workplace (Schein, 1985; Isabella, 1990). They have been distinguished from more fundamental shared 'values and basic assumptions' in societies (Hofstede, 1991; Lundberg, 1985), which, normally unconsciously, govern how realities are perceived and how behaviour is assessed. They lie at the core of behaviour, are resistant to change and differ between nations but are stable within them (Hofstede, 1991; Schein, 1985). Managers in different countries can be expected to hold different underpinning values, different assumptions regarding the environment, and different expectations about relationships among people (Schein, 1985). These can all be expected to result in different business purposes or objectives.

First, they can be expected to affect the underlying expectations about the stakeholders for whom an organization exists. Different managers may hold different views as to who the key stakeholders are (Thomsen and Pedersen, 2000; Whitley, 1992). Owners are the stakeholders given greatest attention in management research, from microeconomic theory to the shareholder value approaches of Rappaport (1986) and McTaggart et al. (1994). Alternative, wider notions of stakeholders may include employees, local communities, 'the national good' or the environment.

Values can also be expected to influence the aims that businesses choose to follow. They can be narrow, simply addressing profit or financial returns, for example, or they can be wide, addressing a range of goals (Hickson and Pugh, 1995, for example). Traditionally, strategy research has seen the concept of 'purpose' as directly linked to that of stakeholders (see, for example, King and Cleland, 1978). Those who believe that only the owners really matter tend to see profitability as the goal (Ansoff, 1965, for instance). Firms where ownership and management are separated, the main context of strategic management research, tend to be profit oriented, but other aims have also been recognized. In firms not constrained by agency interrelationships and contracts, the aims pursued will reflect the life values of those who control the firm. Examples of this might be, for example, orientations towards the pursuit of income and wealth, or love and friendship, or religious aims. So the aims that managers choose to follow may reflect not only their institutional settings but, where they can exercise discretion, their values as well. Aims may be concerned only with financial outcomes (the stereotype often associated with Anglo-Saxon cultures) or may be concerned with wider outcomes, such as the overall strength and scale of the business (Albert, 1994; Whitley, 1999).

Aims and objectives may be short or long term; managers may look towards the quarterly report or the long-term strategic outcome (Whitley, 1999; Hickson and Pugh, 1995). Short-termism has been a concern in the UK and in the US, with Germany and Japan, for example, apparently having longer-term decision-making horizons. Much strategic management literature has long seen this to be an agency problem, where the interests of managers are at variance with those of owners or other stakeholders (Berle and Means, 1932; Fama, 1980). Values research has also shown that orientations towards time are different in different countries, with different cultures seeing time in different ways. If so, the timescales over which managers try to achieve their objectives might vary accordingly. Two contrasting notions of aims will be explored here: the short-term focus often associated with Anglo-Saxon cultures, and the

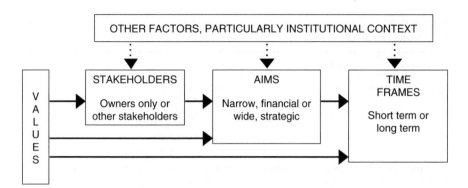

Figure 4.1   Broad analytical model of factors underlying strategic decisions

longer-term time frame associated with some Asian cultures (for example, see Hickson and Pugh, 1995), and with some forms of European capitalism (Calori and de Woot, 1994). Figure 4.1 draws these ideas together into a broad conceptual model. More specific propositions concerning the business purposes that might be expected in the six nations represented in this study are developed in the next section from national values research.

National values and business purposes in six nations

Table 4.1 presents an overview of the quantitative national values research undertaken by Hofstede (1991), Hampden-Turner and Trompenaars (1994), Trompenaars and Hampden-Turner (1997) and Laurent (1983) that is relevant to the perception of stakeholders. These studies have employed structured questionnaires and analysed the resulting data using quantitative techniques to identify similarities and differences between individuals in different countries, in terms of their *average* orientations and predispositions within predetermined categories of values and attitudes. On occasion, the resulting values can be contradictory and difficult to interpret (Smith, 1992; Tayeb, 2000). Most of these findings, however, have received substantive corroboration (Sondegaard, 1994), but the robustness of these approaches has been widely discussed and criticized (Tayeb, 1988; Whitley, 1992).

Japan's tendency towards collectivist values, its greater long-termism, emphasis on employee welfare, its ascribing of status according to position rather than to performance and its way of integrating different modes of thinking rather than adopting 'one best way' all point towards managers holding the needs of a range of stakeholders in mind – including employees within the firm and groups outside. A particularistic way of thinking, however, would indicate no general rules: managers will determine for themselves the stakeholders for whom they

Table 4.1 National values orientations and expectations for stakeholders, aims and time frames in six nations

Values areas	Stakeholders	Aims	Time frames
Japan expectation:	**Owners and employees**	**Diverse, employee welfare**	**Long term**
Based on:	Collectivist (T)	Communitarian (T)	Long term (H)
	Masculine (H)	Masculine (H)	Long horizon (T)
	Task orientation (T)	Task orientation (T)	
		Achieved status (T)	
		Integrational; particularist (T)	
Germany expectation:	**Unclear proposition**	**Profit and growth and other**	**Medium term**
Based on:	Individualist (H)	Individualist (H) and (T)	No proposition (H)
	Communitarian (T)	Communitarian (T)	Long/mixed
	Masculine (H)	Masculine (H)	propositions (T)
	Task orientation (T)	Task orientation (T)	
	No social role (L)	Achieved status (T)	
		No social role (L)	
		Integrational, universalist (T)	
US expectation:	**Owners**	**Profit**	**Short term**
Based on:	Individualist (H) and (T)	Individualist (H) and (T)	Short term (H)
	No social role (L)	No social role (L)	Short horizon (T)
	Masculine (H)	Masculine (H)	
	Task orientation (T)	Task orientation (T)	
		Achieved status (T)	
		No social role (L)	
		Analytical, universalist (T)	
UK expectation:	**Owners**	**Profit**	**Short term**
Based on:	Individualist (H) and (T)	Individualist (H) and (T)	Short term (H)
	No social role (L)	No social role (L)	Short horizon (T)
	Masculine (H)	Masculine (H)	
		Achieved status (T)	
		No social role (L)	
		Analytical, universalist (T)	
France expectation:	**Mainly owners**	**Unclear**	**Medium term**
Based on:	Individualist (H)	Individualist (H)	No proposition (H)
	Communitarian (T)	Communitarian (T)	Long/medium (H)
	Task orientation (T)	Task orientation (T)	
	Social role (L)	Ascribed status (T)	
		Social role (L)	
		Integrational; particularist (T)	
The Netherlands expectation:	**Owners and employees**	**Diverse, including profit and employee welfare**	**Long term**
Based on:	Individualist (H) and (T)	Individualist (H) and (T)	Long term (H)
	Feminine (H)	Feminine (H)	Mixed horizons (T)
	Person orientation (T)	Person orientation (T)	
	No social role (L)	No social role (L)	
		Universalist (T)	

Sources: Derived from Hofstede (1991) (H); Laurent (1983) (L); Trompenaars and Hampden-Turner (1997) (T)

believe the firm exists. France is also integrational and particularist which, together with French social orientation, points towards a variety of stakeholders, even though owners will predominate due to its task orientation. The values data for Germany give mixed propositions, which themselves are not strong. Only weak propositions are possible for the USA, but its strong individualism, universalism and analytical way of thinking point towards owners being the stakeholders that will be the main concern of managers. For the UK, the propositions are unequivocal: owners emerge as the dominant stakeholders and this will be generally accepted in the country. The expectations are entirely different for the Netherlands, however: feminine and person orientations point towards a wide range of stakeholders, particularly those within the firms, such as the employees.

A similar range of propositions is evident concerning business aims. Those for Japan are again clear: strategic aims can be expected. By contrast, financial aims would generally be expected in the UK and USA, with the achievement orientation in the USA generating a particular focus on financial performance. The values research gives an unclear picture of what might be expected in France, but for Germany, although the propositions are mixed, medium-term profit and other performance might be expected. The expectations for the Netherlands are unambiguous; the aims will be diverse and will include the welfare of staff and others. As regards the time frames of business, direct and clear expectations emerge. Long-termism is expected in Japan and the Netherlands while short-termism is associated with the UK and the USA. France and Germany appear to lie midway between these two groups.

Research methodology

The examination and analysis of cases drawn from comparable businesses in different countries were chosen as the appropriate research approach for this study as it explores conceptual linkages between complex phenomena (Eisenhardt, 1989; Yin, 1993). Seven cases were studied in total and these were drawn from two industries; four of the sample firms produced vehicle components (from Japan, Germany, the USA and the UK) and there were three electronics firms (from France, the Netherlands and the UK).

Both of the industries included in the empirical work are global in nature and can be classified as medium to high technology activities. The choice of industries to study reflects the aims of the research: to explore whether institutional factors may intervene between national values and the purposes that firms pursue. One industry, the vehicle components industry, is dominated by large multinational firms from different parts of the world, and it is one of the few such industries that is sufficiently open to enable the data to be gathered for this type of research. The other has many medium-sized, owner-managed firms in different parts of the world. External influencing factors were similar in each industry, as the firms studied within each are rivals with the same internationally based customers.

The firms and the people chosen for interview were matched within the groups as much as possible and particularly by size and organizational type. The respondents in both industries were central to strategic decision-making in their firms. In vehicle components, executives in the large MNEs charged with the coordination of strategic investment decisions were interviewed. The owner managers themselves were interviewed in the medium-sized owner-managed firms studied in the electronics industry.

Data were gathered in two-hour semi-structured interviews in each case. These focused on the strategic issues underlying the future development of the businesses concerned. Each interviewee was given an assurance of full confidentiality. In the findings, the British companies are referred to as Britcom (for the vehicle components company), and Britelec (for the electronics company) and, following the same pattern, the other firms are referred to below as Japcom, Americom, Deutschcom, Franelec and Nethelec.

Interviews were conducted in English and were tape recorded and subsequently transcribed. Protocol analysis was used to analyse the transcribed interviews and notes. The specific propositions, already discussed, were assessed by reference to the interview transcripts and notes (Ericsson and Simon, 1985). Within the aims and context of this study, the method used was as rigorous as possible (Harris, 2000).

Research findings

MNEs in the vehicle components industry

Deutschcom and Japcom barely mentioned the needs of their shareholders and the attention of both was on the future viability of the company as a whole, implying a diversity of important stakeholders. As Japcom noted: 'I think stakeholders these days know they are customers, employees and I think the corporation has to give lots of obligations to these stakeholders.' Both, however, were having to pay greater attention to financial results, though in both cases, these were still relatively unimportant. Germany's high achievement orientation and low 'societal role' for business did not appear to generate an ownership focus in Deutschcom. Unlike the case of Deutschcom (where the propositions were mixed), the findings for Japcom closely corresponded with the quite definitive propositions: there appeared to be various stakeholders and lifetime employees were specifically mentioned as an important stakeholder group which was given special attention.

Owners appeared to be more important for Britcom and Americom, in line with the propositions. They were, however, perceived in different ways. Britcom's managers were attempting to achieve strategic success in the face of short-term profit requirements that they thought their shareholders demanded. They were here, perhaps, confirming a high egalitarian value orientation within a legal and institutional structure that obliged them only to take their shareholders' interests into account. Americom's managers perceived their owners to need both performance within a two-year time frame *and* strategic development within a 15-year horizon.

The aims in both Deutschcom and Japcom appeared to be long-term strategic viability, growth and success, strongly confirming the hypotheses concerning broader stakeholder interests and longer-term, strategic objectives. Neither expressed their aims in a direct, clear or quantifiable way: they were multifaceted. Both felt a need to pay increasing attention to financial performance but this remained unimportant in comparison with longer-term strategic success.

The customer was the critical trigger for the strategic investment discussed with Deutschcom and the gains were regarded as being mainly non-quantifiable. Though they were not quantified, they were considered sufficiently important to justify the investment: 'Our standing will be much better. This is more important than the cost gain. Our customers know they can order small orders and that we can produce them....The time gain, which is quite a lot, could not be evaluated.'

Japcom's executive argued that his company, like most in Japan, had to take wider stakeholder interests into account:

> In Japanese enterprise automobile manufacturers, they have been in Europe for maybe a quarter of a century, losing money. I think it is only recently they started to consider that as an investment. Most recently, and it's only in the last five years, they started to make some profit. And their stakeholders didn't object to anything like that.

Achieving a good 'position in the industry' and also with particular original equipment manufacturer (OEM) customers was the predominant aim in Japcom and this was seen as necessary in order to realize long-term aspirations:

> Again, it's not just the return on capital that is our only criteria. Another good consideration has to be keeping up with this evolution in the automotive industry. To be a successful automotive component supplier you have to be a global corporation. You have to be a partner. I mean automotive companies like Nissan, Toyota, Volkswagen and Mercedes etc. And what they are looking for as a reliable component supplier is someone who can supply and can meet the requirement everywhere in the global arena....The bigger issue is are we going to be keeping up with the business, and surviving in the long term?

Strong, though less unequivocal findings emerged in Britcom and Americom. Britcom was the shortest-term and the most profit focused of all the firms, with stringent return on assets criteria for all investment decisions that were rarely reduced for longer-term strategic considerations: 'On top of this we have a growth target of 10–15 per cent a year on earnings per share. This is a permanent thing. We always want growth.' The managers, however, were also influenced by longer-term strategic criteria that underlay their decisions – in effect, they were pursuing strategic development subject to minimum financial profits and growth targets on a one- to five-year horizon. Americom's executive was even clearer on the need to integrate strategic and financial targets:

> We had those issues with [our Japanese partner], so I think we better be real clear on the strategic objectives and make sure they are compatible. In the financials of the business, your financials need to follow the form of the business. I mean if you get financials that are unbalanced with the business objectives, we are putting in all the money but you are taking all the product, or vice versa, you want to be sensitive to that.... In practice, we don't want to alter the leverage of the company too much, we don't want to give money away or whatever; but at the end of the day there is an internal market and we reckon we can get a lot more than 15 per cent and that justifies us going up on the internal rate of return.... We tend to force ourselves to make strategic decisions on direction, but we are not using 15 per cent as a cut-off.... We have certain decisions that we make using the red, yellow, green analysis where our hurdle rate is much higher.... It is 50 per cent for non-strategic investments.

A more mixed pattern emerged in Americom than Britcom. Like Britcom, the managers aimed to achieve high return on assets (adjusted for risk) over a one- to two-year horizon. They were also, however, continually refining their strategic vision for the company, and were flexible about achieving short-term profit targets in order to realize long-term (15-year) strategic ones. Short-term financial performance could be compromised if it was agreed that 'objective' analysis of the quantified long-term gains exceeded the short-term benefits forgone.

Medium-sized electronics firms

This section considers the responses of the owner managers of medium-sized firms in the electronics industry to allow comparisons and contrasts to be drawn with the previous institutional context of large multinationals where ownership and control were separated. Once again, the stakeholders are considered first to see what interests the owners of the firms recognized in their thinking about the future of their firms.

The owner manager of Nethelec did not readily regard himself as a stakeholder, and made no connection between his own life ambitions and the future of the firm. In discussing the firm's success, he referred to all those working in it, as well as to some outsiders who had strong relationships with the business. When discussing the long-term future, he did not connect the issue of his own retirement to what the firm would do and this appeared to be partly because discussions concerning the future of the firm were normally held with the supervisory board of the firm, which included some senior managers, employees and external supervisors.

Franelec's owner had created his businesses so that he could achieve his personal life vision of becoming a well-off artist and the intended beneficiaries of the success of the business were himself and his family. Similarly, the owner of Britelec recognized himself and his family as the stakeholders and no others. Both Britelec and Franelec had created their businesses so that they could achieve personal life visions: for them, their families were the most important intended other beneficiaries of its success beyond themselves.

None of the owner managers interviewed recognized groups within the wider society, or even the wider society itself, as stakeholders in their firms. This is in contrast to the indications of the national values research for France presented in Table 4.1, where some indications of communitarianism and of managers believing that they have a high social role suggested that social goals might have featured in the thinking of Franelec.

The implications of the national values matched the case study findings to a limited degree in the Dutch case, but did not distinguish between the French and British cases. The conceptualization of the owner as stakeholder can go beyond the individual, with recognition of family and other close friends as primary stakeholders whether or not they are involved in the business. Franelec recognized his family as stakeholders, even though they were not involved in the business. Britelec's family was involved in the business and family members were recognized as stakeholders. Nethelec recognized no family or friends in this way, but he has established a different institutional structure within his firm, with a supervisory board (quite normal for medium-sized privately owned Dutch firms but rare in the UK and France) among whom recognition of personal and family interests may not be acceptable.

Franelec's goals were directly and explicitly related to his own ambitions for himself, and were clearly to make money. Contrary to implications of the values research, he showed no desire for power or influence, asserting his individuality through his intentions to be an artist. He planned to float his business on a bourse as soon as possible:

> I do not want to run a business for the rest of my life, this is just a stage, an interesting stage. What I want is to be a sculptor, but not a poor one. Antibes is

no place to have no money, and we, my wife and my family, are comfortable here. The business is being sold as soon as possible on the NASDAQ.

Britelec, like Franelec, intended to float his business on a stock exchange as soon as possible: '...ultimately the business will be very successful when I've made a lot of money and I mean when I've made several million...then I can retire'. 'Masculine' goals of achievement and acquisition of wealth are clearly visible here, with an explicit focus on the rapid acquisition of wealth for personal material gain: '...it will be very valuable for the company itself to be able to raise money on the flotation, no question, that's why you do it...for the founders to get some money back for all their hard work'.

Nethelec was completely different. He made little reference to goals or aspirations, and never in a personal way. He was concerned with developing good relationships between individuals, and with the learning and growth both of his employees and of his distributors and customers. His was a 'long-term orientation'. He called this 'good business'. For Nethelec, developing a secure, substantial and harmonious organization went beyond the employees of the business:

> ...These distributors are very important to us...we try to look after them.... I worry about them.... We take great care to help the distributors do their business. We have got to know them very well, we bring them here to the factory, and entertain them and look after them regularly for periods when they stay here with us.

Clear differences were seen in the CEOs' overall business aims, and these largely, but not completely, corresponded to a priori expectations of national values. These differences are associated with their fundamental beliefs and life purposes, the kinds of aspects with which values are most associated. Whereas Britelec's aims were highly focused (around financial gain for himself), the aims of Franelec and particularly of Nethelec were more diffuse. For Nethelec, the main aim could be described as 'the growth of the organization as a whole', and included relationships within and outside the firm. Franelec also showed some modest concern for status, in the broadest sense, through his concern that the outside world should perceive him to be doing something worthwhile.

All these owner-managed firms were working to fairly short time horizons. Contrary to some of the values research expectations, Franelec was not concerned about the long-term development of his business. He was seeking a new distribution deal to expand sales massively and a new subcontract deal to cut manufacturing costs, but this was to enable the business to be sold on NASDAQ as soon as possible. Britelec, like Franelec, was also looking to sell his business as soon as possible, and the following quotation illustrates his time frame: 'It may be that you can't sell out for two or three years after that because you'll be locked in various ways but that's okay, I can handle that.'

Nethelec, like the others, needed to make significant and rapid changes in the face of industry pressures, and this clearly limited any long-termism. Some changes were being made gradually. For example, a decision to move his subcontract manufacture away from the Netherlands, while it was a necessary response to the dynamic changes in the industry, had taken four years to debate and organize. He referred continually to building up his firm's capabilities through training, staff development and establishing new offices. There was one 'transforming deal' in the offing, involving a merger with another firm. While Nethelec's pattern of business development had been steady growth, he expressed impatience with his employees and their inability to get things done quickly: 'I try to convince them to look abroad rather than in the Netherlands, to make comparisons between different subcontractors, and to see if things are in control. This is difficult... our people do not shift themselves enough... they have to be kicked...'

Discussion

Table 4.2 summarizes the congruence between the expectations arising from the national values research and the findings from the interview data. Some clear patterns emerge. The clearest pattern is found within the large firm environment of the vehicle components industry. The respondents' expressions of beliefs concerning the key aspects studied – stakeholders, aims and time frames – correspond remarkably closely to what might have been expected from the national values research. In the Japanese and German cases, the perceived stakeholders were more diverse, the aims more diffuse and the time frames were longer. The American and British had narrower views of the relevant stakeholders, more focused aims and shorter-term orientations.

The results from the group of owner managers did not provide such a clear pattern. These entrepreneurial types were driven mainly by their own interests and dreams that they had enshrined in the organizations that they had created. They saw themselves as the main stakeholders. This would have been expected in Britain, but less so in the Netherlands. The results regarding time frames are more surprising. The Netherlands appears as Europe's 'long-term' nation in the values research, but this is much less evident in the case examined here. Nethelec's environment, the rapidly changing world of high technological electronics, dictated the owner manager's concern with the immediate future, although his employees were not well attuned to the demands this entailed.

It was only in their aims that the owner managers of the medium-sized electronics firms revealed orientations that were remarkably close to the patterns

Table 4.2   Congruence between national values and case study observations

Case	Stakeholders	Aims	Time frames
Vehicle components			
Deutschcom:	*Some congruence*: company: owners not mentioned	*Some congruence*: strategic viability, firm growth. Finance	*Strong congruence*: undefined long future
Japcom:	*Strong congruence*: 'the company as a whole'; employees	*Strong congruence*: a strong strategic position	*Strong congruence*: lifetime employment and management
Americom:	*Strong congruence*: owners predominate	*Some congruence*: profits, growth and strategic development	*Unclear*: profits: 1–2 years; growth: 15 years
Britcom:	*Strong congruence*: owners predominate	*Strong congruence*: profits and growth of profits	*Some congruence*: 1–5 years overtly, managers subverted
Electronics			
Britelec:	*Some congruence*: owners mainly, family also	*Strong congruence*: profits and growth of profits	*Some congruence*: 3 years
Franelec:	*Little congruence*: owners only	*Some congruence*: profits and growth of profits	*Little congruence*: 3 years
Nethelec:	*Little congruence*: owners predominate	*Strong congruence*: profits, growth, strategic development	*Little congruence*: profits: 3–5 years; growth: 5–10 years

that might have been anticipated from the national values research. The French and the British were unambiguously mercurial but the Dutch respondent was less so; he was more 'feminine', more people oriented and showed more concern for the strategic development of his firm over time.

This Dutch owner manager, like many other small firm owners in the Netherlands, had chosen to construct an institutional structure akin to those that elsewhere might normally be seen in larger firms where ownership is separated from management. But why should so many Dutch firms do this? And why should French, British and American firms not do so? The answer may well reside in values, as well as, quite possibly, in laws and customs.

A phenomenon that anthropologists have highlighted for decades is relevant here, namely that institutions reflect values and values, institutions. The richness of human behaviour in societies, our cultures, is acting to usurp the rigour that management researchers seek in separating independent from dependent variables. Institutions and values begin to appear as both, in complex ways. The use of national values as data that represent independent variable measures of orientations that may predict behaviours begins to look more problematic.

Conclusions

The exploratory research reported here produced some interesting results from the evidence provided by seven firms in the two industries studied. Findings for the cases which were based on the responses of executives in multinational companies subject to international financial markets mostly match the predictions generated by the national values studies of Hofstede, Laurent and Trompenaars which were derived from investigating the same types of large firms. The enduring popularity of this work on national values, despite its age and the criticisms made of it, becomes a little more understandable. The evidence provided here suggests that national values do have concrete, tangible consequences in terms of the business behaviour manifested when making strategic decisions. This is of real consequence both to researchers and managers. To researchers, it suggests some concrete values variables that may be used in studies that aim to find more confident, generalizable associations between values and behaviour. Such behaviour, however, is not apparent in overt or public data: it is subtle and revealed as personal priorities and ways of thinking that require appropriate in-depth methods of data gathering.

Aspects of this exploratory research were inevitably imperfect. Complete matching of the businesses was impossible, interview interactions can never be value free, and different interpretations are always possible within the coding process (Harris, 2000). Empirical generalization will require the analysis of data from larger numbers of appropriate and matched businesses (Harris, 2000), and it is planned to extend this study to include more firms. For managers, it reveals that the individual values that they are familiar with, in their everyday business dealings, have national dimensions that will place new demands on them when making strategic decisions in multinational environments. A surprising result is that, in spite of globalization in the vehicle components industry, managers' perceived stakeholders and their aims still reflect underlying national values. Such findings merit further research.

The investigation into the owner-managed firms – equally subject to globalization in competitive terms, but less subject to international capital markets – suggests a quite different picture. Their strategic behaviour is *not* predictable from national values research in quite the same manner. This is important because most values research has been based on studies of managers in large companies, mostly with outside shareholders. Less attention has been paid to the values held in private firms in different countries, which are by far the most numerous type of firm worldwide, or to the values of business leaders rather than salaried managers. This study confirms that national values findings are of some assistance in predicting the aims of owner managers, but not their views on stakeholders or their time frames.

Many important similarities and differences in strategic behaviour between countries may be attributable to the institutional and ownership structures of firms, or the characteristics of those who manage them, as new institutional theory would indicate (for example, DiMaggio and Powell, 1983; Scott, 1995; Kostova and Roth, 2002). The values research can lead international business researchers and managers to expectations that are unlikely to be fulfilled in practice in many areas. Further, we begin to see interactions between institutions and national values that are complex and which can generate apparently inconsistent and surprising outcomes. The need for further empirical research in this context thus appears urgent, but the difficulty of doing so, and in particular of separating institutional from national values effects, has been brought sharply into focus.

When engaging in international business by meeting, discussing, negotiating and agreeing with managers in other countries, international managers can prepare themselves for different purposes behind business abroad, and in this, a knowledge of national values gleaned from the popular books of Geert Hofstede and Fons Trompenaars might well help to indicate where these differences might lie. The case examples shown in this chapter help to illustrate how they may be manifested in practice. These differences may be deeply rooted and unlikely to change, and will need to be accommodated by being culturally aware if successful business relationships are to develop over time. But this study shows that international managers should not pay too much attention to the scriptures of the 'values' researchers when preparing for these interactions. The data used by these researchers came from salaried executives in large companies. This does not mean that cultural differences are unimportant when dealing with owner managers in smaller firms. It means that they are more difficult to understand and to deal with on the basis of present research, and that building successful business relations across nations will take time and cultural sensitivity.

References

Albert, M. (1994) 'Strategy Styles and Different Blends of Capitalism', keynote address to the 14th Annual Conference of the Strategic Management Society, September (Paris: Groupe HEC).

Ansoff, H.I. (1965) *Corporate Strategy* (New York: McGraw-Hill).

Berle, A.A. and G.C. Means (1932) *The Modern Corporation and Private Property* (New York: Transaction Publishers).

Calori, R. and P. de Woot (1994) *A European Management Model, Beyond Diversity* (Hemel Hempstead: Prentice Hall).

Carr, C. and C. Tomkins (1998) 'Context, Culture and the Role of the Finance Function in Strategic Decisions. A Comparative Analysis of Britain, Germany, the USA and Japan', *Management Accounting Research*, 9 (1), 213–39.

DiMaggio, P.J. and W.W. Powell (1983) *The New Institutionalism in Organizational Analysis* (Chicago, Ill.: University of Chicago Press).

Eisenhardt, K.M. (1989) 'Building Theories from Case Study Research', *Academy of Management Review*, 14 (4), 532–50.

Ericsson, K. and H. Simon (1985) *Protocol Analysis* (New York: Sage).

Fama, E.F. (1980) 'Agency Problems and the Theory of the Firm', *Journal of Political Economy*, 88, 375–90.

Hampden-Turner, C. and F. Trompenaars (1994) *The Seven Cultures of Capitalism* (London: Pitakus).

Harris, S. (2000) 'Reconciling Positive and Interpretive in International Management Research: a Native Category Approach', *International Business Review*, 9 (6), 755–70.

Hayes, R.H. and W.J. Abernathy (1980) 'Managing Our Way to Economic Decline', *Harvard Business Review*, 58 (4), 67–77.

Hayes, R.H. and J.A. Limprecht (1982) 'Germany's World Class Industrial Competitors', *Harvard Business Review*, 60 (November/December), 42–56.

Hickson, D.J. (ed.) (1993) *Management in Western Europe: Society, Culture and Organization in Twelve Nations* (Berlin: de Gruyter).

Hickson, D.J. and D.S. Pugh (1995) *Management Worldwide: the Impact of Societal Culture on Organisations around the Globe* (London: Penguin).

Hofstede, G. (1991) *Culture and Organisation* (London: McGraw-Hill).

Isabella, L.A. (1990) 'Evolving Interpretations as a Change Unfolds: How Managers Construe Organizational Events', *Academy of Management Journal*, 33 (1), 7–41.

Jacobs, M.T. (1991) *Short-term America: Causes and Cures of our Business Myopia* (Cambridge, Mass.: Harvard Business School Press).

King, W.R. and D.I. Cleland (1978) *Strategic Planning and Policy* (New York: Van Nostrand Reinhold).

Kostova, T. and K. Roth (2002) 'Adoption of an Organizational Practice by Subsidiaries of Multinational Corporations: Institutional and Relational Effects', *Academy of Management Journal*, 45 (1), 215–33.

Laurent, A. (1983) 'The Cultural Diversity of Western Conceptions of Management', *International Studies of Management and Organization*, 13 (1), 75–96.

Laurent, A. (1986) 'The Cross-cultural Puzzle of International Human Resource Management', *Human Resource Management*, 25 (1), 91–102.

Lawrence, P. and V. Edwards (2000) *Management in Western Europe* (Basingstoke: Macmillan).

Lundberg, C.C. (1985) 'On the Feasibility of Cultural Intervention in Organization', in P.J. Frost et al. (eds), *Organizational Culture* (Beverly Hills, Calif.: Sage), pp. 169–85.

McTaggart, J.T., P.W. Kontes and M.C. Mankins (1994) *The Value Imperative: Managing for Superior Returns* (New York: Free Press).

Pascale, R.T. and A.G. Athos (1981) *The Art of Japanese Management* (New York: Simon and Schuster).

Pedersen, T. and S. Thomsen (1997) 'European Patterns of Corporate Ownership', *Journal of International Business Studies*, 28 (4), 759–78.

Pedersen, T. and S. Thomsen (2003) 'Ownership Structure and Value of the Largest European Firms: the Importance of Owner Identity', *Journal of Management and Governance*, 7 (1), 27–55.

Rappaport, A. (1986) *Creating Shareholder Value: the New Standard for Business Performance* (New York: Free Press).

Schein, E.H. (1985) *Organizational Culture and Leadership* (San Francisco: Jossey Bass).

Schneider, S.C. (1988) 'National vs. Corporate Culture: Implications for Human Resource Management', *Human Resource Management*, 27 (2), 231–46.

Schulze, W.S., M.H. Lubatkin and R.N. Dino (2003) 'Exploring the Agency Consequences of Ownership Dispersion among the Directors of Private Family Firms', *Academy of Management Journal*, 46 (2), 179–95.

Scott, R. (1995) *Institutions and Organizations* (Thousand Oaks, Calif.: Sage Publications).

Smith, P.B. (1992) 'Organizational Behaviour and National Cultures', *British Journal of Management*, 3 (1), 39–51.

Sondergaard, M. (1994) 'Research Note: Hofstede's Consequences: a Study of Reviews, Citations and Replications', *Organization Studies*, 5 (3), 447–56.

Tayeb, M. (1988) *Organizations and National Culture: a Comparative Analysis* (London: Sage Publications).

Tayeb, M. (2000) 'Conducting Research across Cultures – Drawbacks and Obstacles', in *Proceedings of the Annual Conference of the British Academy of Management*, September (Edinburgh: British Academy of Management).

Thomsen, S. and T. Pedersen (2000) 'Ownership Structure and Economic Performance in the Largest European Companies', *Strategic Management Journal*, 21 (6), 689–705.

Trompenaars, F. and C. Hampden-Turner (1997) *Riding the Waves of Culture: Understanding Cultural Diversity in Business* (2nd edn) (London: Nicholas Brearly).

Whitley, R. (ed.) (1992) *European Business Systems: Firms and Markets in their National Context* (London: Sage).

Whitley, R. (1999) *Divergent Capitalisms: the Social Structuring and Change of Business Systems* (Oxford: Oxford University Press).

Wright, P., M. Kroll, A. Lado and B. V. Ness (2002) 'The Structure of Ownership and Corporate Acquisition Strategies', *Strategic Management Journal*, 23 (1), 41–53.

Yin, R.K. (1993) *Applications of Case Study Research* (London: Sage).

5

A New Perspective on Parenting Spin-offs for Cluster Formation

Manuel P. Ferreira, William Hesterly and Ana Teresa Tavares

Introduction

The factors propelling the competitiveness of industry clusters have been subject to extensive research. While these factors are reasonably understood, the conditions that lead to the emergence and evolution of clusters still warrant further examination. This chapter proposes that the emergence and development of at least some clusters are endogenously driven by the generation of new insider entrepreneurial spin-offs[1] from incumbent firms. The specific conditions that lead to spin-off opportunities are beyond the scope of this chapter, but because these opportunities exist – for example because of technological or market changes or employee dissatisfaction – new firms will be founded. The majority of these spin-offs shape the cluster's birth, configuration, technological specialization and evolution by remaining in the same region as the parent firm (Arthur, 1990; Zander, 2003). Hence, knowledge of the genesis of inter-firm ties in a cluster may permit a better understanding of the formation and evolution of the inter-firm organizational forms that prevail in clusters. This line of enquiry builds on recent research on how the emergence and growth of clusters are essentially an entrepreneurial process and on research studying entrepreneurship as a regional phenomenon associated with unusual innovativeness and dynamism (for example Saxenian, 1994; Zander, 2003).

Clusters represent a pool of available resources (for example human resources and suppliers) upon which new firms can draw and so they are important in the founding of new firms (Marshall, 1920; Arthur, 1990; Porter, 1998). Moreover, clusters ease the identification of opportunities for firms to 'pursue collective strategies in conjunction with the competitive strategies of the individual members' (Gulati, 1998, p. 305). Clusters also facilitate the identification of new opportunities because clients are likely to look at firms in the cluster for specific technological expertise. Finally, the cluster makes the development of the entrepreneur's support network easier because the entrepreneur's pre-existing relationships with other firms in the cluster lower entry barriers and increase access to intangible resources such as business expertise (Saxenian, 1994).

The theme of this chapter is twofold: first, it proposes that clusters evolve endogenously through entrepreneurial spin-offs and second, it explores the characteristics of leader firms (here called flagships) and their role in clusters. The idea of endogenous evolution primarily serves to highlight the relationships between the new spin-offs and parent firms and other offspring and how such ties may carry substantial networks benefits. These parent–progeny (Klepper, 2001; Phillips, 2002) and progeny–siblings relationships can be crucial to overcome the potential liabilities of newness and smallness (Stinchcombe, 1965; Hannan and Freeman, 1977) and the absence of legitimacy (Carroll, 1984) often characterizing small and new spin-offs. They increase the likelihood that the spin-offs will be successful as they help to identify opportunities and secure start-up resources (Singh et al., 1986; Oviatt and McDougall, 1995; Higgins and Gulati, 2003). Hence, while contributing to the research on the evolution of clusters as a function of entrepreneurial activity and to the literature on the value of networks in supporting entrepreneurial dynamism and success, the chapter shows that some leader firms actually have a primary role in cluster evolution because these are the firms that will gestate more, and more successful, entrepreneurial spin-offs. The leaders are parent firms that generate a larger number of spin-offs because they offer greater network benefits to their offspring. Moreover, leader firms should be easily identifiable because they are larger, well-performing, deeply embedded and extensively connected higher-status central firms.

Understanding industry clusters may be important for the location decisions of multinational corporations (MNCs). MNCs increasingly seek knowledge from industry clusters (Tallman et al., 2004) to augment their own knowledge capabilities (Tallman and Fladmoe-Lindquist, 2002). As much of the knowledge accessed is location-bound, it requires a fair degree of local embeddedness for effective absorption. Issues such as the understanding of inter-firm dynamics in the relevant cluster, the extent to which networks of firms in the cluster are more closed or open and the patterns of inter-firm knowledge flows are essential aspects that require scrutiny by MNCs. By and large, MNCs may understand these issues by studying the genesis of the ties and configurations of firms in the cluster.

The remainder of this chapter reviews literature on cluster dynamism through entrepreneurial action. A model termed 'motherhood' is then advanced which is distinct from the traditional parent–progeny literature and is based on the social network benefits that some leader firms offer their offspring. The chapter concludes with a discussion of cluster evolution, implications for theory and policy, and directions for future research.

Clusters and entrepreneurship

The focus on clusters highlights spin-off activity because clusters tend to be rich in innovative activity and inter-firm collaboration (Porter, 1998, 2000; Sandee and Rietveld, 2001). The entrepreneurial activity and the pattern of entrepreneurial spin-offs in a cluster highlight the potential network benefits of a parent–progeny model led by one, or a few, leader firms.

Clusters defined

An industry cluster can be seen as 'a geographically bounded concentration of similar, related or complementary businesses, with active channels for business transactions, communications and dialogue, that share specialized infrastructures, labor markets and services, and that are faced with common opportunities and threats' (Rosenfeld, 1997, p. 10). Porter (1998, p. 78) defined clusters as a 'geographic concentration of interconnected companies, and institutions in a particular field' in a bounded geographical area with unusual competitive success. Hence, clusters are characterized by the concentration of horizontally and verti-cally interlinked firms in a delimited geographic location. Saxenian (1990, 1994) further argued that the region's relational networks tie together individuals, firms and institutions (see also Sandee and Rietveld, 2001) and that these regions have a competitive advantage that emerges from their local network structures, local culture and specialized institutional framework. According to Tallman et al. (2004), the binding glue among clustered firms is their shared architectural knowledge, which, following Marshall (1920), is 'in the air'.

From a strategic and managerial stance, it is important to assess how much of the knowledge within the cluster can be accessed at a distance (using electronic means or through inter-firm cooperative agreements, for instance) and how much it requires co-location and hence FDI. While the traditional view has assumed that mere co-location would suffice to absorb some of the knowledge that 'is in the air', it seems more reasonable to believe that such capture will not be viable without an appropriate degree of local embeddedness partly due to already existing inter-firm ties. That is, insider firms seem to have an advantage over outsiders and new entrants (Phillips, 2002; Garvin, 1983).

Entrepreneurial activity

'Entrepreneurship' is defined here as the identification and exploitation of previously undetected or unexplored opportunities that lead to the creation of new organizations (Gartner, 1988; Hitt et al., 2001). 'Entrepreneurial spin-offs' are those new firms, typically also small, that are created by employees who identify an opportunity for brokerage between two separate firms or a new technological or market opportunity and thus exit the parent firm to create their own business (Garvin, 1983; Klepper, 2001; Phillips, 2002).

This chapter does not address the causes of entrepreneurial activity or why some employees decide to exit the parent firm (see Cooper, 1985; Brittain and Freeman, 1986; Wiggins, 1995; Klepper, 2001 for a review of these motives). However, it does depart from the stylized fact that each exit corresponds to an opportunity detected for an entrepreneurial endeavour. Existing studies on spin-offs and new firm formation found that in some instances employees exit their parent firm and risk setting up their own business either with the expectation of a greater financial reward or due to dissatisfaction in the workplace, perhaps induced by the parent's inability to exploit an emerging opportunity (Cooper, 1985; Klepper, 2001; Phillips, 2002). This chapter also does not support the reductionist approach suggested in studies that view entrepreneurial spin-offs as a 'brain drain' – it is fairly clear across many European clusters that spin-offs do not all cut the ties to their parent; it would destroy the social fabric that underlies social networks in the cluster if they did.

Multiple factors may account for some regions favouring entrepreneurship (Aldrich and Wiedenmayer, 1993) and being more innovative than others. The cluster's environment has specific social, cultural, relational, infrastructural, institutional, economic, financial and technological idiosyncrasies that are hard to generalize. Entrepreneurial activity is likely to be intensive in clusters because of the relative abundance of specialized institutions as well as public and private agents (Porter, 2000). Entrepreneurial activity in clusters is also eased by traded and non-traded interdependencies (Storper, 1995) and shared architectural knowledge (Tallman et al., 2004) that facilitates the flow of people, information, know-how and business among firms. Despite being hard to quantify, these benefits have been identified reasonably clearly through qualitative work in various locations (Saxenian, 1994; Porter, 1998). MNCs also seem to search these locations particularly to benefit from this pool of favourable physical and institutional infrastructure and the knowledge that evolves idiosyncratically across such a geographic space (Kogut, 1991).

Genealogies and family trees

In examining the evolution of clusters, some scholars have advanced the importance of parenting processes (Klepper, 2001) and identified firms' family trees showing how many firms in clusters originated from one, or a few, parent firms (Saxenian, 1990). Phillips (2002) presents, to our knowledge, the most recent study on firm genealogies and specifically the effect of progeny on both offspring and parents' survival. Yet many of the existing studies (for example Brittain and Freeman, 1980; Carroll, 1984; Hannan and Freeman, 1989; Phillips, 2002) focused on the transfer of parental organizational practices and forms, skills, routines and blueprints to the new firm, and how this transfer impacted the likelihood of success of both parent and offspring. Essentially, these studies suggest that new firms' capabilities are determined by prior history and work experience of the founder in the parent firm. This history and experience is leveraged when identifying new business opportunities and managing operations (Shane, 2000; Burton et al., 2002) and has a deep impact on their survival (Helfat and Lieberman, 2002).

Firm genealogies are the outcome of successive parenting processes. Hendry et al. (2000) noted that clusters might begin through the presence of a firm that generates spin-offs (see also Arthur, 1990). In fact, there is much anecdotal evidence that in several clusters, many of the firms are genealogically tied to one (original) firm. For example, Dalum (1995) noted that most firm genealogies were tied to one manufacturer of offshore radio equipment in a radio communications cluster in Denmark. Saxenian (1994) described how, in Silicon Valley, many employees exited Fairchild in what she termed the 'family tree' of Fairchild Semiconductors. The offspring that originated from the Springfield Massachusetts metalworking sector (Forrant and Flynn, 1998) is yet another example of a family tree. These spin-offs tend to co-locate in proximity to the parent, possibly to avoid the burden of relocating families and moving away from social contacts and the comfort of a familiar environment (Zander, 2003).

Hence the founding of new spin-offs is a major way in which clusters emerge and evolve. As Garvin (1983, p. 3) noted, 'a high rate of new firm formation appears to have been vitally important to the success of many of our most progressive, technology-based industries'. Moreover, while it is likely that some of the new firms are insiders to the cluster (that is, founded by employees exiting incumbent firms) it is less clear which firms are more likely to gestate the greatest number of spin-offs and what the benefits are for both the spin-off and the parent of this entrepreneurial cluster activity.

Leading evolution

A more complete understanding of why clusters may emerge, expand and succeed requires an examination of the determinants of success and specifically of the entrepreneurial activity that occurs inside the cluster. In particular, several authors have noted how insider spin-off firms, which are better embedded in the social and business structure of the cluster, are likely to have an a priori advantage over other firms exogenous to the cluster. For example, Phillips (2002) noted that spin-offs are more likely than *de novo* start-ups to have trustworthy relationships with other agents, be better embedded, more cognizant of inter-firm relationships and better informed about market opportunities. Garvin (1983, p. 10) referred to the advantage of individuals currently working in the cluster compared to individuals from outside as 'intimate familiarity with the market', possibly because these individuals were socialized 'in the same country club' (Sull, 1999). Firms embedded in the cluster have advantages over outsider start-ups because they have better access to information due to their more extensive connections to other incumbent firms (Rowley et al., 2000). This should be a concern for foreign MNCs in that it may prevent them from developing ties to the local institutions, knowledge and agents required for operating in the host region. The importance of local adaptation to all firms seeking to locate in certain regions is important, but it is all the more critical the more closed are the inter-firm ties binding existing firms together. Strong ties between local agents make new entries more hazardous.

Mothering spin-offs

Parenting models of entrepreneurship and cluster growth have been identified before. The term 'motherhood' is used here to distinguish the present conceptualization from prior work on parenting processes. A parenting process such as the one proposed (see also Ferreira, 2002; Ferreira et al., 2005a, b) is based on the network benefits of (a) spinning-off from certain mother, leader firms and (b) spawning new entrepreneurial spin-offs. This conceptualization contrasts with other analyses observing the transfer of knowledge, routines, skills and procedures from the parent to spin-offs (Brittain and Freeman, 1980; Carroll, 1984; Hannan and Freeman, 1989), which often invoke path dependencies and a certain fatalism. It also contrasts with studies referring to entrepreneurial spin-offs as parasites that deplete the parent's knowledge and envisage spin-offs as a dreadful outcome. In contrast, the argument here is that the likelihood of entrepreneurial success is at least partly determined by the content and perhaps the structure of the networks of relationships spin-offs have at inception. Moreover, this chapter complements Burt's (1992) claim that entrepreneurs with a network rich in structural holes have greater chances of identifying entrepreneurial opportunities by suggesting that entrepreneurs benefit not only from their direct ties (most notably ties to the parent) but also from access to other firms that these direct ties facilitate. In this regard, the network of direct and indirect ties of the new spin-off eases entrepreneurial activity. The parenting process suggested in this chapter primarily reflects these network benefits.

The parenting variant theorized here (that is, motherhood) relates primarily to entrepreneurial activity in highly interlinked networks. Newly created spin-offs lack legitimacy, reputation and resources (Stinchcombe, 1965; Stuart et al., 1999) and need to transact with other firms to access these. However, other firms are likely to be reluctant to engage in exchanges with new spin-offs (Gulati, 1998; Hite and Hesterly, 2001; Podolny, 2001). Ties to the parent reduce these uncertainties and the costs of searching for partners and resources and provide stability to the spin-off. It is worth noting that the present focus is only on those spin-offs that maintain good relationships with the parent. The chapter does not deal with hostile spin-offs where a disgruntled employee exits and does not maintain good relationships with the parent.[2] Rather, the focus is on how the entrepreneurial spin-offs, spawned from certain leader firms, gain from reputation spillovers, identification and legitimacy. In addition, these spin-offs will probably not only gain access to the mother firm, but also to the latter's other offspring and the wider network of the mother more generally. That is, at the moment of founding, the spin-off is immediately embedded in a network that connects mother, siblings and other indirect ties which are going to be important in terms of access information, resources, markets and technologies as well as bestowing credibility, legitimacy, social endorsement and identification of opportunities (Hitt et al., 2001). As Hite and Hesterly (2001) suggest, offspring from the same parent share some sense of identification and cohesiveness between them. The motherhood process is thus based on the network advantages that insider spin-offs have in adhering to an existing network from their inception.

The motherhood conceptualization is complementary to other work on parent–progeny effects in that the technical expertise generated and the social connections established by the employees (or entrepreneurs) and the parent firm, ensure a position for the spin-offs in the parent's network, and simultaneously reduce the spin-offs' liabilities. Moreover, this perspective is complementary to the adoption of blueprints identical to those of the parent, because this mimicry also increases the legitimacy of the spin-off.

Some mother firms will gestate a higher rate of entrepreneurial spin-offs because their spin-offs have a higher likelihood of success that accrues from network benefits. For example, spin-offs from successful parents have a reputation benefit that facilitates access to finance, attracting customers and employees, interactions with local institutions and so forth. These spin-offs will also benefit from exchanging and identifying with other offspring. However, the cluster environment created by the motherhood process is likely to be averse to start-ups created by outsiders to the cluster, and they will have a lower likelihood of survival and success (Klepper, 2001).

Contrary to conventional wisdom, it is suggested that mother firms gain several benefits from nurturing new spin-offs. Entrepreneurial spin-offs reduce the parent's resource uncertainties as they are often founded as a result of the identification of a resource gap in the parent's value chain. Parent firms may devote their resources to their core activities and outsource either less important or complementary activities to spin-offs. Another benefit for the mother firm comes in the form of reduced transaction costs. The mother's exchanges with spin-off progeny are likely to involve higher mutual trust and easier interaction; as a result larger amounts of information will be exchanged, while the benefits of intertemporal cooperation due to geographical proximity possibly constrain opportunistic behaviours (Williamson, 1985). This is even more likely when inter-firm exchanges are 'regulated' by social norms derived from prior acquaintance, as it is easier to trust people (prior employees) with whom there is a previous history of interface (Burt, 1992, 1997; Gulati, 1995) and personal cohesive ties (Shah, 1998). These ties reduce uncertainty and promote trust (Granovetter, 1973; Benjamin and Poldony, 1999) and are sources of relational stability (Kale et al., 2000). Moreover, the spin-offs populate the mother's network, improving its key position in the cluster by increasing its centrality, reputation, visibility and status. Finally, spin-offs, particularly those located on the boundaries of the industry, technology and/or market, are likely to bring new technological and commercial opportunities to the mother.

The leader firms in clusters

The network benefits of a parenting model with the characteristics highlighted above, suggest that it is important to identify who are the likely leader parent firms. These are 'flagship firms' who by their characteristics and actions play a dominant role in the activity of the cluster (see also Ferreira et al., 2005a). The term 'flagship' was used by Rugman and D'Cruz (2000) and Dunning (2001) to refer to MNCs that were leaders in vertical or horizontal clusters and led other firms by coordinating and managing the value-added chain of the firms in the cluster. This terminology is adapted here to refer to flagships as firms that are more likely to generate more, and probably also more successful, entrepreneurial spin-offs. Flagships are thus mother firms that through their path (technologies, markets and businesses) shape the cluster's evolution through the gestation of entrepreneurial spin-offs that will be positioned upwards and downwards in the flagship's value chain.

The chapter will now briefly illustrate some of the major characteristics of flagship firms in the specific context of the network benefits they offer (intended or not) to their entrepreneurial spin-offs. For illustrative purposes, issues like flagships' age, size, status, centrality and connectedness are discussed here as characteristics that highlight the potential to offer social network benefits to the offspring. These characteristics may help explain how and why some firms will be more likely than others to generate more new spin-offs. By identifying some characteristics of flagship firms in the cluster, this chapter further complements existing research on the generation of entrepreneurial spin-offs that has been based essentially on the innovative ability, flexibility and supply uncertainties of the parent firms and the learning opportunities provided by the parent to the spin-off.

The age of parent firms is an important driver of their ability to generate spin-offs, but whether to be younger or older is of greater benefit is subject to debate. Younger parents were suggested to be more innovative, flexible (Phillips, 2002), adaptive (Nelson and Winter, 1982; Hannan and Freeman, 1984) and based on novel technologies (Shane, 2000; Hite and Hesterly, 2001) than comparatively older firms, and therefore to present greater opportunities for spin-offs. The traditional view that younger firms are more fertile grounds for the generation of entrepreneurial spin-offs is based on the idea that innovation activity is a sine qua non and *ex ante* condition for entrepreneurial behaviour. Not only could entrepreneurial employees detect new market niches such as unexplored supply opportunities (Cooper, 1985) but younger parents would also provide employees with more learning opportunities and with clearer models to follow when setting up their own small firms. Having less defined markets and product portfolios, lower control mechanisms, less formalization, bureaucracies and embedded routines, provides more flexibility to younger parent firms and more opportunities for spin-offs.

In the context of a motherhood process, however, it is important to see how the parent's age may influence the extent of network benefits to their spin-offs. Spin-offs from older parents could have a social capital advantage based on a positive inherited reputation, visibility and legitimacy and on the possibility of engaging in exchanges with the parent's prior (and future) offspring as well as with other firms in the parent's network. Hence spinning-off from older firms may also increase the likelihood of success of the spin-offs and this greater likelihood of success may encourage more spin-offs. In sum, it seems that younger firms may provide greater opportunities for spin-offs, but better-established mother firms may provide the most benefits for spin-offs once the social capital, legitimacy, and reputation and networking benefits are appreciated.

The size of the parent firm is another driver of its ability to generate spin-offs. Larger parent firms may offer more network benefits to their offspring than smaller firms for a variety of reasons. They can sustain the high costs of innovative endeavours that may create opportunities for entrepreneurial spin-offs (Arrow, 1983). Larger firms are also typically involved in a variety of projects, carry broader product lines and have higher production capacity that may provide entrepreneurial opportunities to detect unfulfilled activities in the parent's value chain. More important, however, are the non-trivial network-based advantages that a large parent may provide. Spin-offs from such parents have an advantage compared to spin-offs from smaller parent firms based on inherited reputation and legitimacy spillovers from the parent and also benefit from the more extensive network of ties that connects the large parent firm to other firms inside and outside the focal cluster. This perspective contrasts to Birch's (1987) and Cooper's (1985) proposal that smaller firms were more likely to generate more new spin-offs, possibly due to the learning possibilities for employees, smaller firms' supply insufficiencies, or because smaller firms provide entrepreneurs with clearer models to follow when setting up their own small firms. Instead, flagships are seen as likely to be medium to larger firms, which are also more likely to generate a higher number of new spin-off opportunities primarily because they offer better resource and network protection than smaller firms.

The status[3] and centrality[4] of parent firms may also be determining factors of the ability to generate more, and more successful, spin-offs. Central firms may occupy structural holes (Burt, 1992, 1997) when, for example, they bridge technological, geographic and/or product markets (Bonacich, 1987; Freeman, 1978; Granovetter, 1983) and connect firms that would not be tied otherwise (Brass, 1984; Burt, 1992; Hite and Hesterly, 2001). Central firms have more control over the flow of resources, privileged access to others, wider sources of information and contracts and are bound to be more innovative (Levinthal, 1997) and have higher status (Bonacich, 1987). For instance, the most central firms seem to be the innovators in Silicon Valley (Saxenian, 1994). When these firms engage in innovation projects for which they have unsatisfied resource needs, they provide opportunities for new spin-offs. Innovations developed by the parent firm that do not require distinctive resources or capabilities and are not based in complementary assets, are more likely to lead to spin-offs (Klepper, 2001).

Entrepreneurial spin-offs benefit from being generated by central, high status,[5] parent firms (Higgins and Gulati, 2003). Central firms are generally better known in the industry, have connections to firms and networks in other domestic and foreign markets (Burt, 1992) and are sought after by more and more varied potential partners. These relationships generate a larger volume of activity with new client orders that require higher production volume. Hence, not only are central firms better connected to other firms and more aware of shifts in the industry and of the competitors' moves (Gulati, 1998), but more fundamentally, spin-offs will benefit from easier access to start-up resources, greater reputation and status spillovers (Stuart, 2000; Podolny, 2001) that will ease the establishment of ties to other incumbent agents. In addition, spin-offs from more central firms are immediately incepted into an extensive network. These high-status mother firms are more likely not only to generate more spin-offs but also spin-offs that have an initial higher likelihood of survival and growth (Larson, 1992; Hite and Hesterly, 2001; Hitt et al., 2001), mainly as the mothers provide the spin-offs with the status, legitimacy and inherited reputation needed for transacting with other incumbent firms (Higgins and Gulati, 2003). These ties function as 'reputation referrals' that help others to evaluate spin-offs. Finally, if the parents are well connected and have more cooperative interactions with other firms, novel needs for recombinations of existing skills or resources (Schumpeter, 1976) may emerge and these are opportunities for new spin-offs to assume a brokerage role between firms (Burt, 1992; Walker et al., 1997). Hence, the connectedness of the mother is another possible indicator of their fertility for spin-offs.

In sum, flagships are likely to be larger, older, central, high status, and more connected parent firms. Jointly, these characteristics seem a good predictor of the ability to be a 'flagship'.

Discussion, conclusion and implications

This chapter departs substantially from previous research on clusters and entrepreneurship, especially on parent–progeny relations, by highlighting the network benefits that some parent firms provide to their entrepreneurial spin-offs. For example, while Phillips (2002) would seem to have suggested that parenting would result in negative disruptions in the parents' social structure, sense-making ability, socialization and market positioning, this chapter emphasizes the positive effects of parenting in terms of resource dependency, survival hazards, positioning in the industry, innovativeness, reputation and ability to attract the best employees. It focused on highlighting the network benefits – the social capital between parents and spin-offs, status, legitimacy and reputation spillovers – for spin-offs but also for parent firms.

A large number of new (and typically small) firms are indeed founded by employees that exit an incumbent firm to create their own businesses (Freeman, 1986; Saxenian, 1994; Hendry et al., 2000; Phillips, 2002). These entrepreneurial spin-offs need to discover ways to improve their likelihood of success. Ties to other (incumbent) firms are important vehicles of information, opportunities and market access and are crucial for the acquisition of resources necessary for the firm's survival and growth (Larson, 1992; Gulati, 1998; Hite and Hesterly, 2001; Hitt et al., 2001). Such ties provide the new firms with start-up resources, legitimacy and 'borrowed' reputation for transacting with incumbent firms (Higgins and Gulati, 2003). Thus, at the moment of founding, one of the most important assets of the entrepreneurs is the number and quality of their ties to adjoining agents and specifically, to the parents and their networks. The spin-off inherits, intendedly or perhaps more plausibly, unintendedly, from the parent not only some level of reputation, status, identification, legitimacy, but also the pool of network ties of the parent. These are ties to other offspring of the parent as well as to other firms in the parent's business network. These benefits are particularly well exploited when the spin-off locates in the same geographic location (Zander, 2003) and in the same or related activities upwards or downwards in the value chain (Saxenian, 1994; Enright and Roberts, 2001) of the parent. In this familiar business and geographic environment, the spin-off can engage in exchanges of inputs, outputs and information, for example with the same clients, suppliers and institutional agents of the parent.

Isomorphism and decline or realignment of clusters?

Parenting models have significant initial imprinting conditions upon the spin-offs' founding that affect the role and development of the spin-off (Stinchcombe, 1965; Gulati, 1998) and possibilities of the entire cluster. For instance, it is likely that initial imprinting conditions lead firms to exhibit similar routines, organizational practices, structures, market orientation and location to those of the parent (Stinchcombe, 1965; Brittain and Freeman, 1980; Hannan and Freeman, 1989; Burton et al., 2002; Phillips, 2002; Zander, 2003), suggesting that the contextual environment of the initial network is a powerful determinant of the evolution of spin-offs. However, the ties that bind may also blind, particularly in closely knit networks, by isolating spin-offs (Prusak and Cohen, 2001) from external agents. For example, managers tend to mimic parent firms and similar others and to restrict themselves to local searches for opportunities (Cyert and March, 1963; Katz and Gartner, 1988), ignoring the opportunities outside their immediate landscape (Gulati and Gargiulo, 1999). This means that while closed networks may be more advantageous for new spin-offs (Coleman, 1988; Larson, 1992) because they provide a munificent environment for resources, knowledge, learning and legitimacy, simultaneously reducing transaction costs and improving performance, these networks may also induce rigidities (Leonard-Barton, 1992). In short, mimicry may jeopardize the evolution and technological upgrade of the cluster because if all firms behave in a similar manner, it is less likely that the clustered firms will be able to make substantial innovations or appropriate the rents from innovation (Ferreira et al., 2005c). In this view, it seems that the evolution of the cluster in a certain geographic location becomes largely dependent on the entry of outsider start-ups for their innovative capacity. Some of these outsider entries may be by MNC subsidiaries. The similarity between parent and progeny is important for the legitimacy of spin-offs and may help explain higher rates of success for insider spin-offs than for outsider start-ups, as noted before.

The arguments presented here offer a complementary perspective by noting that rather than observing mimicry effects, the realignment of clustered firms as they adjust to market and technological shifts is driven by a few flagship firms. This view seems more realistic given the evidence that the evolution of clusters is not deterministically driven by isomorphic behaviours and that not all clusters are doomed to failure, as should be the long-term effect of mimicking behaviours. A motherhood model, in the terms illustrated, helps explain how clusters may realign led by a few major leader mother firms (flagships) that gestate entrepreneurial spin-offs. As flagships generate spin-offs, a network of largely cooperative firms emerges and the cluster will most likely evolve into the areas of most intense entrepreneurial activity because these are the areas where more new spin-offs are being originated, possibly as a result of technological and market changes or of the strategy of flagship firms as they experiment across boundaries. Employees of these flagships enjoy the social benefits of spinning out of leader firms. Hence, a parenting process such as that described in this chapter encompasses the evolution of the cluster through new spin-offs that are gestated as the flagships move across space.

Future research may address questions such as why do incumbent firms not internalize activities to reduce uncertainty, therefore actually reducing the number of entrepreneurial spin-offs? Using selected case studies of clusters, future empirical research may also examine which spin-offs perform better, those spawned from flagships or from other firms. These studies will allow remaining doubts on the existence of an advantage for insiders vis-à-vis outsiders to be addressed. The motherhood model only implies higher chances of survival for insiders, that is, for firms originating from parent firms already in the cluster. Outsider firms may require substantial local adaptation, and this will tend to be more so the more closed the inter-firm ties binding existing firms together. For foreign MNCs this should be a concern, as it may prevent them from developing ties to access local institutions, knowledge and agents. By the same token, it might be relevant to assess whether non-central firms may become more central (perhaps even becoming a true flagship) by generating spin-offs. How can firms, particularly MNC subsidiaries, with their liability of foreignness, become central drivers in an already established cluster?

The implications of this study extend across practitioners and academia to government policies and strategies. For the practitioner, it shows a significant way of founding firms and the benefits for larger, older, central, higher-status firms of supporting a hub of smaller innovative spin-offs that tap into novel market opportunities. These firms benefit from developing parenting into a fully fledged strategy, rather than an occasional event. For the academic, it proposes a different model of firm founding, one that looks beyond resource dependencies and also beyond the 'losses' for the parent emerging from a 'brain drain'. For governments and public policy makers, this chapter suggests that rather than discretely supporting new firms in 'strategic' activities, or activities that explore the nation's comparative advantage, a more efficient strategy may be to support selected firms in identified clusters that have the potential for gestating a higher number of, and more successful, spin-offs. For public policy, it is important to consider how the design of employment contracts may severely hinder entrepreneurial employees from exiting their parent firms, thus restricting the possibilities for founding new firms. Employment contracts in the USA are much less rigid than in many European countries (where social welfare concerns predominate over an economic efficiency rationale) but even so, many US firms tend to design contracts that prevent employees from using their acquired knowledge elsewhere.

To conclude, this chapter advanced a model of network benefits for the gestation and success of spin-offs by parent firms and discussed some of the characteristics of these parent firms, which were called 'flagships' in view of their capacity to influence and mould the cluster. It contributes to a better understanding of endogenous evolution of networks and clusters beyond explanations based on exogenous determinants. It also helps to explain why insider spin-offs may have a higher likelihood of survival and success than outsider start-up firms: parent firms act as a protective and munificent umbrella abundant in resources, ties with other firms, reputation and legitimacy that benefit spin-offs.

Acknowledgements

Manuel Ferreira acknowledges the partial financial support of the Foundation for Science and Technology – MCT, Portugal (grant: SFRH/BD/880/2000). Ana Teresa Tavares acknowledges financial support from Centro de Estudos Macroeconómicos e Previsão (CEMPRE). She is also supported by the Fundação para a Ciência e a Tecnologia, Portugal, through the Programa Operacional Ciência, Tecnologia e Inovação (POCTI) of the Quadro Comunitário de Apoio III, which is financed by FEDER and Portuguese Funds.

Notes

1. It is worth noting at the outset that, in some instances, the existence of opportunities leads incumbent firms to diversify into new businesses or geographies by spinning out a division, for example, which is made formally independent from the corporate firm, but still continues to hold equity ties and possibly control over the subsidiary's operations. This chapter does not focus on these corporate spin-offs, rather the focus is on entrepreneurial spin-offs. Entrepreneurial spin-offs are firms that are constituted by employees who exit the parent to set up their own firm.
2. Although maintaining good relationships with the parent firm may not be necessary, an absolute, and publicly visible, clash will hinder the spin-off's ability to benefit from the support of other members of the parent's network.
3. 'Status' refers to the social capital of the firm in the network, its visibility and recognized importance (Podolny, 1993).
4. 'Centrality' refers to the strategic location the firm occupies in the network. Centrality gives the firm the ability to impact the network through its resource links to other firms, within and outside the network, by exercising the power to control resources, transmit information and bridge gaps between them and their clients and suppliers (Freeman, 1978).
5. Status and centrality are distinct concepts. Status may emerge independent of centrality through, for example, innovation, participation in highly visible projects, leadership of trade and commercial associations, and so forth.

References

Aldrich, H. and G. Wiedenmayer (1993) 'From Traits to Rates: an Ecological Perspective on Organizational Founding', *Advances in Entrepreneurship, Firm Emergence and Growth*, 1, 145–95.

Arrow, K. (1983) 'Innovation in Large and Small Firms', in J. Ronen (ed.), *Entrepreneurship: Price Institute for Entrepreneurial Studies* (Lexington, Mass.: Lexington).

Arthur, W. (1990) 'Silicon Valley Locational Clusters: When do Increasing Returns Imply Monopoly?', *Mathematical Social Sciences*, 19, 235–51.

Benjamin, B. and J. Poldony (1999) 'Status, Quality, and Social Order in the California Wine Industry', *Administrative Science Quarterly*, 44, 563–89.

Birch, D. (1987) *Job Creation in America: How Our Smallest Companies Put the Most People to Work* (New York: Free Press).

Bonacich, P. (1987) 'Power and Centrality: a Family of Measures', *American Journal of Sociology*, 92, 1170–82.

Brass, D. (1984) 'Being in the Right Place: a Structural Analysis of Individual Influence in an Organization', *Administrative Science Quarterly*, 29, 518–39.

Brittain, J. and J. Freeman (1980) 'Organizational Proliferation and Density Dependent Selection', in J. Kimberly and R. Miles (eds), *The Organizational Life Cycle* (San Francisco: Jossey Bass).

Burt, R. (1992) *Structural Holes: the Social Structure of Competition* (Cambridge, Mass.: Harvard University Press).

Burt, R. (1997) 'The Contingent Value of Social Capital', *Administrative Science Quarterly*, 42, 349–65.

Burton, M., J. Sorensen and C. Beckman (2002) 'Coming from Good Stock: Career Histories and New Venture Formation', in M. Lounsbury and M. Ventresca (eds), *Research in the Sociology of Organizations* (New York: Elsevier Science), Vol. 19, pp. 229–62.

Carroll, G. (1984) 'Organizational Ecology', *Annual Review of Sociology*, 10, 71–93.

Coleman, J. (1988) 'Social Capital in the Creation of Human Capital', *American Journal of Sociology*, 94, S95–S120.

Cooper, A. (1985) 'The Role of Incubator Organizations in the Founding of Growth-oriented Firms', *Journal of Business Venturing*, 1 (1), 75–86.

Cyert, R. and J. March (1963) *A Behavioral Theory of the Firm* (New Jersey: Prentice Hall).

Dalum, B. (1995) 'Local and Global Linkages. The Radiocommunications Cluster in Northern Denmark', *Journal of Industry Studies*, 2, 89–109.

Dunning, J. (2001) 'Regions, Globalization and the Knowledge Economy'. Chapter 6 in *Global Capitalism at Bay?* (London: Routledge).

Enright, M. and B. Roberts (2001) 'Regional Clustering in Australia', *Australian Journal of Management*, 26, Special Issue, 66–85.

Ferreira, M. (2002) 'From Dyadic Ties to Networks: a Model of Surrogate Motherhood in the Portuguese Plastics Molds Industry', Academy of Management meeting, Denver, Colorado, published in the best papers proceedings.

Ferreira, M., W. Hesterly and A. Tavares (2005a) 'Evolution of Industry Clusters through Spin-offs and the Role of Flagship Firms', Workshop on Multinationals. Clusters and Innovation: Does Public Policy Matter? Porto, Portugal.

Ferreira, M., W. Hesterly, A. Tavares and S. Armagan (2005b) 'Network and Firm Antecedents of Spin-offs: Motherhooding Spin-offs', working paper, the University of Utah.

Ferreira, M., D. Li and S. Tallman (2005c) 'Innovation, Knowledge Sharing, and Clustered Firms' Ability to Capture Rents from Innovation', working paper, the University of Utah.

Forrant, R. and E. Flynn (1998) 'Seizing Agglomeration's Potential: the Greater Springfield Massachusetts Metalworking Sector in Transition, 1986–1996', *Regional Studies*, 32 (3), 209–22.

Freeman, J. (1978) 'Centrality in Social Networks: Conceptual Clarification', *Social Networks*, 1, 215–39.

Freeman, J. (1986) 'Entrepreneurs as Organizational Products: Semiconductor Firms and Venture Capital Firms', in *Advances in the Study of Entrepreneurship, Innovation, and Economic Growth* (Greenwich: JAI Press Inc.).

Gartner, W. (1988) 'Who is an Entrepreneur? Is the Wrong Question', *Entrepreneurship Theory and Practice*, 13 (4), 47–68.

Garvin, D. (1983) 'Spin-offs and the New Firm Formation Process', *California Management Review*, January, 3–20.

Granovetter, M. (1973) 'The Strength of Weak Ties', *American Sociological Review*, 78, 1360–80.

Granovetter, M. (1983) 'The Strength of Weak Ties: a Network Theory Revisited', in P. Marsden and N. Lin (eds), *Social Structure and Network Analysis* (Thousand Oaks, Calif.: Sage).

Gulati, R. (1995) 'Does Familiarity Breed Trust? The Implications of Repeated Ties for Contractual Choice in Alliances', *Academy of Management Journal*, 38 (1), 85–112.

Gulati, R. (1998) 'Alliances and Networks', *Strategic Management Journal*, 19 (4), 293–317.

Gulati, R. and M. Gargiulo (1999) 'Where do Networks Come From?', *American Journal of Sociology*, 104 (5), 1439–93.

Hannan, M. and J. Freeman (1977) 'The Population Ecology of Organizations', *American Journal of Sociology*, 83, 929–64.

Hannan, M. and J. Freeman (1984) 'Structural Inertia and Organizational Change', *American Sociological Review*, 49, 149–64.

Hannan, M. and J. Freeman (1989) *Organizational Ecology* (Cambridge, Mass.: Harvard University Press).

Helfat, C. and M. Lieberman (2002) 'The Birth of Capabilities: Market Entry and the Importance of Prehistory', *Industrial and Corporate Change*, 11 (4), 725–60.

Hendry, C., J. Brown and R. DeFillipi (2000) 'Regional Clustering of High Technology-based Firms: Opto-electronics in Three Countries', *Regional Studies*, 34 (2), 129–44.

Higgins, M. and R. Gulati (2003) 'Getting Off to a Good Start: the Effects of Upper Echelon Affiliations in Interorganizational Endorsements and IPO Success', *Organization Science*, 14 (3), 244–63.

Hite, J. and W. Hesterly (2001) 'The Evolution of Firm Networks: from Emergence to Early Growth of the Firm', *Strategic Management Journal*, 22, 275–86.

Hitt, M., R. Ireland, S. Camp and D. Sexton (2001) 'Introduction to the Special Issue Strategic Entrepreneurship: Entrepreneurial Strategies for Wealth Creation', *Strategic Management Journal*, 22, 479–91.

Kale, P., H. Singh and H. Perlmutter (2000) 'Learning and Protection of Proprietary Assets in Strategic Alliances: Building Relational Capital', *Strategic Management Journal*, 21, 217–37.

Katz, J. and W. Gartner (1988) 'Properties of Emerging Organizations', *Academy of Management Review*, 13 (3), 429–41.

Klepper, S. (2001) 'Employee Startups in High-tech Industries', *Industrial and Corporate Change*, 10 (3), 639–74.

Kogut, B. (1991) 'Country Capabilities and the Permeability of Borders', *Strategic Management Journal*, 12, 33–47.

Larson, A. (1992) 'Network Dyads in Entrepreneurial Settings: a Study of the Governance of Exchange Relationships', *Administrative Science Quarterly*, 37, 76–104.

Leonard-Barton, D. (1992) 'Core Capabilities and Core Rigidities: a Paradox in Managing New Product Development', *Strategic Management Journal*, 13, 111–25.

Levinthal, D. (1997) 'Adaptation on Rugged Landscapes', *Management Science*, 43 (7), 934–50.

Marshall, A. (1920) *Principles of Economics*, 8th edn (London: Macmillan).

Nelson, R. and S. Winter (1982) *An Evolutionary Theory of Economic Change* (Cambridge, Mass.: Belknap Press).

Oviatt, B. and P. McDougall (1995) 'Global Start-ups: Entrepreneurs on a Worldwide Stage', *Academy of Management Review*, 9 (2), 30–43.

Phillips, D. (2002) 'A Genealogical Approach to Organizational Life Changes: the Parent–Progenitor Transfer among Silicon Valley Law Firms, 1946–1996', *Administrative Science Quarterly*, 47, 474–506.

Podolny, J. (1993) 'A Status-based Model of Market Competition', *American Journal of Sociology*, 98, 829–72.

Podolny, J. (2001) 'Networks as Pipes and Prisms of the Market', *American Journal of Sociology*, 107 (1), 33–60.

Porter, M. (1998) 'Clusters and the New Economics of Competition', *Harvard Business Review*, Nov/Dec, 77–90.

Porter, M. (2000) 'Location, Competition, and Economic Development: Local Clusters in a Global Economy', *Economic Development Quarterly*, 14 (1), 15–34.

Prusak L. and D. Cohen (2001) 'How to Invest in Social Capital', *Harvard Business Review*, 79 (6), 86–94.

Rosenfeld, S. (1997) 'Bringing Business Clusters into the Mainstream of Economic Development', *European Planning Studies*, 5 (1), 3–23.

Rowley, T., D. Behrens and D. Krackardt (2000) 'Redundant Governance Structures: an Analysis of Structural and Relational Embeddedness in the Steel and Semiconductor Industries', *Strategic Management Journal*, 21, 369–86.

Rugman, A. and J. D'Cruz (2000) *Multinationals as Flagship Firms: Regional Business Networks* (Oxford: Oxford University Press).

Sandee, H. and P. Rietveld (2001) 'Upgrading Traditional Technologies in Small-scale Industry Clusters: Collaboration and Innovation Adoption in Indonesia', *The Journal of Development Studies*, 37 (4), 150–72.

Saxenian, A. (1990) 'Regional Networks and the Resurgence of Silicon Valley', *California Management Review*, Fall, 90–112.

Saxenian, A. (1994) *Regional Advantage: Culture and Competition in Silicon Valley and Route 128* (Cambridge: Harvard University Press).

Schumpeter, J. (1976) 'The Process of Creative Destruction', Ch. VII in *Capitalism, Socialism and Democracy* (London: George Allen and Unwin).

Shah, P. (1998) 'Who Are Employees' Social Referent Others? Using a Network Perspective to Determine Referent Others', *Academy of Management Journal*, 41 (3), 249–68.

Shane, S. (2000) 'Prior Knowledge and the Discovery of Entrepreneurial Opportunities', *Organization Science*, 11 (4), 448–69.

Singh, J., D. Tucker and R. House (1986) 'Organizational Legitimacy and the Liability of Newness', *Administrative Science Quarterly*, 31 (2), 171–94.

Stinchcombe, A. (1965) 'Social Structure and Organizations', in J. March (ed.), *Handbook of Organizations* (Chicago: Rand McNally).

Storper, M. (1995) 'The Resurgence of Regional Economics, Ten Years Later: the Region as a Nexus of Untraded Interdependencies', *Journal of European Urban and Regional Studies*, 2, 191–221.

Stuart, T. (2000) 'Interorganizational Alliances and the Performance of Firms: a Study of Growth and Innovation Rates in a High-technology Industry', *Strategic Management Journal*, 21 (8), 791–811.

Stuart, T., H. Hoang and R. Hybels (1999) 'Interorganizational Endorsements and the Performance of Entrepreneurial Ventures', *Administrative Science Quarterly*, 44, 315–49.

Sull, D. (1999) 'The Dynamics of Standing Still: Firestone Tire and Rubber and the Radial Revolution', *Business History Review*, 73 (3), 430–64.

Tallman, S. and K. Fladmoe-Lindquist (2002) 'Internationalization, Globalization, and Capability-based Strategy', *California Management Review*, 45 (1), 116–35.

Tallman, S., M. Jenkins, N. Henry and S. Pinch (2004) 'Knowledge, Clusters, and Competitive Advantage', *Academy of Management Review*, 29 (2), 258–71.

Walker, G., B. Kogut and W. Shan (1997) 'Social Capital, Structural Holes and the Formation of an Industry Network', *Organization Science*, 8 (2), 109–25.

Wiggins, S. (1995) 'Entrepreneurial Enterprises, Endogenous Ownership, and the Limits to Firm Size', *Economic Inquiry*, 33, 54–69.

Williamson, O. (1985) *The Economic Institutions of Capitalism: Firms, Markets, Relational Contracting* (New York: Free Press).

Zander, I. (2003) 'The Micro-foundations of Cluster Stickiness: Entering the Mind of the Entrepreneur', 4th IB research forum at Temple University, Philadelphia.

6

Towards an Explanation of MNE FDI in the City of London Financial Services Cluster

Naresh R. Pandit, Gary A.S. Cook and Pervez N. Ghauri

Introduction

Research on the foreign direct investment (FDI) activities of multinational enterprises (MNEs) has a long and rich tradition (Dunning, 2003). Research on the advantages, disadvantages and processes that arise in business clusters has a similar tradition (Marshall, 1890; Porter, 1998). While it is clear that there is a considerable amount of MNE FDI in clusters (Kozul-Wright and Rowthorn, 1998), and that this activity is increasing (Nachum, 2003), the body of research on this interface is small (Birkinshaw and Solvell, 2000). However, it is growing fast in the face of increased globalization, deregulation and advances in information and communication technology all of which have begun to prompt a re-evaluation of the spatial organization of MNE activity both by academic scholars and strategic managers. This chapter asks two related questions to contribute to this small but growing area:

1. Drawing from the extant literature on the MNE FDI/clusters interface, what theoretical reasons might explain the high level of MNE FDI in the 'City of London' (a generic term used to include its extension into north and west of London and Canary Wharf to the east) financial services cluster?
2. What are the general attractions of the City that managers in this cluster perceive and how do these relate to the theories identified earlier?

The chapter is structured as follows. The literature on the MNE FDI/clusters interface is reviewed next before providing a concise history of the City, emphasizing the rise of MNE FDI in the post-war period. The methodology of a study which investigated the general attractions of the City, based on postal questionnaire and interview data collected in 2002, is then outlined. The penultimate section presents the empirical findings and discusses them in relation to the literature on the MNE FDI/clusters interface before conclusions are drawn in the final section.

Literature on the MNE FDI/clusters interface

A better understanding of agglomeration is desirable from the perspective of MNE managers because performance may improve if certain activities are located in clusters where higher levels of productivity (Henderson, 1986; Porter, 1998) and innovation (Baptista and Swann, 1998; Porter, 1998) may be achievable. A better understanding of agglomeration will also help managers to decide which activities not to locate in clusters. Unless an activity needs to be located in a cluster, it will pay the MNE to move it elsewhere because clusters are usually expensive and congested locations (Swann et al., 1998). These reasons, coupled with the trends of increased globalization, deregulation and advances in information and communication technologies, mean that MNEs are increasingly employing cluster-based thinking to inform their investment and location decisions (Enright, 1998). At one extreme, there are MNEs that locate entire activities, including headquarters, in a cluster (Birkinshaw, 1996) and at the other, there are MNEs that place only certain activities in clusters while moving other activities to non-clustered locations (Enright, 2000).

There is a growing body of more specific evidence that shows that MNEs are attracted to clusters (Gong, 1995; Head et al., 1995, 1999; Wheeler and Moody, 1992) and that MNE FDI in clusters is increasing (Nachum, 2003). This evidence suggests that 'liability of foreignness' (Zaheer, 1995) – disadvantages faced by firms in foreign locations due to unfamiliarity and inferior access to local assets – is being compensated by the advantages of cluster location. These advantages may be categorized into those that are available to all firms at a location ('general cluster advantages') and those that are of particular benefit to MNEs ('MNE cluster advantages'). General cluster advantages include advantages that are directly related to the co-presence that exists within a cluster which are referred to as economies of agglomeration. These can emanate on the demand or supply side and are extensively detailed in Porter (1998), Swann et al. (1998) and Pandit and Cook (2005). These go beyond so-called 'fixed effects' (Swann et al., 1998) – advantages that exist at a location that are not a function of the co-presence of related firms and institutions (such as climate, time zone and cultural capital). But what, then, are the advantages that accrue to MNEs in clusters?

At a general level, a large literature exists that attempts to explain MNE FDI in terms of the benefits that certain locations provide for inward investing MNEs. Dunning (1993) presents an FDI typology differentiating between investments that are 'natural-resource seeking', 'market-seeking', 'efficiency-seeking' and 'strategic-asset seeking'. More recently, he has drawn from economic geography (Dunning, 1998) to elaborate the location element of his 'OLI' framework by incorporating clusters thinking.

Birkinshaw and Hood (2000) find that it is rational for MNEs to locate in clusters as subsidiaries located in clusters make greater strategic contributions to parent companies than other subsidiaries. Enright (1998) elaborates a typology of such contributions. 'Listening posts' aim to absorb knowledge from the cluster and then disseminate it within the wider enterprise (Dupuy and Gilly, 1999). Nachum and Keeble (2003) state that the ability to tap into cluster-specific knowledge is particularly important when significant knowledge is tacit. 'Stand-alone corporate portfolio investments' serve as centres for particular business activities, perhaps benefiting from the reputation spillover of a particular location. Nachum (2000a, p. 370) supports this line of thinking by commenting on the increased importance and autonomy of foreign subsidiaries:

> The hierarchical structure, which was common amongst most TNCs in the past, has become inadequate in the more recent decades when knowledge creation by all parts of the TNC has become essential for competitive success... Greater autonomy for the affiliates is increasing the potential for local linkage formation and the transfer of technology and skills between the affiliates and other firms in the near locality, sometimes independent from the headquarters and the TNCs as a whole.

Another type is the subsidiary that 'supplies products and activities' for the MNE's other activities and finally there is the subsidiary which absorbs 'skills and capabilities' from the cluster and then transfers these to the wider enterprise. Beaverstock's (1994) study of multinational banks elaborates this type of MNE FDI by finding that such firms benefit from the ability to transfer skills and capabilities between subsidiaries in their worldwide operations through international personnel movements. This may be particularly the case when an industry has more than one prominent location and so the MNE may benefit from locating in all prominent locations in order to pick up skills and capabilities in one to pass on to the others. Nachum and Keeble (2003) point further to the advantage of a subsidiary absorbing a cluster's culture and then disseminating it to its other parts.

A further motivation for MNE managers to locate strategic business units in clusters is provided by Harrison (1994). He argues that a cluster location may enable MNEs to concentrate on their core competences and outsource non-core activities to specialist suppliers that are geographically proximate. Nachum (2000a, p. 370) provides support for this argument, finding that: 'In the process of internal reorganization of the production and externalization of certain activities, TNCs have come to rely heavily on the supply of goods and services from other firms and have become considerably more dependent on linkages with them.' Similarly, Nachum and Keeble (2003) argue that MNEs will locate in clusters to benefit from the highly specialized, non-standard inputs that are available there.

Although this typology encourages us to think of MNEs 'taking' from clusters, one should guard against such a conclusion. Studies by Dunning (2000), Head et al. (1995), Nachum (2000a) and Wheeler and Moody (1992) show that MNEs can play a major role in cluster development and evolution. Indeed, Birkinshaw and Hood's (2000) analysis of the characteristics of 229 foreign-owned subsidiaries located in clusters finds that such subsidiaries are more embedded and more internationally oriented than subsidiaries that are not located in clusters. Another caveat is that, as with most typologies, the types should not be thought of as mutually exclusive (Markusen, 1996). An MNE may invest in a cluster for more than one reason, although it is likely that one reason will dominate the others.

Before reporting the advantages of the City of London financial services cluster and exploring the reasons why MNEs are attracted there, the City will be introduced and the activity which takes place there will be described, emphasizing its MNE dimension.

The City of London

The City of London is best understood as a wholesale financial services centre (Coggan, 2002) with core activities in banking, insurance and fund management supported by a panoply of activities including legal services, accounting, management consultancy, advertising, market research, recruitment, property management, financial printing and publishing and the provision of electronic information (IFSL, 2004). Technically, the 'City of London' refers to the 'square mile' around the Bank of England. Although this remains the geographic core of the cluster, developments to the east, west and north have extended the centre to the extent that the term 'the City' is now often used to refer to the cluster as a whole and not just the square mile (Golding, 2001). There are five distinctive sub-concentrations (see Figure 6.1). First, Canary Wharf to the east, which is the home of some of the largest investment banks. Second, the very dense 'square mile' that is the original City of London featuring banks, insurance and law firms. Third, a less dense West End concentration featuring banks near Mayfair and advertising in Soho. Fourth, an incipient concentration north of the City featuring services such as architecture and business support. Finally, a concentration that lies in-between the City and the West End consisting of law firms located in close proximity to the law courts. Collectively these interdependent sub-concentrations employ some 369,000

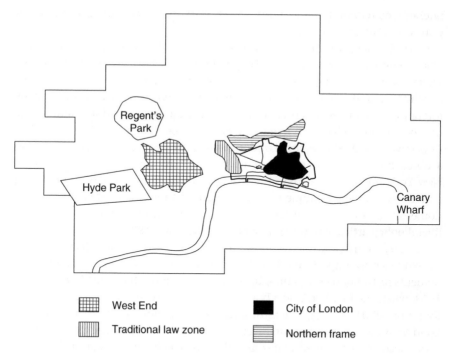

Figure 6.1 The London financial services cluster
Source: Taylor et al. (2003)

people (Corporation of London, 2004) and make up the City of London financial services cluster.

The cluster fits the generic definition arrived at by the Department of Trade and Industry after an extensive review of the clusters literature: 'A geographic concentration of competing, collaborating and interdependent companies and institutions which are connected by a system of market and non-market links' (DTI, 1998). This definition has at least four strengths. Firstly, it does not relate to a single industry; rather it merely requires that companies in a cluster are interdependent in some way. Secondly, a cluster is defined not just in terms of companies but also supporting institutions. Thirdly, non-market linkages are emphasized. These, borne out of a common culture and trust, are known to be important with respect to productivity and innovation. Finally, the definition encourages us to think of clusters as complex systems of industrial organization that confer sustainable competitive advantage to incumbents. A weakness of the definition is that it is imprecise in at least two important ways: it provides little guidance on the required quantity or quality of incumbents and linkages in a cluster and it provides no guidance on the geographic scope of a cluster. A rebuttal is that as clusters are complex and polymorphous phenomena (Gordon and McCann, 2000; Markusen, 1996) any generic definition will necessarily be vague.

Three financial centres are ranked together as the most important in the world: London, New York and Tokyo (Roberts, 1994; Sassen, 1991, 1999). There exist three major differences between London and the other two (Nachum, 2003). First, the share of financial services activity controlled by foreign ownership is much lower in New York and Tokyo (for example, the number of foreign banks in London, New York and Tokyo was 573, 275 and 93 respectively in 2000). Second, London is more international in its outlook with a much higher percentage of foreign business. In contrast, the strengths of New York and Tokyo relate to the strengths of their domestic economies and currencies. London's unique position is that its strength is independent of its domestic economy and currency. Third, the UK and so London has a more liberal policy attitude to foreign ownership (Morgan, 1997).

The City's current attractiveness as a centre for MNE FDI and its position as the world's most important international financial services is the result of developments in the post-war period, in particular the growth of the 'Euromarkets'; 1963, when the first Eurodollar bond was issued by Warburgs, was according to Kynaston (2001, p. 275), 'the most important year since 1914 in the history of London as an international financial center'. In 1957 'Regulation Q' had been introduced in the United States and this artificially capped the interest rate that could be paid on dollar deposits in the USA. In response, dollar deposits searched for better returns and found them at European banks trading in the more loosely regulated City of London. By the end of 1964, Kynaston (2001) estimates that the majority of 44 foreign dollar issues worth $681m had been made in London. Very importantly, currency and location had been decoupled (HM Treasury, 2003); the City's strength would now be independent of the strength of the UK economy and currency. The size of London's Euromarkets increased in the 1970s as US banks used them to recycle large 'petrodollar' surpluses of the OPEC countries. The parallel developments of investment banking and investment institutions in the late 1960s and 1970s further enhanced the City's strength. The ground for London's role as an international financial services centre and so its attractiveness to MNE FDI had been prepared. A subsequent development in the late 1970s and 1980s – deregulation – then triggered a substantial rise in MNE FDI in the City (Augar, 2000; Coggan, 2002; Golding, 2001; Hamilton, 1996; Kynaston, 2001).

Exchange controls were abolished in 1979, and full competition was introduced to the banking sector by 1980. These changes paved the way for foreign, mainly US, banks to take over British firms and so establish their European time zone wholesale operations in the City. As a result, 'foreign firms' investment came to dominate London's wholesale markets – 'the City as FDI' (HM Treasury,

2003, p. 31). The term 'Big Bang', although initially used to refer to the deregulation in 1986 of the London Stock Exchange when trading was automated,
has become associated with the general modernization and deregulation of
London's financial markets brought on by the 1986 Financial Services Act. It
was the first major deregulation of this type in Europe: 'This focus on competitiveness meant that foreign investment was encouraged, resulting in most of
the leading wholesale institutions being foreign owned' (HM Treasury, 2003,
p. 31). Clark (2002, p. 438) concludes:

> London is an 'industrial district' that has attracted and retained firms whose
> home location could place them elsewhere in the world (in the US and
> Europe for example). Indeed, for many such firms, locating and developing
> a significant presence in London has been a conscious locational choice
> made both in relation to competitors and related firms, and in relation to
> the preferences and needs of UK and European customers.

Clark's advocacy of London as a rational choice for MNE FDI is supported
by Nachum's (2000b) analysis of the profitability and failure of City firms
between 1975 and 2000. She finds that the profit margin of British financial
services firms was 0.132 compared with 0.147 for foreign financial services
firms, and that of 313 failures over the period, 214 were British and 99 foreign.
Accordingly, in line with Enright (2000) and contrary to Porter (1990), it seems
that the conditions within a cluster that attract foreign companies will not
necessarily foster local companies to the same extent. While the City of
London attracts many world-class foreign financial services firms, it has not
spawned nearly as many domestic equivalents.

The empirical research being carried out by the present authors on the
attractions of the City of London financial services cluster for MNEs began
with a study of the general advantages of a City location (reported below)
together with a review of the relationship between these reasons and the literature on the motives for MNE FDI in clusters, as outlined earlier. This is a part of
a research programme which will subsequently compare and contrast these
advantages for MNEs and non-MNEs.

Methodology

Data on the advantages of financial services clustering in the City of London
were collected via a postal questionnaire survey and in-depth face-to-face
interviews. For the questionnaire survey, 1500 questionnaires were posted to
companies engaged in banking, investment banking, insurance and fund
management and to companies providing related support: legal services,
accounting, management consultancy, advertising, market research, recruitment,

property management, financial printing and publishing and the provision of electronic information. The firms included in the sampling frame were those known to be operating within a 500-metre buffer extending beyond the boundaries of the City of London and Canary Wharf. The sample was selected using a stratified method; 100 per cent of the largest 350 financial services firms were selected and these were identified primarily from a database supplied by the specialist information provider Market Locations. The remaining 1150 firms were drawn at random (using a random number generator) from the rest of the Market Locations database. A total of 310 usable questionnaires were returned, a response rate of just over 20 per cent.

Respondents were asked to rank the importance of a factor from 1 (not important) to 5 (very important) with an option of 0 if not applicable. Factors are presented in total score rank order which is simply the sum of recorded scores for a given factor. For example, a factor which received two ranks of 1 (not important), two of 2 and two of 5 (very important) would receive a total score of 16. A benchmark for interpreting these total scores is the mean of the total score across all questions, which is 855. The 95 per cent confidence interval around this average is 808–901. Accordingly, a rule of thumb in comparing the relative importance of each factor is that any total score below 808 is relatively unimportant and any total score above 901 is relatively important. The heavy black lines in the tables that follow divide factors into groups where there is no statistically significant difference in the total score within groups but there is a statistically significant difference between groups (based on the 'conservative' sign test). This indicates that factors within two heavy black lines were regarded as being of roughly equal importance by respondents, but either side of a black line there is a difference in the degree of importance attached to a factor.

An interview survey was designed to provide qualitative evidence complementing the quantitative data gathered by the postal questionnaire. Senior executives in leading organizations within key subsectors were identified using 2001/2 sources, for example *The Banker*, London Investment Banking Association (LIBA), International Financial Services, London (IFSL), and invited to participate. While most firms were large by international and London standards, prominent small, specialized organizations were included. In total, 39 interviews were conducted across seven sectors. The interview data were coded numerically and sorted by both sector and location variables.

Results

Table 6.1 shows that no less than six advantages score more than 901, indicating that the cluster is attractive for many reasons.

Table 6.1   General advantages of a City of London location

How important are each of the following benefits of your location?

	1	2	3	4	5	0	Total
Your address is important to being perceived as credible	18	23	63	111	91	2	1152
You benefit from a strong, skilled labour supply	21	22	62	95	85	22	1056
You benefit from being close to market-leading customers	18	46	66	88	77	12	1045
Your customers external to London find it easier to locate you	32	42	72	98	46	15	954
You benefit from being near professional bodies	36	59	79	68	52	11	923
Knowledge transfer from the City's 'financial atmosphere'	28	45	75	72	57	28	916
You benefit from being near leading competitors	49	58	63	73	41	23	851
Customers external to London find it easier to interact with you	45	58	87	62	35	19	845
Ability to find firms who will supply bespoke services	34	75	83	56	36	22	837
It is the best place to be to take market share from rivals	37	60	74	65	39	32	834
Proximity to a relevant exchange or physical marketplace	55	36	70	44	57	45	798
Ability to benchmark against competitors	67	68	72	43	23	33	706
Local rivalry among competitors is a powerful spur	63	70	69	44	18	42	676
Ability to access real time information on market trends	80	65	49	44	27	41	668
Support from local government	119	66	33	13	11	64	457
Access to venture capital	113	46	31	13	11	90	405

Reputation

The importance of a credible address stands apart at the head of these advantages and indeed has the fifth highest total score of all factors in the questionnaire. It is also one of the most consistently mentioned advantages in the interview survey where the executives stated that a firm's address signals that it is a serious player and as such, the address acts as a strong brand. For example, a City location turns a law firm into a 'City law firm'. Similarly, insurance companies gain prestige when in close proximity to Lloyd's of London. What is more, positive feedback was mentioned whereby a location's reputation attracts reputable firms that further enhance the reputation of the location. This excerpt from an interview with the senior manager of a law firm summarizes very clearly the importance of a 'City' address and associated branding:

> Geographically we're a bit pompous...Things would have to change dramatically before we would leave the City...the reason we have an office in the City now is that this is the biggest legal market in the UK and one of the biggest legal markets in the world. We want to be part of that.

Also, if a bank wanted to be perceived as an 'international bank' it had to be in London. Here is a typical comment from a bank executive:

> We're here for two reasons – one is that we have an ambition to be an international bank and you can't be an international bank unless you have something in London. The other is that the exposure to London markets and London personnel and the ways of doing things in London is something we want to gain experience of and communicate through the rest of the...Group.

These findings are in line with Clark (2002, p. 440) who maintains that 'a firm's reputation may depend upon the reputation of its financial center as much as its own competence'.

The search for reputation via foreign cluster location seems to fit under Enright's (1998) 'stand-alone corporate portfolio investment motive' when the subsidiary serves as the centre or one of a few centres of corporate activity and signals clearly that the firm is a serious global player in the industry. However, the second quotation above indicates multiple motives. In addition to the 'stand-alone corporate portfolio investment motive', the respondent is suggesting the 'skills and capabilities' motive, a point that is elucidated in the next section on labour supply.

Labour supply

The second highest rated advantage of a London location is the ability to tap into a strong, skilled labour supply from both domestic and international pools. Positive feedback can be observed again as the attractiveness of the labour pool increases as the labour pool itself increases in size. The interview data corroborate the questionnaire data. A typical response from a senior banker is as follows:

> ...there is a skills base, people both front and back office, that exists in London that you'd probably have difficulty finding elsewhere in the volumes you need to support the industry. So because the industry's grown up and evolved in the City then around it you have a large pool of skilled

resource in the areas you need it and some of those areas are quite specific. So that's the major point.

A feature of this advantage is the ability of staff to gain experience in London and transfer best practice internationally. Evidence from the interviews does suggest that labour market turnover (estimated to be 25 per cent annually) was an important mechanism to achieve this, whether that be the specificities of particular labour market processes or tacit and formal knowledge brought about via new cultural working practices or management structures.

These advantages clearly relate to Dunning's (1993) general 'strategic asset seeking' motive for MNE FDI and to Enright's (1998) 'listening post' and 'skills and capabilities' motives for MNE FDI in clusters.

Proximity to related firms and institutions

The defining characteristic of a cluster is, of course, the close proximity of related firms and institutions. Proximity to customers, in the physical sense and in the sense of being on the beaten track, are the third and fourth most important general advantages in Table 6.1. Proximity to professional bodies is ranked fifth and the knowledge spillovers that occur when physically close to related firms and institutions is the sixth most important advantage. All four of these proximity-related advantages score more than the benchmark of 901 and taken together rack up a sizeable score of 3838.

The questionnaire asked why proximity was advantageous (Table 6.2). The importance of maintaining personal contact and being able to interact face to

Table 6.2 The importance of close proximity to other firms

How important are each of the following reasons for having a location in close proximity to other firms in London?

	1	2	3	4	5	0	Total
It is easier to build and maintain personal contacts	12	15	46	123	101	7	1177
The ability to have face-to-face contact	14	15	37	108	117	12	1172
It is easier to build relationships of trust and cooperation	17	33	71	98	73	13	1053
It is easier to communicate because we have a common understanding of the business	27	33	67	108	51	17	981
We generally have complementary expertise with such firms	24	47	101	80	34	19	911
Multidisciplinary teams can be assembled more quickly	30	46	73	86	41	27	890

face is clear. In the questionnaire survey as a whole, these were the second and third most highly ranked factors. The compactness of the City also aids the ability to establish relationships of trust. The existence of common understanding and complementary expertise are classic characteristics of dynamic clusters and are much in evidence here.

The importance of face-to-face contact was underscored by the interview survey, which cast light on why it is important. The executives of several firms emphasized the importance of a face-to-face meeting for conducting complex transactions where it is important to fashion agreement while reducing the chances of misunderstandings or creating antagonism. At the stage when deals are being transacted, a crisis can emerge at any time and there may be a need for a meeting to sort the matter out quickly and satisfactorily. One firm suggested that this requirement meant that it was important for senior staff to be based in London. Similarly, several firms cited the need to be close to regulators, including the Bank of England, in order to have the ability to meet face to face to resolve important issues and to cement an ongoing relationship. The overall impression gained in the interviews is that there is a deep-rooted need to conduct certain business face to face. As one manager remarked: 'Face-to-face is very important, absolutely; you're never going to replace face-to-face contact. You can't pick up body language; you can't build relationships truly over the phone and with video-conferencing.'

An important benefit of the density of information which physical propinquity allows is that knowledge flows more easily and this is the sixth advantage in Table 6.1, scoring 916. One respondent bemoaned the demise of the 'City lunch' which was seen as a powerful way of ensuring people knew what the key developments in the market were. Another manager explained:

> You want to be able to meet with your biggest customers over lunch – take the head of x out to lunch and see what he thinks – and it's being able to say to someone – look I'm going to be walking past your building this morning. I'll just pop in and see what you're doing about this, that and the other – again it boils down to human contact – if you want to keep your finger on the pulse and in the loop – you can't get that from the trade press and so ... actually a lot of that comes from dinner parties and cocktail parties – it's informal but that's what you miss if you're not in the loop.

An important advantage of being close to other firms in the same line of business is the ability to work out solutions and share risk. Being close to other types of firm which provide complementary services is also important because it enables multidisciplinary teams to assemble quickly to meet client needs. It is also convenient for clients, particularly those who travel some distance to London, to be able to see a range of their advisers quickly and efficiently. It was judged to be less likely that a client would have a pure financing or pure legal requirement. The following quotation illustrates this:

> There is an awful lot of business that is done which is joint business between institutions. There is more and more now of large transactions which are done jointly and the risk is spread then between different organizations. So there's a need not only for you to get yourself together with a client but to get those proposing the solution together.

From the discussion in this subsection, a picture emerges of the complex nature of wholesale financial services. The production of mergers and acquisitions, initial public offerings and other wholesale financial services is horizontally multidisciplinary, involving banks, legal firms, insurance firms, accountants and so on; vertically multi-actor, involving suppliers, customers and regulators, and fundamentally bespoke. Employing Dunning's (1993) and Enright's (1998) typologies, it can be concluded that the investments of financial services MNEs in the City are not only 'market seeking' but more importantly 'marketplace-seeking' (Enright, 2000). In short, the nature of the business severely limits where it can occur and so the choice for financial services MNEs is not whether or not to locate in the City but rather to locate there and continue to be involved in the industry or not locate there and exit the industry. Similarly, in their study of MNE participation in the Central London media cluster, Nachum and Keeble (2003, p. 187) find that 'cluster participation enriches affiliates' opportunities, access to resources, and flexibility in ways that are difficult to emulate from a distance'. Also, in his study of the interest rate swaps (derivatives) industry in Australia, Agnes finds that:

> ...the globalization of financial services has not undermined the importance of local embeddedness in world financial centers...Dealing networks are underpinned by social relationships, requiring face-to-face interaction that is facilitated by spatial proximity. Although the global swaps industry is dominated by multinational banks, the centrality of these embedded networks *impedes* globalization in interest rate swaps dealing. (Agnes, 2000, p. 347, emphasis added)

Conclusion

This chapter has focused on the extraordinary concentration of MNE FDI in the City of London financial services cluster. It has examined the small but growing literature that suggests motives for MNE location in clusters and has attempted to relate these motives to the findings of a study which investigated the general advantages of location in the City of London financial services cluster. The primary conclusion is that the managers of MNEs are likely to have multiple motives for locating activity in the cluster and these essentially relate to the complex nature of the production of certain financial services. This is not to say that such firms need to locate lock, stock and barrel in the cluster. Rather, the senior executives need to continually assess which activities they need to locate there and which they do not (Buckley and Ghauri, 2004). Clark (2002) corroborates this, finding that in the wholesale financial services industry, 'Firms assess and re-assess time-after-time the costs and benefits of particular locations. This is especially true of Anglo-American "bulge-bracket" financial houses that maintain and manage their global operations on a daily basis' (Clark, 2002, p. 437).

An example of this process is the movement of activity out of the City's core during the 1970s. During that decade, London companies such as Clerical Medical, Sun Life and Nat West Life moved the less knowledge-intensive aspects of their business out of London to Bristol to save costs (Pandit and Cook, 2003). Similarly, certain investment banking activity is now moving out of London to India. Research by IFSL (2005) finds that such 'offshoring' is most appropriate when the activity in question is characterized by no face-to-face servicing requirement, low social networking requirements, high information content, a work process that is telecommutable and internet enabled, high wage levels relative to the destination country and low set-up barriers.

Just over a decade ago, O'Brien declared the 'end of geography' in financial services, stating:

> Geographic location no longer matters in finance, or much less than hitherto . . . For financial firms, this means that the choice of geographical location can be greatly widened, provided that an appropriate investment in information and computer systems can be made . . . There will be forces seeking to maintain geographical control . . . Yet, as markets and rules become integrated, the relevance of geography and the need to base decisions on geography will alter and often diminish. (O'Brien, 1991, pp. 1–2)

While this may have great applicability to *retail* financial services, this study finds that wholesale financial services remain sticky in increasingly slippery space. Thus, as Enright (2000, pp. 115–16) states:

> as transportation and communications improve, as technology becomes more widely dispersed, and as barriers to trade and investment fall, some

industries become more dispersed over geographic space. In other industries and activities, however, the same forces foster geographic concentration by allowing firms and locations to exploit specific sources of competitive advantage over even wider geographic areas...This logic concludes that as competition globalizes, the geographic or location-specific sources of competitive advantage will tend to become more, not less, important.

While London's initial advantage may have been one of historical legacy as 'the center of Empire' (Clark, 2002), a London location continues to be important in order to have face-to-face contact and build trusting relationships that enable important inter-firm linkages among local firms, particularly those with complementary expertise, which above all translate into the ability to provide high-level services to clients.

While the findings support the continued importance of clusters in the finance industry, questions regarding the particular benefits of locating in clusters for MNEs and non-MNEs remain. In particular, how and why are the advantages, disadvantages and processes that arise in the London cluster similar and different for MNEs and non-MNEs? Also, to what extent do the answers to the question above support, contradict or extend the theoretical explanations identified in the early part of this chapter? These questions will be addressed in forthcoming research.

Acknowledgements

This research was funded partly by the UK Economic and Social Research Council and partly by the Corporation of London. We would like to acknowledge input from Jon Beaverstock, Helen Greenwood, Kathy Pain and Peter Taylor. None of these are responsible for any remaining errors.

References

Agnes, P. (2000) 'The "End of Geography" in Financial Services? Local Embeddedness and Territorialisation in the Interest Rate Swaps Industry', *Economic Geography*, 76 (4), 347–66.

Augar, P. (2000) *The Death of Gentlemanly Capitalism* (London: Penguin).

Baptista, R.M.L.N. and G.M.P. Swann (1998) 'Do Firms in Clusters Innovate More?' *Research Policy* 27, 527–42.

Beaverstock, J.V. (1994) 'Re-thinking Skilled International Labor Migration: World Cities and Banking Organizations', *Geoforum*, 25 (3), 323–38.

Birkinshaw, J.M. (1996) 'How Multinational Subsidiary Mandates Are Gained and Lost', *Journal of International Business Studies*, 27 (3), 467–96.

Birkinshaw J.M. and N. Hood (2000) 'Characteristics of Foreign Subsidiaries in Industry Clusters', *Journal of International Business Studies*, 31 (1), 141–54.

Birkinshaw, J.M. and O. Solvell (2000) 'Preface', *International Studies of Management and Organization*, 30 (2), 3–9.

Buckley, P.J. and P.N. Ghauri (2004) 'Globalization, Economic Geography and the Strategy of Multinational Enterprises', *Journal of International Business Studies*, 35, 81–98.

Clark, G.L. (2002) 'London in the European Financial Services Industry: Locational Advantages and Product Complementarities', *Journal of Economic Geography*, 2, 433–54.

Coggan, P. (2002) *The Money Machine: How the City Works* (London: Penguin).

Corporation of London (2004) *City Economy Digest*, Issue 1, February (London: Corporation of London).

Department of Trade and Industry (DTI) (1998) *Our Competitive Future: Building the Knowledge Driven Economy*, Cmnd 4176 (London: HMSO).

Dunning, J.H. (1993) *Multinational Enterprises and the Global Economy* (Reading, Mass.: Addison-Wesley).

Dunning, J.H. (1998) 'Location and the Multinational Enterprise: a Neglected Factor?', *Journal of International Business Studies*, 29 (1), 45–66.

Dunning, J.H. (2000) 'The Eclectic Paradigm as an Envelope for Economic and Business Theories of MNE Activity', *International Business Review*, 9, 163–90.

Dunning, J.H. (2003) 'The Key Literature on IB Activities: 1960–2000', in A.M. Rugman and T.L. Brewer (eds), *The Oxford Handbook of International Business* (Oxford: Oxford University Press).

Dupuy, C. and J.P. Gilly (1999) 'Industrial Groups and Territories: the Case of Matra-Marconi-Space in Toulouse', *Cambridge Journal of Economics*, 23 (2), 207–25.

Enright, M.J. (1998) 'Regional Clusters and Firm Strategy', in A.D Chandler, O. Solvell and P. Hagstrom (eds), *The Dynamic Firm: the Role of Technology, Strategy, and Regions* (Oxford: Oxford University Press).

Enright, M.J. (2000) 'Regional Clusters and Multinational Enterprises', *International Studies of Management and Organization*, 30 (2), 114–38.

Golding, T. (2001) *The City: Inside the Great Expectation Machine* (London: Prentice Hall).

Gong, H. (1995) 'Spatial Patterns of Foreign Investment in China's Cities, 1980–1989', *Urban Geography*, 16 (3), 198–209.

Gordon, I.R. and P. McCann (2000) 'Industrial Clusters: Complexes, Agglomeration and/ or Social Networks?', *Urban Studies*, 37 (3), 513–32.

Hamilton, A. (1996) *The Financial Revolution* (London: Penguin).

Harrison, B. (1994) *Lean and Mean: the Changing Landscape of Corporate Power in the Age of Flexibility* (London: The Guilford Press).

Head, K., J.C. Ries and D.L. Swenson (1995) 'Agglomeration Benefits and Location Choices: Evidence from Japanese Manufacturing Investments in the United States', *Journal of International Economics*, 38, 223–47.

Head, K., J.C. Ries and D.L. Swenson (1999) 'Attracting Foreign Manufacturing: Investment Promotion and Agglomeration', *Regional Science and Urban Economics*, 29 (2), 197–218.

Henderson, J.V. (1986) 'Efficiency of Resource Usage and City Size', *Journal of Urban Economics*, 19, 47–70.

HM Treasury (2003) *The Location of Financial Activity and the Euro* (London: HM Treasury, Whitehall).

International Financial Services London (2004) 'International Financial Markets in the UK', May (available at www.ifsl.org.uk).

International Financial Services London (2005) 'Offshoring of Services: Impact and Implications', March (available at www.ifsl.org.uk).

Kozul-Wright, R. and R. Rowthorn (1998) 'Spoilt for Choice? Multinational Corporations and the Geography of International Production', *Oxford Review of Economic Policy*, 14 (2), 74–92.

Kynaston, D. (2001) *The City of London*: Vol. IV: *A Club No More 1945–2000* (London: Pimlico).

Markusen, A. (1996) 'Sticky Places in Slippery Space: a Typology of Industrial Districts', *Economic Geography*, 72, 293–313.

Marshall, A. (1890) *Principles of Economics* (London: Macmillan).

Morgan, G. (1997) 'The Global Context of Financial Services: National Systems and the International Political Economy', in G. Morgan and D. Knights (eds), *Regulation and Deregulation in European Financial Services* (Basingstoke: Macmillan Business).

Nachum, L. (2000a) 'Economic Geography and the Location of TNCs: Financial and Professional Service FDI to the USA', *Journal of International Business Studies*, 31 (3), 367–85.

Nachum, L. (2000b) 'Global Financial Centers in an Era of Globalization', Geneva Association for the Study of Insurance Economics, Working paper 233.

Nachum, L. (2003), 'Liability of Foreignness in Global Competition? Financial Service Affiliates in the City of London', *Strategic Management Journal*, 24, 1187–208.

Nachum, L. and D. Keeble (2003) 'Neo-Marshallian Clusters and Global Networks: the Linkages of Media Firms in Central London', *Long Range Planning*, 36, 459–80.

O'Brien, R. (1991) *Global Financial Integration: the End of Geography* (London: Pinter/Royal Institute of International Affairs).

Pandit, N.R. and G.A.S. Cook (2003) 'The Benefits of Industrial Clustering: Insights from the British Financial Services Industry at Three Locations', *Journal of Financial Services Marketing*, 7 (3), 230–45.

Pandit, N.R. and G.A.S. Cook (2005) 'The Clustering of the British Financial Services Industry', in B. Johansson, C. Karlsson and R. Stough (eds), *Entrepreneurship, Spatial Industrial Clusters and Inter-Firm Networks* (Cheltenham: Edward Elgar).

Porter, M.E. (1990) *The Competitive Advantage of Nations* (London: Macmillan).

Porter, M.E. (1998) 'Clusters and Competition: New Agendas for Companies, Governments, and Institutions', in M.E. Porter (ed.), *On Competition* (Boston, Mass.: Harvard Business School Press).

Roberts, R. (ed.) (1994) *Global Financial Centers*. Vol. II: *London, New York, Tokyo* (Aldershot: Edward Elgar).

Sassen, S. (1991) *The Global City: New York, London, Tokyo* (Princeton: Princeton University Press).

Sassen, S. (1999) 'Global Financial Centers', *Foreign Affairs*, 78 (1), 75–87.

Swann, G.M.P., M. Prevezer and D. Stout (eds) (1998) *The Dynamics of Industrial Clustering: International Comparisons in Computing and Biotechnology* (Oxford: Oxford University Press).

Taylor, P.J., J.V. Beaverstock, G.A.S. Cook and N.R. Pandit (2003) *Financial Services Clustering and its Significance for London* (London: Corporation of London).

Wheeler, D. and A. Moody (1992) 'International Investment Location Decisions', *Journal of International Economics*, 33, 57–76.

Zaheer, S. (1995) 'Overcoming the Liability of Foreignness', *Academy of Management Journal*, 38 (2), 341–63.

7
International Entrepreneurship and Managing Network Dynamics: SMEs in the UK Advertising Sector

Dev K. Boojihawon

Introduction

The accelerating pace of internationalization of small and medium-sized enterprises (SMEs) is now a widely acknowledged phenomenon. Ongoing globalization seems to stimulate SMEs to internationalize, relying less on a predetermined sequence of events or 'steps' and opting for more innovative network-based approaches to enter and expand into foreign markets (Wright and Dana, 2003). Small service firms are no exception to this trend. Their internationalization processes, however, have not been adequately studied. Yet the international growth of small service firms seems to be increasingly determined by their ability to be entrepreneurial and competitive internationally by using innovative ways to network.

This chapter explores how network relationships impact on service SMEs' ability to implement international entrepreneurial initiatives and strategies. The focus of this essay extends Boojihawon's (2004) findings, which outlined the detailed case of the network orientation a small advertising agency adopted, in order to internationalize. This chapter conducts similar in-depth analyses of three small and medium-sized advertising agencies (SMAs) and examines their entrepreneurial ways of exploiting changing network relationships for international advantage. In particular, this research focuses on how management in these firms use network relationships and positions to pursue foreign market opportunities and/or to service international clients. It is argued that there is much to be learned from further research examining network theory in the context of entrepreneurial small service firms.

The chapter is organized as follows. Its theoretical bases are drawn from literatures on international entrepreneurship, the network view of internationalization and the internationalization of services. Based on this review, a conceptual framework is proposed which supports the key research questions. The research methods utilized are then discussed followed by the presentation of three cases. The final part of the essay considers avenues for further research and managerial insights based on the findings.

Literature review

International entrepreneurship and services

International entrepreneurship (IE) is a rapidly maturing field of study and, until recently, has benefited enormously from contributions from various disciplines (Acs et al., 2003). The guiding definition of IE adopted in this study is that of McDougall and Oviatt (2000, p. 903) who define 'international entrepreneurship' as a 'combination of innovative, proactive, and risk-seeking behavior that crosses national borders and is intended to create value in organizations'.

The full scope of IE remains undefined and continues to be debated (see Young et al., 2003). However, as interests grow, some researchers advocate extending the traditional domain of IE studies (Welch and Welch, 2004) to encompass 'sweeping transformations' shaping the contemporary international business environment (Wright and Dana, 2003, p. 136). These authors explain that international entrepreneurship adopts many guises globally and needs to be studied in a more holistic manner. With ongoing globalization, the new paradigm of IE is moving away from a focus on the firm, towards a focus on relationships within multipolar networks involving a multipolar distribution of power and control.

Wright and Dana (2003) suggest that the ongoing impact of globalization is characterized by two dramatic trends: (1) the demise of the nation state as the relevant unit around which international business activity is organized and conducted; and (2) the demise of the stand-alone firm, with a hierarchic distribution of power and control, as the principal unit of business competition. In adjusting to these trends, small firms in all sectors display complex internationalization behaviour (Fletcher, 2001). In services, in particular, such behaviour is driven by an increasing need to serve customers in the global environment, to bring products to market more quickly, to maintain service quality in several countries simultaneously, to lower costs in each country focusing on their core competencies or reduce promotion costs by marketing globally under one brand. Strategically, SMEs are utilizing network relationships to internationalize more effectively than they could on their own. In this process, they are even prepared to trade off some of their autonomy and control to achieve world-scale competitiveness.

In essence, small service firms are now open to diverse 'pathways' to internationalize their activities (Fletcher, 2001). Facilitated by Internet technology, they can easily tap into global sources of supply for requisite resources. They can enter collaborative arrangements – especially with larger firms – to leapfrog into new international markets (referred to as 'symbiotic' arrangements). This collaboration is stimulated by serendipitous or critical events (Spence, 2003) that provide them with additional human or financial resources, such as changes in ownership/management or being taken over by another company with international networks.

In sum, the internationalization alternatives facing small service firms have changed subject to their own entrepreneurial capabilities. However, research investigating the international entrepreneurial behaviour of management in small service firms is nascent and demands further attention. This study contributes to addressing this research lacuna, and draws on the network school of internationalization to develop its conceptual framework. This is discussed below.

Networks, services and the internationalization process of small firms

The internationalization process of small firms has been studied from several perspectives. Recent studies on small business internationalization have observed the important influence of international network connections as key levers enabling and accelerating the internationalization process (Welch and Welch, 2004; Johanson and Vahlne, 2003; Andersson, 2000; Sadler and Chetty, 2000; Chetty and Blankenburg Holm, 2000; Coviello and Munro, 1995, 1997). These studies argue that networks offer a wealth of internal and external linkages and opportunities, the effective exploitation of which depends on the entrepreneurial capabilities of the firms' key decision-makers and their organizational characteristics. Research, however, still remains vague on the entrepreneurial actions and processes utilized by small firms to tap into their rich web of network relationships to gain the necessary information, support and assistance needed to internationalize (Nummela, 2004; Johanson and Vahlne, 2003).

The above studies also highlight that network relationships are highly context-dependent and dynamic. For the newly internationalizing firm, such relationships in foreign markets come in diverse guises, they are established and developed through bilateral or even multilateral interactions, they change over time, they are used in various ways for different purposes and they are uncertain and time-consuming, often requiring considerable resource commitment to succeed. For the small entrepreneurial firm, interrelationships among a set of network partners can alter not only the range of international strategic options available, but also the resource base and mechanisms available for their pursuit. From an internationalization perspective, however, the patterns and impact of network relationships on small firms are complex and not fully understood (Coviello and Munro, 1995; Johanson and Vahlne, 2003).

Following the network school, this chapter adopts the view that 'internationalization' is the result of 'a mixture of strategic thinking, strategic action, emergent developments, chance and necessity' (Johanson and Vahlne, 1990, p. 22). In so doing, internationalization is argued to be 'an entrepreneurial process that is embedded in an institutional and social web which supports the firm in terms of access to information, human capital, finance, and so on' (Bell et al., 2003, p. 341). During this process such relationships change over time. They are used for different purposes, as the firm needs different resources in different phases. Relationships are established and dissolved simultaneously as strategic priorities change. In essence, the nature of network relationships established in a given context might dictate the direction of current and future strategic options (Madsen and Servais, 1997; Coviello and McAuley, 1999).

However, empirical research on the usage of networks by SMEs in the internationalization process has been quite scattered and largely of an exploratory nature (for an extensive review, see Coviello and McAuley, 1999; Nummela, 2004). As such, more research employing a networking perspective to examine the internationalization process of entrepreneurial firms is warranted. Given the salience of network relationships to the small firm, there is a need to examine the ongoing influence of network partners as it evolves internationally. There is an even greater need to understand the organizational and growth management issues faced by small entrepreneurial firms as such relationships mature, and their international involvement deepens over time. With these arguments in mind, the next section reviews research analysing the significance of network effects on the internationalization of small service firms.

Internationalization and service SMEs

One of the main criticisms of the internationalization literature argues that extant theories do not adequately reflect the internationalization behaviour and patterns of service industries. Limited academic attention has been attributed to service firms and industries despite their increasingly active involvement in international trade (Clark and Rajaratnam, 1999; Bryson, 2001; Selstad and Sjøholt, 2004). Overall, internationalization research and literature draw primarily from the internationalization experiences, processes and patterns of small and multinational manufacturing firms and lack an explicit service focus (see Boojihawon, 2004 for a comprehensive review).

Referring to the services' internationalization literature, in particular, very limited empirical attention has been devoted towards the analysis of small service firms. For instance, out of 16 articles (1999) on small firm internationalization, comprehensively reviewed by Coviello and McAuley, only two focused on service organizations (Bjorkman and Kock, 1997; O'Farrell and Wood, 1998). Some studies in their sample also examined software/information technology firms, although it may be argued that software firms are not in the service industry (Bell, 1995). In essence, all these authors have observed the relative lack of empirical evidence on service SMEs' entrepreneurship and internationalization. The same group of authors also highlight some evidence illustrating the influence of network relationships on small service firm internationalization. For instance, O'Farrell and Wood (1998) and Korhonen et al. (1996) found that cooperative relationships were used by 34 per cent of service SMEs at some point in the internationalization process. Also, Scandinavian researchers such as Sharma and Johanson (1987) found that some professional service firms, for example technical consulting firms, operate in networks of connected relationships between organizations. These relationships become 'bridges to foreign markets' and provide firms with the opportunity and motivation to internationalize.

The conclusion of these studies calls for further research examining the role of networks in small service firms' abilities to undertake international entrepreneurial initiatives across borders. These arguments lend support to the argument that the network approach can provide valuable insights into the nature and dynamics of internationalization in service industries. It allows for a more plausible description of the process as it is directly linked to the strategic direction and provides the firm's managers with a way of doing business.

Internationalization and service characteristics

Service firms tend to adopt different internationalization approaches when compared to their manufacturing counterparts because of several characteristics that are unique to services (Erramilli, 1990; Bryson, 2001; Ochel, 2002; Selstad and Sjøholt, 2004). The focus of this study is on advertising services.

Advertising is a 'communication tool delivering controlled messages to many people simultaneously and at a low cost per message'; it is expected to influence the attitudes, intentions and behaviour of targeted audiences (Wilmhurst, 1985, p. 58). Advertising services are packages of activities that are offered by advertising agencies to their clients that have creativity and innovation at their heart, making such advertising services entrepreneurial by default.

Another important feature in the provision of advertising services relates to the extent of customer participation in the creative process. An advertising agency can only create an appropriate campaign if the client communicates its needs, and is prepared to provide relevant (often confidential) information that defines the creative process. The necessity of this cooperation implies that the service outputs are typically unique. It also means that neither of the two parties can precisely predict whether or not the campaign will be successful. Boojihawon (2004) further discusses the implications of other service characteristics such as 'intangibility', 'heterogeneity' and 'perishability' on the internationalization process of service firms. In contrast, other related arguments assert that the influence of these characteristics on internationalization is, in fact, sector-specific given the increasingly blurred distinctions between 'goods' and 'service' offerings as manufacturing firms incorporate greater amounts of service components in their outputs. Therefore, we need to understand the development of the international activities of service firms as a whole, and also the differences in such activities between given service sectors (Hellman, 1994).

The UK advertising sector is the chosen context for this study as it is one of the world's dominant centres for media and advertising activities. London holds the largest concentration of advertising agencies by far, including both large and small firms. In fact, the entire value chain of film and TV production – film production, post-production, film distribution, sales agents, design, photography, music and advertising – is all located within one square mile in a small district known as Soho (Nachum and Keeble, 2003). These authors posit that in such a geographical setting, local networking and inter-firm linkages have a strong influence on the competitive advantage of individual firms and their economic success. The UK advertising sector, therefore, has two features of particular relevance to this study. Firstly, it contains large numbers of both large (multinational) and small firms, thus allowing ample scope for firms of different size to engage in networks entrepreneurially, and secondly, it is characterized by a striking geographical concentration, providing an appropriate platform for the examination of the behaviour of firms in network relationships. The conceptual framework underpinning this study is explained in the next section.

Conceptualization and method

As mentioned earlier, this research aims to explore how small service agencies utilize their network relationships entrepreneurially to enhance their internationalization capabilities. A framework for analysis is presented in Figure 7.1. The framework takes a processual perspective on the network-based internationalization 'pathways' adopted by small service firms. It argues that networking may be an important strategic element in the growth and international development of such firms. The emphasis is on the entrepreneurial capabilities of these firms to exploit network relationships (interorganizational or interpersonal) developed through international transactions or emerging through serendipitous events. Altogether, the framework takes a holistic view of international entrepreneurship, and argues that international initiatives can develop as a result of strategic as well as informal, unstructured interaction of the firm with its network's actors. Relationships with these actors play an instrumental role in the firm's ability to carry out its international initiatives.

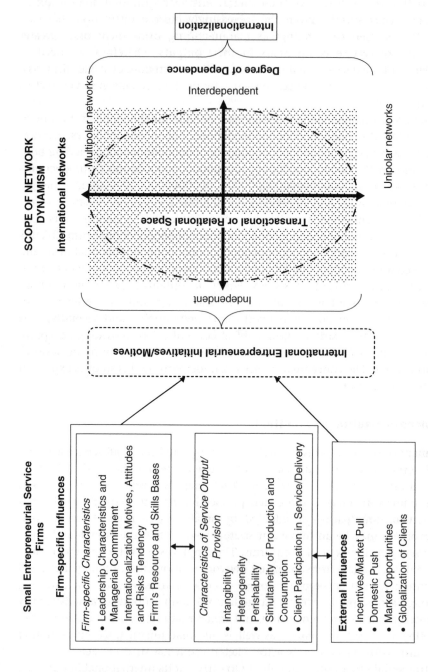

Figure 7.1 International entrepreneurship and network dynamics: a conceptual framework

On the left-hand side of the framework, it is argued that an interactive combination of firm-specific influences and external industry characteristics can affect the motives for international entrepreneurial initiatives and the ways in which they are executed. At the firm level, Cicic et al. (1999) and Ibeh and Young (1999) suggest that individual and firm-level factors (identified as firm-specific characteristics in Figure 7.1) are antecedents to small service firms' entrepreneurial export orientation. Also as mentioned earlier, service products are characterized by distinct features that can invariably affect the mode of international expansion adopted by small service firms (for example, intangibility and heterogeneity). Additionally, external industry-level factors (market pull from overseas, domestic push from saturation of home markets, etc.) are also expected to influence the motives to internationalize for these entrepreneurial service SMEs.

These influences in turn affect the types of relationships management can engage in, as given in the right-hand side of the framework. This shaded area defines a space in which the scope of networking strategies for internationalization is defined by a range of options to integrate networks that vary in their levels of international involvement; from unipolar through to multipolar networks (represented vertically here, see Wright and Dana, 2003; Dana et al., 2004), and which are also defined by varying degrees of dependence from complete independence to tight interdependence (represented horizontally here, see Etemad et al., 2001). This 'scope of network dynamism' maps out a transactional or relational space in which small service firms can build 'ties' (Granovetter, 1985) or create relationships to carry out their international activities. On this basis, two research questions govern the focus of this framework:

1. How do firm-specific and industry characteristics influence international entrepreneurship in small service firms? And,
2. How do small service firms entrepreneurially utilize network relationships to undertake international activities?

Methodology

The research reported in this chapter draws from the empirical data of a major process-oriented examination of the international strategy of advertising agencies based in the UK. The study was qualitative in approach and 19 case studies were conducted. The case method was appropriate given the limited amount of empirical work investigating the international entrepreneurial behaviour of small service firms. The method was useful for developing a detailed understanding of the phenomena and provided the flexibility to explore concepts, or insights that changed, or emerged, during the data collection process. This flexibility added to the richness and quality of the data as the research process unfolded (Yin, 1994). This was beneficial as the researchers wanted to 'get close' to the socially constructed realities and experiences of the advertising agencies and their international strategy processes.

The following sampling frame was adopted. The companies approached were from the list of the top 300 advertising agencies in the UK, compiled by Campaign (2000). The agencies were selected on the basis of their degree of international involvement, level of fee income and the extent to which they were servicing international clients. These criteria provided coherence throughout the case research design and analysis, as they would intentionally limit the variance in the sample, thereby making cross-case analysis meaningful (Yin, 1994). The case study sampling process was expected to recruit between 15 and 25 firms, with the possibility of securing multiple respondents in each of them. From the list of the top 300 agencies, those with fee income of less than £3 million were screened out because of their small size and strong domestic orientation. This left about 150 agencies to choose from. All of these agencies were randomly approached on a convenience basis, keeping in mind the requirement of 'theoretical saturation' (Eisenhardt, 1989) that underpins qualitative inquiry. A sample of 19 agencies agreed to participate in the study, six of which were small and medium-sized advertising companies (SMAs). Only three of these are analysed and presented for the purpose of this chapter. It is important to note that the three cases described here are not necessarily representative of all the SMAs but do allow for some theoretical generalizations (Eisenhardt, 1989).

In-depth interviews were used as the primary mechanisms to explore issues, events, feelings, knowledge and experiences in detail around the issues of interest. The interviews were semi-structured but non-directed. The respondents principally comprised senior-level managers with significant experience and involvement in strategic decision-making in their respective agencies. The interviews lasted between 45 minutes and 2½ hours. Each interview was taped, transcribed and complemented with notes and memos that were taken during discussions. A total of approximately 600 pages of data were assembled through this process. The initial insights from the data were revealed during the interview process and the analysis became more fine-grained and systematic as the fieldwork progressed. Once this had been developed, attention was directed towards the elements of international entrepreneurial behaviour of each firm based on the conceptual framework. Qualitative data were content-analysed using the NVIVO software package and the procedures recommended by Miles and Huberman (1994) and Shaw (1999), who emphasize the use of matrices and diagrams for reducing and visualizing data. In the section below, the international entrepreneurial behaviour and the distinct networking strategies of three SMAs are delineated.

Findings

AccentUK

AccentUK was established in 1990 (see Figure 7.2). It was a full service agency founded by four partners, each with an average of 15–25 years of international experience working in multinational advertising agencies like Publicis, Grey Worldwide and Ogilvy and Mather. Currently, its fee income amounts to over £4.8 million and it employs 21 professionals.

AccentUK was founded with a corporate vision of creating a respected, medium-sized agency. The agency was deliberately kept small as management wanted to maintain hands-on involvement in the service delivery process. In so doing, it aspires to its mission of 'helping clients build better successful brands with great creative work and strong insightful strategies'. The agency targets mainly 'secondary and tertiary brands' for its business (basically brands that come second or third to leading brands in the market), and wants to be recognized for the quality of its creative work and client servicing.

Throughout the early 1990s, the company undertook various international advertising projects through clients' invitations to launch pan-European campaigns. But such businesses were few, and in several instances, they had to decline clients' offers as they had insufficient capabilities to meet their expectations. For instance, management could not maintain the same level of hands-on involvement in international campaigns. Nonetheless, the partners were determined to expand internationally. During the late 1990s, they approached several agencies in Europe in the hope of local partnerships. Their efforts materialized and they started servicing foreign clients in five international markets, namely France, Germany, Belgium, Italy and the USA (New York) through partnership arrangements. However, business was inconsistent and the overseas partners did not offer adequate scope for further international penetration.

In 2000, AccentUK joined BRUSSELINKS, an independent international network, regrouping a close-knit group of owner-driven entrepreneurial advertising agencies, covering over 20 markets in Europe. BRUSSELINKS was founded in the 1980s in Switzerland as a limited stock company, with its equity shared by its members. Currently, BRUSSELINKS is Europe's second largest independent network. It represents 12 multinational clients in three or more markets. It defines itself as an 'unconventional European network' with the resources and flexibility to tailor itself to the needs of its clients.

Note that internationalization did not take place in incremental 'stages'; Figures 7.2–7.4 are presented in this manner for analytical purposes. AccentUK agreed to an equity arrangement with BRUSSELINKS and almost instantly leapfrogged its way into several international markets. The partners were confident in this strategy as there were limited financial and strategic risks attached

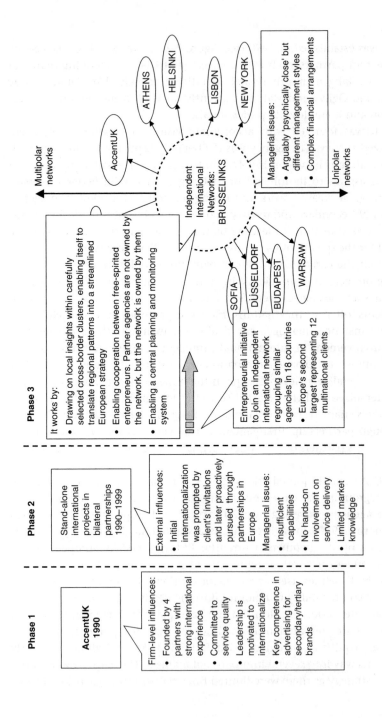

Figure 7.2 AccentUK

to the venture – BRUSSELINKS was not going to share AccentUK's equity, but vice versa. There were also significant similarities in the background and experience of the firms forming the network.

AccentUK now works primarily with sister agencies with contact established through BRUSSELINKS' headquarters (HQ). New and existing businesses are handled through proactive use of established network relationships or cross-referrals based on flexible, non-binding contractual agreements. The interviewee at AccentUK explains:

> International businesses are handled in three ways in the network: first, through the HQ going European-wide or global; second, at a satellite-level where two or more partner agencies collaborate to pitch for a big international account at their own discretion and third at a local level, basically foreign market servicing of domestic clients.

Furthermore, the organization of the network is structured to promote flexibility and coordination to avoid the red tape and bottlenecks involved in multinational agency structures. However, handling international business in this network is not entirely problem-free. AccentUK encounters frequent challenges in liaising with partner agencies coming from arguably 'psychically close' cultures but with their different management styles. Even though the agencies share more or less the same philosophies at corporate level, they are very often not organized or managed in the same way. There are different approaches to handling international business, different styles of management and different strategic approaches. There are also significant differences in accounting for profitability. Partners often end up in conflict because of the lack of precise guidelines in handling financial arrangements in completed international projects.

Contactpoint

Four entrepreneurs founded Contactpoint in 1971 (see Figure 7.3). Its current annual fee income approximates to £6m and it employs about 42 people. These partners had planned to go international from the very outset, but no significant opportunities appeared. In 1980 they seized a unique chance to sell out when a multinational agency network (Intermedia) showed interest. Intermedia offered Contactpoint a strong partnership and promised access to a global network of offices and clients. Intermedia is a multinational agency with a global network of 359 offices in 100 countries, employing more than 8500 people.

Interestingly, however, Contactpoint decided to change its strategic orientation following the acquisition. Based on its core competences, it chose to service only business-to-business (B2B) clients and projects (for example advertising

114

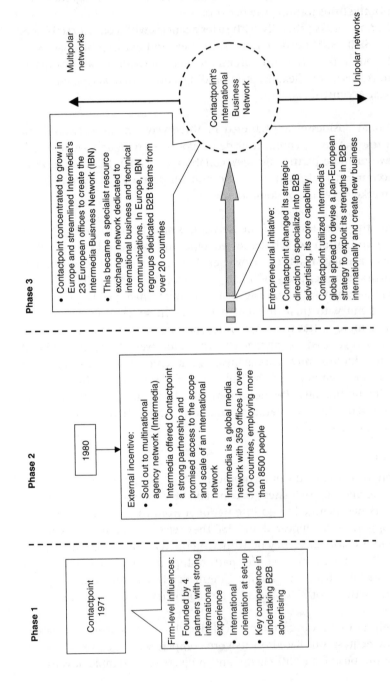

Multipolar networks

Unipolar networks

Phase 3

- Contactpoint concentrated to grow in Europe and streamlined Intermedia's 23 European offices to create the Intermedia Buisness Network (IBN)
- This became a specialist resource exchange network dedicated to international business and technical communications. In Europe, IBN regroups dedicated B2B teams from over 20 countries

Contactpoint's International Business Network

Entrepreneurial initiative:

- Contactpoint changed its strategic direction to specialize into B2B advertising, its core capability
- Contactpoint utilized Intermedia's global spread to devise a pan-European strategy to exploit its strengths in B2B internationally and create new business

Phase 2

1980

External incentive:

- Sold out to multinational agency network (Intermedia)
- Intermedia offered Contactpoint a strong partnership and promised access to the scope and scale of an international network
- Intermedia is a global media network with 359 offices in over 100 countries, employing more than 8500 people

Phase 1

Contactpoint 1971

Firm-level influences:

- Founded by 4 partners with strong international experience
- International orientation at set-up
- Key competence in undertaking B2B advertising

Figure 7.3 Contactpoint

only complex industrial and technological products). This gained the full support of Intermedia as it had been unsuccessful in penetrating B2B markets. B2B campaigns are distinct because they must speak to a knowledgeable target audience, often about highly complex products and services.

Contactpoint also devised a pan-European strategy to penetrate B2B markets across Europe by exploiting Intermedia's global spread. Contactpoint's managers focused their growth on Europe and reorganized Intermedia's 23 European offices to create the Intermedia Business Network (IBN), a specialist B2B resource exchange network. In Europe, IBN regrouped B2B teams from over 20 European countries. Through IBN, Contactpoint operates as a B2B specialist with its own in-house design and creative teams, media planners, print-buying experts, and undertakes responsibility for the overall marketing communications of its clients. Contactpoint is able to offer 'international advertising' rather than 'literal' translations for international markets. In other words, it checks its creative works for cultural acceptability, provides information on local markets, media and list sourcing. It is capable of liaising with local experts who understand the complexities of B2B advertising and use their knowledge to create well-branded campaigns that work locally.

The international strategy of IBN centres not only on servicing Intermedia's existing international clients, but also on stretching the network's international capability and experience to accommodate new businesses. It benefits both through its own initiative to appoint new clients, and through referrals by Intermedia. Furthermore, irrespective of how the client is appointed, Contactpoint directly coordinates its works through IBN's offices. The local managers of those offices have immediate control of the businesses and departments but they are ultimately responsible for reporting to Contactpoint in the UK.

This networking strategy has been very successful for Contactpoint and it is actively planning to replicate this process across Intermedia's American and Asia-Pacific networks. The difficulty in this process is that creativity is impaired because this loose network structure makes it difficult for managers to align advertising professionals to produce good ideas.

Finewaters

Finewaters is small agency with fee income of about £4.8m and 35 employees. Four partners established it in 1989 (see Figure 7.4). Similar to AccentUK, all the partners had worked for multinational agencies like Abbott Mead Vickers BBDO and EuroRSCG. Despite launching at the height of London's recession, Finewaters has enjoyed spectacular growth. The agency has produced some widely recognized campaigns, mostly for the big blue chip companies, like Toshiba, Daewoo Cars and Pizza Hut among others.

This agency's initial internationalization opportunity came about with the success of its first international appointment to Pizza Hut in 1992. Its

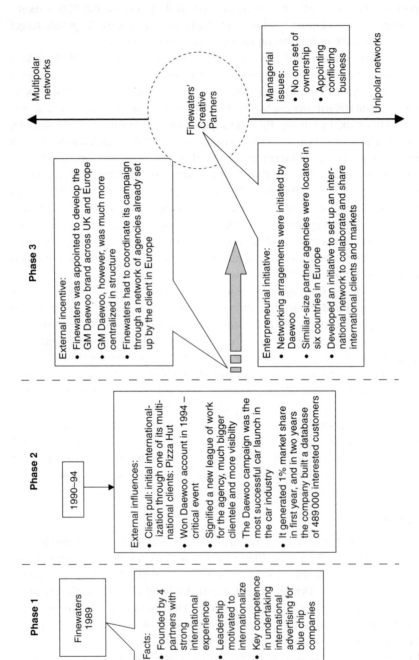

Figure 7.4 Finewaters

successful campaign here attracted Daewoo Cars in 1994, which in turn became instrumental in furthering its international expansion. The interviewee recalls:

> ... The first of those was probably a few years ago when we won business from Pizza Hut. Then, about two years after that, the company won the Daewoo Car business and that was a huge step forward for the company because what happened was very innovative and built the company's reputation a great deal... Daewoo was also particularly awkward from the point of view that we had to suddenly deal with a, culturally, very different company (Korean). The difference is that we had to work at a much more fundamental level to get their trust in that respect. We did hire somebody who could speak the language but it was the cultural issues that were the biggest ones to deal with. And then they were very different projects from what we were used to handle (bigger and more complicated) but that's a question of degree rather than anything else.

The Daewoo campaign was the most successful car launch in the industry. Following this success, Finewaters was appointed by General Motors (GM), which later acquired Daewoo, to develop the GM Daewoo brand across UK and Europe. GM Daewoo, however, wanted to work in a more centralized way and Finewaters was asked to coordinate its campaign through a network of agencies already set up in Europe by GM.

The networking arrangements were initiated and directed by GM Daewoo. In total, six agencies were coordinated across France, Germany, Switzerland, Italy, the Netherlands and Sweden to manage Daewoo's pan-European campaign. All these agencies were of similar sizes, had a reputation for consistent creativity in their respective markets and were commonly ranked among the most competitively awarded agencies.

Furthermore, while GM Daewoo's campaign was ongoing, these collaborating agencies developed enough trust in each other to start sharing other international businesses: '... the French agency needed to come to the UK and asked for our collaboration. Then the Spanish and Italian agencies came with similar needs and we helped them to service their clients in the UK.'

Although frequent, most of these collaborations took place in a fairly haphazard manner. They decided to give them form by creating their own independent international network called Creative Partners. This network shares similar characteristics to BRUSSELINKS, in the AccentUK case above, but was much smaller in size. Currently, their shared clientele includes Prudential Europe and Bananalotto. The network is also looking to expand in the USA. However, the biggest managerial challenge for Finewaters relates to handling partners' insecurities in undertaking competing international businesses. The advertising firms in the Creative Partners network are not governed through single ownership; each conducts business for clients competing in common markets or industries, so cross-border referrals between partners can lead to potential conflicts of interests in the portfolio of clients they represent.

Discussion and conclusion

Overall, the cases illustrate that network relationships act as effective 'bridges' to hasten the internationalization of SMAs (Sharma and Johanson, 1987), motivating and enabling them to adopt innovative ways to undertake new businesses, or service existing clients, internationally. However, in contrast to the conclusion of Johanson and Mattsson (1988), successful internationalization in the three cases depended less on success within domestic markets, but more on the agencies' abilities and initiatives to exploit the wealth of relationships accumulated within given international networks, irrespective of the individual firm's size-related, or resource-related, limitations. The next subsections consider the research questions underlying this study.

Firm- and industry-level influences on international entrepreneurship

As argued earlier, understanding the international entrepreneurial behaviour of small service firms requires an understanding of their key managerial and service characteristics, as well as those of the industry in which they are embedded. As illustrated, all three cases comprised internationally experienced managers in the advertising industry. They were entrepreneurial in attitude and motivated to internationalize their activities while maintaining the quality of their service delivery process. These firm-specific features are the essential ingredients that differentiated their service outputs from the competition and also influenced the type of network relationships with which they would get involved. AccentUK and Finewaters, for example, chose to work with like-minded partners sharing similar backgrounds, creative assets and enthusiasm for service quality. These observations concur with those of Scholhammer and Kuriloff (1979) and O'Farrell and Wood (1998) who argue that a small firm's managerial style, independence, ownership, scale and scope of operations, influence the nature and extent of their international involvement. This chapter further emphasizes that these dimensions are unique for service SMEs and are defined by the industry context in which they are embedded.

The cases also indicated some managerial challenges that affected the way in which network relationships were established and evolved in each case firm. In all three scenarios, although the firms had entered promising network arrangements, the successful implementation of entrepreneurial initiatives depended on how the relationship dynamics between the different partners evolved and how subsequent processual activities were managed once the relationships were established. For instance, AccentUK experienced conflicting cultures among collaborating agencies, although this was not an issue at the start. Contactpoint faced difficulties in maintaining consistent quality in creative outputs and Finewaters had to continuously handle its partners' insecurities in order to internationalize further. In general, there is limited empirical evidence in the literature that examines the post-managerial and organizational implications once network relationships are established. From a practical viewpoint, the management of established network relationships is instrumental to the firm's success and warrants more attention. Managers must be astute when international partners are negotiating for greater control of shared projects. Relatedly, they must understand the issues linked to managing relationships in cross-cultural contexts as well as how to secure their advantage in multiple complex relationship structures.

International entrepreneurship and network dynamics

The cases illustrate that growth prospects in international networks rely on network dynamics. In all three scenarios, international expansion was unstructured and relied on a mixture of serendipitous events occurring through interaction and the entrepreneurial ability of the firm's management to take advantage of such opportunities. For AccentUK and Finewaters, international expansion was achieved through the member agencies' own initiatives and intelligence to make proactive use of established network relations (via BRUSSELINKS or Creative Partners), or through cross-referral based on inter-firm agreements. Similarly, Contactpoint relied on clients' cross-referrals from its parent, or pitched for new projects on its own. As such, this study supports the findings of Coviello and Munro (1995, 1997) and Chetty and Blankenburg Holm (2000) that network relationships create synergistic benefits for member partners, but there is limited evidence here to suggest or identify processes of how entrepreneurial initiatives are pursued and realized beyond their initial stages. Related to this, managers must understand the benefits and risks associated with externalizing their businesses or projects with overseas partners. This is crucial for service firms like SMAs since they trade off their control for shared profits, potentially weakening their position in a relationship.

Throughout, this chapter has emphasized that network relationships are dynamic and the cases also illustrated that such relationships changed with the circumstances underpinning them. The interesting illustration here is that of Finewaters which moved from interdependently supporting the GM Daewoo brand across Europe to eventually creating its own independent international network to further its international capability. Network relationships change continuously with circumstances, and such change affects the nature of opportunism inherent within them. The managers of small firms need to understand how to manage this change process consistently to the firm's advantage.

References

Acs, Z., L.P. Dana and M.V. Jones (2003) 'Towards New Horizons: the Internationalization of Entrepreneurship', *Journal of International Entrepreneurship*, 1, 5–12.

Andersson, S. (2000) 'The Internationalization of the Firm from an Entrepreneurial Perspective', *International Studies of Management and Organisation*, 30 (1), 63–92.

Bell, J. (1995) 'The Internationalization of Small Computer Software Firms – a Further Challenge to "Stage Theories" ', *European Journal of Marketing*, 29 (8), 60–75.

Bell, J., R. McNaughton, S. Young and D. Crick (2003) 'Towards an Integrative Model of Small Firm Internationalization', *Journal of International Entrepreneurship*, 1, 339–62.

Bjorkman, I. and S. Kock (1997) 'Inward International Activities in Service Firms – Illustrated by Three Firms from the Tourism Industry', *International Journal of Service Industries Management*, 8 (5), 362–76.

Boojihawon, D.K. (2004) 'International Entrepreneurship and Network Relationships: the International Marketing Communications Sector', in M.V. Jones and P. Dimitratos (eds), *Emerging Paradigms in International Entrepreneurship* (Cheltenham, UK: Edward Elgar Publishing).

Bryson, J.R. (2001) 'Services and Internationalization: Annual Report on the Progress of Research into Service Activities in Europe in 1998', *The Services Industries Journal*, 21 (1), 227–40.

Campaign (2000) *Report: Worldwide Advertising*, London, UK.

Chetty, S. and D. Blankenburg Holm (2000) 'Internationalisation of Small to Medium-sized Manufacturing Firms: a Network Approach', *International Business Review*, 9 (1), 77–93.

Cicic, M., P.G. Patterson and A. Shoham (1999) 'A Conceptual Model of the Internationalisation of Services Firms', *Journal of Global Marketing*, 12, 81–105.

Clark, T. and D. Rajaratnam (1999) 'International Services: Perspectives at Century's End', *Journal of Services Marketing*, 13 (4/5), 298–310.

Coviello, N.E. and A. McAuley (1999) 'Internationalisation and the Smaller Firm: a Review of Contemporary Empirical Research', *Management International Review*, 39, 223–56.

Coviello, N.E. and H.J. Munro (1995) 'Growing the Entrepreneurial Firm: Networking for International Market Development', *European Journal of Marketing*, 29 (7), 49–61.

Coviello, N.E. and H. J. Munro (1997) 'Network Relationships and the Internationalisation Process of Smaller Software Firms', *International Business Review*, 6 (4), 361–84.

Dana, L-P., H. Etemad and R.W. Wright (2004) 'Back to the Future: International Entrepreneurship in the New Economy', in M.V. Jones and P. Dimitratos (eds), *Emerging Paradigms in International Entrepreneurship* (Cheltenham: Edward Elgar).

Eisenhardt, K.M. (1989) 'Building Theories from Case Study Research', *Academy of Management Review*, 14, 532–50.

Erramilli, M.K. (1990) 'Entry Mode Choice in Service Industries', *International Marketing Review*, 7 (5), 50–62.

Etemad, H., R.W. Wright and L-P. Dana (2001) 'Symbiotic International Business Networks: Collaboration between Small and Large Firms', *Thunderbird International Business Review*, 43 (4), 481–99.

Fletcher, R. (2001) 'A Holistic Approach to Internationalisation', *International Business Review*, 10, 25–49.

Granovetter, M.S. (1985) 'Economic Action and Social Structure: the Problem of Embeddedness', *American Journal of Sociology*, 91 (3), 481–510.

Hellman, P. (1994) 'The Internationalisation of Finnish Financial Service Companies', *International Business Review*, 5 (2), 191–208.

Ibeh, K.I.N. and S. Young (1999) 'The Contingency Model of Export Entrepreneurship: a Proposed Conceptual Framework for Initial Export Venturing', Strathclyde International Business Unit, Working Paper Series, 5, 1–25.

Johanson, J. and L.G. Mattsson (1988). 'Internationalisation in Industrial Systems – a Network Approach', in N. Hood and J.E. Vahlne (eds), *Strategies in Global Competition* (London: Croom Helm).

Johanson, J. and J.E. Vahlne (1990) 'The Mechanism of Internationalisation', *International Marketing Review*, 7 (4), 11–24.

Johanson, J. and J.E. Vahlne (2003) 'Business Relationship Learning and Commitment in the Internationalisation Process', *Journal of International Entrepreneurship*, 1, 83–101.

Korhonen, H., R. Luostarinen and L.S. Welch (1996) 'Internationalisation of SMEs: Inward–outward Patterns and Government Policy', *Management International Review*, 36 (4), 315–29.

McDougall, P.P. and B.M. Oviatt (2000) 'International Entrepreneurship: the Intersection of Two Research Paths', *Academy of Management Journal*, 43 (3), 902–6.

Madsen, T.K. and P. Servais (1997) 'The Internationalisation of Born Globals: an Evolutionary Process?', *International Business Review*, 6 (6), 561–83.

Miles, M.B. and M.A. Huberman (1994) *Qualitative Data Analysis: an Expanded Sourcebook* (Thousand Oaks: Sage Publications).

Nachum, L. and D. Keeble (2003) 'Neo-Marshallian Clusters and Global Networks: the Linkages of Media Firms in Central London', *Long Range Planning*, 36, 459–80.

Nummela, N. (2004) 'Is the Globe Becoming Small or Is the Small Becoming Global? Globalisation and Internationalising SMEs', in M.V. Jones and P. Dimitratos (eds), *Emerging Paradigms in International Entrepreneurship* (Cheltenham, UK: Edward Elgar).

Ochel, W. (2002) 'The International Competitiveness of Business Service Firms: the Case of Germany', *The Services Industries Journal*, 22 (2), 1–16.

O'Farrell, P.N. and P.A.Wood (1998) 'Internationalisation by Business Service Firms: towards a New Regionally Based Conceptual Framework', *Environment and Planning*, 30, 109–28.

Sadler, A. and S. Chetty (2000) 'The Impact of Networks on New Zealand Firms', *Journal of Euromarketing*, 9 (20), 37–58.

Schollhammer, H. and A.H. Kuriloff (1979) *Entrepreneurship and Small Business Management* (Chichester: John Wiley).

Selstad, T. and P. Sjøholt (2004) 'Service Industries in the Global Economy', *Norwegian Journal of Geography*, 58, 136–40.

Sharma, D. and J. Johanson (1987) 'Technical Consultancy in Internationalisation', *International Marketing Review*, Winter, 20–9.

Shaw, E. (1999) 'A Guide to the Qualitative Research Process: Evidence from a Small Firm Study', *Qualitative Market Research: an International Journal*, 2(2), February, 59–70.

Spence, M. (2003) 'International Strategy Formation in Small Canadian High-technology Companies', *Journal of International Entrepreneurship*, 1 (3), 277–96.

Welch, C.L. and L.S. Welch (2004) 'Broadening the Concept of International Entrepreneurship: Internationalisation, Networks and Politics', *Journal of International Entrepreneurship*, 2, 217–37.

Wilmhurst, J. (1985) *The Fundamentals of Advertising* (Oxford: Butterworth-Heinemann Ltd).

Wright, R.W. and L-P. Dana (2003) 'Changing Paradigms of International Entrepreneurship Strategy', *Journal of International Entrepreneurship*, 1, 135–52.

Yin, R. (1994) *Case Study Research Design and Methods* (Thousand Oaks: Sage).

Young, S., P. Dimitratos and L-P. Dana (2003) 'International Entrepreneurship Research: What Scope for International Business Theories?', *Journal of International Entrepreneurship*, 1, 31–42.

8

Cross-border Management Issues in International Law Firms

Susan Segal-Horn and Alison Dean

Introduction

This chapter focuses on the organizational changes arising from the creation of large cross-border legal service organizations and alliance networks. We address the management issues faced by legal professional service firms (PSFs) in responding to the demands placed upon their existing organizational structures and processes by the most recent phase in their international expansion. This phase of their growth has been intended to implement global strategies and to create global organization structures. In particular, our findings relate to the larger law firms for whom the requirement to build integrated global networks is a competitive and client expectation. To put the issue of firm size into perspective, the largest UK law firm at which we conducted interviews operated in 24 countries, had over 350 partners (of whom nearly 50 per cent were located outside the UK) and had fee income in excess of £450 million; a smaller firm studied still operated in 15 countries, had almost 3000 professional staff and over 300 partners, with fee income in excess of £280 million.

Arising from this focus on larger firms is a set of issues that involve unlocking managerial, cultural and organizational barriers to integration across jurisdictions. The work described here is part of an ongoing study of the globalization of UK City law firms. Sample firms have taken different routes to globalization, either growth by acquisition or growth via alliance building and networks. These approaches do not appear to be country specific; they are firm specific. Despite this, there is significant similarity in the mechanisms adopted for the development of cross-border integration of activities and integration of organizational practices and cultures across national boundaries and legal jurisdictions. In this chapter, we use data from two top 10 firms that had pursued different routes to international expansion: one by acquisition, the other by building an alliance network. Interestingly, subsequent to our data collection, the network builder had begun consolidation by finalizing outright acquisition of many of its long-term international network partners.

Law is an under-researched industry. This research adds to knowledge of the legal services industry, explores globalization in a PSF context and further extends the global strategy literature into the services domain.

Industry context

Professional services have changed in a variety of ways in the last decade. Changes in their competitive environment resulting from a combination of international competitors, client expectations and globalization of products and markets, have led larger PSFs to expand their existing activities and their product and client portfolios beyond national boundaries by developing global strategies. PSFs have therefore begun building integrated global networks. In most service industries, including professional services, the initial push for global strategies has been from the demand side. Customers or clients who are already global themselves require service providers and PSF providers to be available to provide client services seamlessly in all the countries in which they have a presence (Segal-Horn, 1993). Some clients, although by no means all, prefer one-stop shopping for professional services. PSFs have had to reorganize themselves to provide services on this basis. On the supply side, pressure within PSFs has arisen from high costs, recruitment and retention issues for quality professional staff, growing problems in finding senior professional staff who are also competent managers, pressure on fees and the changing nature of competition within professional services. This is enhanced by the importance of trust and relationships within PSF/client relations. Therefore, the globalization of the marketplace for professional services is both supply and demand led.

These changes have come somewhat later to law firms than to other PSF sectors, such as accounting and business advisory services. However, law firms now appear to be following similar supply and demand-led pathways to these other PSF sectors. These changes are predominantly driven by the largest US and UK law firms since these two legal jurisdictions constitute the largest legal markets, form the basis of international law and contain the two dominant global firm clusters. However, global strategies carry with them other strategic, organizational and operational requirements that legal PSFs were not originally designed to meet. It is important to emphasize that although many large legal PSFs have had international networks for some years, they have not been globally integrated networks. This is the significant recent shift that this research is reviewing. Global strategies for legal PSFs require structural change, internal cultural change and a reappraisal of professional practice. These responses have both managerial and organizational implications. This chapter therefore focuses on managerial responses to the strategic issues arising from the emergence of a global market for legal services and the creation of large cross-border legal service organizations and alliance networks.

Literature review

The theoretical underpinnings of this chapter are derived from existing literatures on PSFs and global and international strategy. While there is some location specificity (Ghemawat, 2003) with regard to legal jurisdictions affecting international law firms, the relevant focus within the international and global strategy literature is on differing types of international organizational structure and management (Bartlett and Ghoshal, 1993; Yip, 1996) and the management of MNCs, rather than internationalization as such. The management of the international PSF requires management of cross-border networks (Ghoshal and Bartlett, 1990; Hedlund, 1994; Malnight, 1996); HQ–subsidiary relationships (Birkinshaw, 2001); internal knowledge management and capture of intellectual capital (Teece, 2000; Szulanski, 2003; Fosstenløkken et al., 2003; Robertson et al., 2003) and effective global account management (Birkinshaw et al., 2001).

Summarizing the general thrust of a deep literature suggests that firms implementing global strategies need to understand and pursue a paradigm shift. The shift needed is from a local national emphasis that maximizes country differences, to a paradigm that emphasizes global commonalities and minimizes country differences within the organization. 'Managerial roles, organizational tasks and even the underlying rationale and purpose of the firm' (Bartlett and Ghoshal, 1993, p. 25) would have to shift in order for cross-border coordination to be effectively implemented. Current barriers to cross-border, intra-firm integration include the dominance of domestic culture and processes; national culture and identity; autonomous national firms and business units; national performance review and compensation; local accounting and information systems; local-for-local-only skills and expertise; poor global account management for multi-local customers, and local branding and advertising (Yip, 1996, 2005). An especially important barrier within knowledge-based PSFs is poor knowledge management and transfer. Barriers to the appropriation, transfer and dissemination of intra-organizational knowledge require 'a departure from the logic of hierarchical organization' (Hedlund, 1994, p. 73) towards the N-form (network) organization, which enables easier knowledge combination within differing parts of the firm. Other attributes of the N-form are temporary groupings of people; lateral communication; interdependence of staff; interdependence of technologies, and the potential for scope rather than scale economies. We would therefore expect to find evidence for such shifts within our sample interview data.

We also draw on literature at the intersection of PSF and international and global strategy literatures (Van Maanen and Laurent, 1993; McLaughlin and

Fitzsimmons, 1996; Løwendahl, 2000; Grosse, 2000; Aharoni and Nachum, 2000; Segal-Horn, 2005) to provide a context for the study of the globalization of legal PSFs and for exploring their internal changes. Within the PSF and international strategy literatures, while studies have been conducted on the internationalization of a number of service industries, for example accounting, financial services, advertising and management consultancy (Daniels et al., 1989; Segal-Horn, 1993; Terpstra and Yu, 1998; Kipping, 2002), law firms have received less specific attention. More general studies have focused on PSF management (Maister, 1993; Lorsch and Mathias, 2001; Greenwood and Empson, 2003) and the globalization of PSFs (Nachum, 1998, 1999; Løwendahl, 2000; Løwendahl et al., 2001).

Research related to law firms has focused on the globalization of the law itself (Shapiro, 1993), the feasibility of international expansion of law firms from a geographical perspective (Beaverstock et al., 1999, 2000; Chang et al., 1998), context change in US law firms (Ramcharran, 1999; Silver, 2000; Spar, 1997) and archetype shift in law firms (Greenwood and Hinings, 1993, 1996; Cooper et al., 1996; Morris and Pinnington, 1998, 1999; Pinnington and Morris, 2002, 2003).

Arising from this literature, we would expect to find archetype shift in large law firms given the changing industry context and structure discussed above, for example multinational clients, large cross-border mergers of law firms and the internationalization of legal business. According to Pinnington and Morris (2003, p. 85), 'evidence of change to more business-like ways of operating' in PSFs is now common. This is likely to include 'more formalized management practices and defined management roles' (Pinnington and Morris, 2003, p. 86). We would therefore expect to find evidence for an archetype shift to MPB (managed professional business) law firms within our sample interview data, or at least sedimentation showing coexistence of MPB and P^2 (that is, traditional professional partnerships) characteristics.

This chapter therefore contributes to the development of PSF literature at the intersection of PSF management and the globalization of PSFs by addressing the managerial issues arising from globalization of legal PSFs.

Research questions

Firm data, industry data and supplementary interview data in this study all provide strong evidence of the growth of global law firms, although these are mainly headquartered and parented in the USA and the UK at this time. These are the two largest industry locations for legal services in the current world market. Our interview data with very large UK law firms have provided evidence that senior managers within such law firms perceive continued international expansion as a defensible and advantageous strategy for legal PSFs. Our research questions arise from such international growth and change.

Given this industry change and the shift in the size and shape of law firms, the following research question arises:

1. What have been the managerial and organizational implications of the globalization of legal PSFs?

International and global strategy literature suggests that cross-border integration and coordination are the key to successful implementation of a globalization strategy (Ghoshal and Nohria, 1993; Bartlett and Ghoshal, 1993). We therefore ask two further questions:

2. What have been the main types of managerial and organizational responses to international integration and global coordination within legal PSFs?
3. What are the key implementation issues that have arisen for legal PSFs and how have they approached them?

Methodology

This study uses qualitative case-based research. As explained in the literature review section, there is little specific research directly related to the study of law firms. There is still less research relating to either the internationalization or globalization of law firms. Therefore we regarded this research as exploratory in nature, seeking to elicit the views of lawyers within their frames of reference, as well as those of other professionals working within law firms, without imposing our preconceptions. The most appropriate method to achieve this was in-depth personal interviews (Jones, 1985). Our interest was in finding out from the perspective of the industry participants what major changes had occurred in the last ten years (the time period most respondents regarded as relevant) and how they and their firms had responded. We were particularly concerned with internal changes as part of understanding how firms perceived and managed the process of globalization. We explored the views of managers concerning significant internal organizational changes made within the last five years and particular difficulties related to such changes.

The data relate to a particular sector of the legal PSF industry, namely very large firms. Our data are drawn solely from UK rather than US firms (although one interview was carried out with a US lawyer at a US law firm operating in London as part of contextual triangulation of issues). This UK emphasis reflects the different historic internal practices between UK and US firms, such as 'lockstep' versus 'eat-what-you-kill' remuneration. We have sought to control for these differences by focusing on UK firms, since such differences may give rise to different potential organizational barriers (not least, financial ones) attached to continued international growth and cross-border integration for US and UK firms respectively. We have focused on the large City law firms whose activities are corporate client based and who, following their clients and as a defensive move against competitors, are developing global strategies for increasingly global markets. In this chapter, we use data from two top 10 firms that had pursued different routes to international expansion: one by acquisition, the other by building an alliance network.

In-depth semi-structured interviews (Yin, 1984; Lee, 1999) were conducted with senior partners, partners, associates and non-legal professionals at UK City law firms ('Magic Circle' and secondary tier), chosen from the top 10 of the Legal 500 (Legal500.com). Clients and non-UK partners of UK firms (German, Swedish and Spanish) were also interviewed. All interview data are treated as confidential. The interviews were guided by a short series of topic questions identified from the experience of other PSFs, a survey of articles in the financial and trade press (for example, *The Lawyer, Legal Week, Legal Business*), and the literature on PSFs and the internationalization/globalization of service industries. The topic guide for interview questions was piloted with lawyers to ensure common understanding of the terminology used. This pilot process was immensely helpful in making the questions more precise to survive the detailed legal scrutiny of our interviewees. The topic guide is provided in Appendix 8.1.

All interviews were recorded and transcribed. Each interview lasted between two and two and a half hours. Respondents were encouraged to speak as much or as little as they wished about industry and organizational characteristics and issues. We only probed to seek clarification and to explore their comments further where more detail was required. Content analysis of the interview transcripts was carried out initially to identify themes and then responses were sorted and coded by theme and each theme allocated to one of seven managerial challenges (see Table 8.1). While the questions in our topic guide were derived from the relevant literatures, we allowed the themes to emerge from the interviewees' responses.

Content analysis (Krippendorff, 1980) was conducted independently by both authors. Within the context of the research aim and following Miles and Huberman's (1994) framework, we both noted dominant themes in the data and drew links with previous literature. From this, organizational implications, managerial responses and implementation issues arising from the pursuit of internationalization strategies were identified. We then each compared our independent analyses. Inter-research differences were resolved through discussion and reference back to the transcriptions, as suggested by Miles and Huberman (1994).

Findings

The increasingly competitive marketplace for legal services and the internationalization of the marketplace for such services have prompted a decline in professionally autonomous lawyers and an increase in managed firms. The managing partner has replaced the senior partner. Globalization of legal services has led to firms developing international strategies which have had a profound impact on the organization structure of the legal PSF. Irrespective of the initial difference in international growth strategy (whether through acquisition or alliance), similar strategic and operational issues were found to apply to the management of practice areas across different national legal jurisdictions and the development and coordination of compatible (and occasionally common) cultures, systems and processes.

This section outlines our findings in relation to our three research questions. We have organized them into sections on the managerial issues arising from the creation of large cross-border legal service organizations; the firm responses to these issues, and remaining implementation issues within the firms. Quotations from interview transcripts are used to illustrate the nature of these management issues and the tone of the responses.

Managerial issues: seven challenges

This section addresses the first research question concerning the managerial and organizational implications of globalization. The 'challenges' given below are those that were identified as significant by the interviewees themselves. We summarize the seven managerial challenges in Table 8.1. We now explore these in more detail.

Challenge 1

The globalization of law firms has fuelled the shift to the managed firm and a decline in professionally autonomous lawyers and partners. This shift from PSF

Table 8.1   The seven managerial challenges

Challenge	Theme 1	Theme 2
1	Shift to the managed firm	Decline in professional autonomy
2	Partner firm selection	Management of merger process
3	HQ–subsidiary relationships	Centralization/decentralization issues
4	Identification of firm-wide values	Building shared corporate culture
5	Common technology platforms	Global know-how (KM) systems
6	Creation of common HRM systems	Integration of HRM practices
7	Professional trust-building	Working relationship networks

to managed partnership has required the overlay of management structures on partnership autonomy. According to our respondents:

> If you become the size we have become as a result of our 'multinationalization', which is roughly 500 partners, you can't act in the same way as we did when I first came to the firm when we were 27 partners. We clearly have become a much more...stratified organization and we have formal committees and people with responsibility for managing it, and we have a clear hierarchy...we are much closer to a management structure and some people like that more than others but it has inevitably changed the way we operate.

> In the old traditional days, a partner was broadly left to get on and develop his or her practice pretty much as he or she saw fit whereas nowadays when we're focused on a few, much bigger, clients, there's clearly much more discussion about the kind of work, the kind of clients, the kind [of clients] that should be taken on. There's more effort to ensure that you have people focused in the right direction, you can't have everyone decide that they really want to focus on Merrill Lynch and poor old Morgan Stanley and Goldman Sachs are out in the cold.

> And whilst you are all opening post together in the morning all around the table you can organize things, you know what is happening...once it gets to something bigger, you have got to have proper systems.

One of the big management challenges for law firms at the moment is therefore to what extent professional managers manage the firm and to what extent lawyers manage the firm.

Challenge 2

In the pursuit of faster growth to include other international jurisdictions, organic growth has largely been replaced by cross-border partnership or by acquisition as forms of growth.

> When we merge we're very careful to merge with a firm that has a reasonably close fit and a similar culture but there are always issues in each different jurisdiction, people with different ways. The local market demands different types of lawyers and in Germany they like much more formality than we might have here in the UK...so we find with a German transaction they are much more formal towards the client and the manner of presenting their advice than we're used to but that's what the German market wants.

> The key thing has been to...see it as more of a partnership. With the first merger...although classically we talked about a merger of equals...there

was a real feeling and the process was very much we're taking over, here it is, these are the processes. As we went through the other mergers we became much more sensitive to establishing a joint team who would work together on the merger so from both sides we established a formal merger integration team which had members from both teams.

We've pulled this firm together, we do have pretty good global processes and practices but it's still going to be two to three years of post-merger integration until we have a completely integrated firm.

In extending the network, two challenges emerge. These are first, the search for the right partner firm or firms for acquisition and, second, the management of the merger process to achieve post-merger integration of national and organizational cultures and multi-jurisdiction capability.

Challenge 3

With acquired firms, offices and staff in a large number of countries, the role of the centre or corporate headquarters has become more complex.

There's a mismatch. I think there is a tendency here to underestimate that mismatch. There is a huge need for actually people here in the centre, leaders here to communicate better with for example, the German firm. There's a need for people to travel there and to engage and to understand what's happening and that's not happening to the extent that is necessary.

It's very difficult to come from an office which is very important and big but still smaller than London.

...every firm should see benefits...It should have an improved perception of itself from its clients, because it had thought about the need to have a European solution and that it should also be able to come together with other members and provide a seamless European service...judged as to whether or not we could convert it into an integrated European law firm.

This challenge concerns HQ–subsidiary issues in managing the global firm. It includes clarifying the relationship between the centre and the periphery and managing the tensions of centralization and decentralization within cross-border firms.

Challenge 4

This is about the identification of firm-wide value systems to underpin the development of a shared corporate culture. This may also be an explicit part of partner selection.

Everyone felt that it was very important to have key principles that we all agreed to as an integrating mechanism across the firm because we'd never had explicitly articulated values. I was involved in gathering the information and coming up with that, I was quite surprised at how similar the value systems were. There were differences but there were definitely core things that we really did share with some of the merged firms.

You have the problem that the values are expressed in English and a big part of the firm does not have English as its mother tongue.

I have been on a number of cross-border transactions where because of the different cultures your instructions or comments on something has been interpreted in a completely different way, so people for example, might not have done the things when you wanted them to because you didn't say, 'I want it right now', so we are trying to bridge that gap.

The implementation of a common set of core firm values is an important building block in order to integrate cross-border firms. HR processes are important as the visible manifestation of the underlying philosophies and attitudes of the integrated firm. They make values explicit as operational practice.

Challenges 5–7 are all concerned with operational issues. Integration across different national jurisdictions causes particular difficulties in the creation of consistency, standards and uniformity of practice and approach throughout the integrated firm. It is not surprising that 5–7 are all about systems issues and human resource management issues since PSFs are predominantly dependent on these two sets of resources for service delivery.

Challenge 5

The creation and integration of common technology platforms and common systems practices are important both for the delivery of complex 'products' and to deliver standardized products more efficiently and cheaply. This must also include global know-how systems for accessing legal precedent.

One of the things that differentiates us from our competitors...I haven't seen it elsewhere, but I think one of the reasons why our mergers have been as successful as they have been...one of the reasons why we were able to do them very quickly and why they were successful was that IT and bringing everyone onto a common technology platform was one of the key aspects of the merger process. Right from day one we have had a common IT platform so everyone uses the same e-mail system, access to the same know-how database.

We were the first global law firm to implement that process which means that we have one global finance system that is a real time system with access to information all around the world, everybody has the same access, 'One source of truth' as they call it.

Technology gives you speed, through templates and common working practices which technology often drives so you get consistency and through global know-how systems you get access to the best knowledge...very, very quickly.

The challenge is therefore in using such common platforms to enable knowledge capture, knowledge transfer and a knowledge management capability.

Challenge 6

This concerns the creation and integration of common human resources management (HRM) practices to coordinate staff across the firm and across projects.

Through the merger process there were agreements made about which of those practices these firms would start to take on so that we would have much more common practices but because it really happened through informal agreements, and each firm that we merged with had a slightly different agreement as to over what period they would phase in a certain practice, it was quite mixed in different parts. So we've now started to look at each practice separately and establish what should be the global things that we all adopt right across the firm no matter which office you're in and then what aspects of the HR practices we can be flexible about so that people can adapt those to their local circumstances.

The other area of ongoing integration is really through our HR processes and systems...the power of those as an integrating mechanism. As we've merged with a number of firms we've encouraged those firms to adopt many of our HR processes – like all following the same appraisal and development process for partners or following the same appraisal process for associates. I talked about the common training programmes, having a similar philosophy to remuneration...that doesn't mean it will be exactly the same or work exactly the same in different jurisdictions but an overall approach, a common view around recruitment...but also then trying to establish common criteria that we're looking for to ensure consistency in quality.

All the partners used to earn basically the same...Now...there's a country factor. These German partners will get paid less than previous partners broadly because they make less money, because Germany is a less efficient legal market and even more so in Stockholm...

> We want a lock-step system because it encourages team working, but if you have that system...things like having a proper appraisal system and doing things the same way in different jurisdictions become a bit more important.

This challenge concerns the people management systems of a large organization in which staff are the main resource and professional expertise is the main vehicle for value creation. Important concerns include the integration of practices between firms such as reward systems, performance management and how the profits of the international firm are divided.

Challenge 7

This highlights the importance within PSFs of building professional trust and strong working relationships. This is especially important the larger and more complex the firm has become.

> I spent a little while in Italy and not necessarily that there was much UK work for me to do in Italy when I was there but I met all the tax people, I could put names to faces, and if you had a transaction with Italian tax advice, and you've got a face in your head, it's so much easier to pick up the phone and it's so much easier if you think they're not quite doing what they should be doing to say it to someone if you've met them rather than someone you don't know.

> One of the big tricks of this is to get people to know each other, and to start spending weekends together, and partying together...that is where a lot of the benefits come from.

> We do have global training programmes where associates from all across the world at key points in their careers will all come together and receive common training.

This challenge is about the enhancement of knowledge, development of trust and dissemination of organizational culture and values. In achieving this, the role of common training programmes, partner retreats, social events and secondments is recognized as central.

Firm responses

This section addresses the second research question concerning the main managerial and organizational responses to the requirement for international integration and global coordination within legal PSFs. From our findings, as illustrated by the quotations from the respondents given above, a number of common responses have emerged as solutions to these challenges presented by the implementation of global strategies. They include the following:

- Professional autonomy is increasingly delegated from individual partners to firm-wide, cross-border committees. Concerns were expressed by existing partners that collegiality among the partners might be lost in this process of growth and restructuring.
- Merger teams and common procedures to ease practice integration with acquired firms are regarded as very important in developing trust between partner firms. This is especially important in PSFs where trust is a key element of the lawyer–client relationship.
- Merger and alliance partners are carefully chosen according to the perceived match between values, aspirations and outlook with the parent or lead firm. However, the implicit expectation of acquiring firms is that the merged/ partner firms adopt the culture of the parent firm. Tensions arise from this.
- Consistency is required in formal knowledge management systems. This is most commonly supported by the installation of compatible IT systems, practice management and finance systems, an organization-wide intranet and access to standard procedures and protocols.
- Accessing professional knowledge within inter- and intra-firm international networks is critical to the efficient and effective functioning of the international firm and to client satisfaction. Therefore the creation of inter- and intra-firm networks (for example working groups across practice areas) at both practice and interpersonal levels is essential to maintaining service levels. Such networks are supported by working groups across practice areas, international secondments and recruitment of multilingual lawyers.
- Consistency in cross-border service delivery is dependent upon developing harmonized human resource practices, hiring policies (including direct entry at senior levels known as 'lateral hires') and cultural awareness training. Once again, building relationships and trust across the organizational networks (for example through professional development, secondments and social activities such as sports weekends) are key.

Remaining implementation issues

Pinnington and Morris (2003, p. 85) point to 'evidence of change to more business-like ways of operating' in PSFs, including more formalized management practices and defined management roles. Our data confirm this shift to the managed firm. However, this shift is a necessary but not sufficient condition for cross-border integration of the global firm. Many of the approaches adopted by legal PSFs as solutions to potentially incompatible historic internal practices leave unresolved issues in the management of cross-border integration.

Therefore in addressing the third research question concerning key implementation issues that have arisen for legal PSFs and how have they approached them, we identify problems relating to effective implementation. These include:

- Dealing with centre–periphery issues involving the locus of control over the single, integrated firm
- Challenging the perceptions among merged firms of the corporate centre as dominant with themselves on a lesser footing
- Managing issues of autonomy and control affecting the international offices of merged or partner firms
- Addressing barriers to integration arising from organizational cultural, rather than national cultural, differences
- Using non-legal professionals to develop the business support functions of the organization and its effect on the management hierarchy and reward systems

These are among the managerial issues that remain to be met in achieving the stated objective identified by interviewees of creating the globally integrated PSF.

Arising from the literature on global MNC strategy and structure discussed in the literature review, many of the current implementation issues in achieving cross-border, intra-firm integration have been successfully recognized by sample firms, according to the interviewees. However they have not yet been fully addressed. We do see some evidence in globalizing law firms of aspects of the N-form organization such as temporary groupings of people within project teams; lateral communication within practice areas and within experience levels; interdependence of staff (that is, use of staff local-for-global); interdependence of technologies through common platforms and systems, and potential for scope rather than scale economies (with shared client referrals). However, in the shift away from PSF and towards managed global service business, we see the continuation of top-down hierarchy, centralization and standardization, exacerbated by lack of clarity in the relationship between parent firm HQ and acquired partner firms as subsidiaries.

Limitations of the research

Clearly the research has many limitations that affect the generalizability of these findings. Among these limitations were problems of access so the sample data were limited to two case studies and these were both UK firms. We were dependent upon the views of interviewees in the interpretation of industry and firm issues; even when interviewing non-UK respondents, interviews were all conducted within the UK and we relied upon the firms to recommend interviewees at the various levels, thus creating potential gatekeeper issues. Many of these problems are common to exploratory case-based research. In further development of this research, additional interviews would be sought outside the UK and among a wider informed community of clients and non-lawyers. Despite these limitations, the research has added to our knowledge and perspective of the legal services industry and our understanding of the impact of globalization in a PSF context. It has extended the literature of international and global strategy further into the services sectors and beyond its normal domain of manufacturing industries.

Conclusion

The nature of the client expectations from cross-border legal service, greater levels of competition between firms and greater price and cost pressures are such that firms have little option in their global strategies other than to pursue the effective provision of integrated organizational processes to generate 'seamless' services. What we have been exploring in this chapter are the managerial and organizational issues that are inherent in this shift from the international firm to the integrated global firm.

We conclude that many of the significant management problems experienced currently within large legal PSFs have been associated with the changes brought about by their cross-border integration efforts. However, we contend that these managerial issues result more from other general factors than from the experience of globalization itself. We therefore wish to emphasize two points. First, many managerial issues in such firms have occurred as part of the profound shift in the nature of the PSF, in response to competitive industry dynamics, from the traditional partnership towards a managed hierarchy within what is now a service business. Second, if we look once again at Table 8.1 and consider this list of the core management issues for global law firms (our 'challenges'), what emerges is a set of issues that appear to have less to do with globalization than with overall growth in the size of firm. These management issues that we have identified may thus result more from problems associated with growth and the increased size of law firms than from internationalization per se.

Finally, although showing awareness of the need for local jurisdiction responsiveness and autonomy, the drive by international law firms to achieve an integrated, 'seamless' cross-border service appears to be leading them towards constructing old-fashioned centralized global hub operations rather than more flexible transnational structures in their international organization.

Appendix 8.1 Topic guide

1. What major changes have affected law firms in the last 10 years? (for example, what about international expansion?)
2. In what manner (please describe) has globalization affected your law firm? (for example, what has been the impact of non-UK firms operating in the UK and/or UK firms operating overseas?)
3. What sort of management structure is appropriate for an international law firm? Who are the appropriate people to manage an international law firm?
4. How does this differ from what has historically been the firm's structure?
5. Is your firm a limited liability partnership (LLP)? If not, do you see it moving in that direction?
6. What has been the impact of internationalization/globalization on lawyers' professional lives? (for example, effect on remuneration issues; effect on culture of the firm)
7. Have the key resource requirements changed in the last 10 years? (for example information technology/information systems (IT/IS) or professional staff?)
8. Who do you see as your main competitors now compared with 10 years ago? (for example multidisciplinary firms (MDFs))
9. To what extent has the client base changed over the last 5–10 years? (for example, is it more international?)
10. To what extent is cross-border capability important to clients and what impact has it had on client relationships and the client base?

References

Aharoni, Y. and L. Nachum (eds) (2000) *The Globalization of Services: Some Implications for Theory and Practice* (London: Routledge).

Bartlett, C.A. and S. Ghoshal (1993) 'Beyond the M-form: towards a Managerial Theory of the Firm', *Strategic Management Journal*, 14 Special Issue, Summer, 23–46.

Beaverstock, J., R. Smith and P. Taylor (1999) 'The Long Arm of the Law: London's Law Firms in a Globalizing World Economy', *Environment and Planning*, 31(10), 1857–76.

Beaverstock, J., R. Smith and P. Taylor (2000) 'Geographies of Globalization: US Law Firms in World Cities', *Urban Geography*, 21 (2), 95–120.

Birkinshaw, J. (2001) 'Strategy and Management in MNE Subsidiaries', in A.M. Rugman and T.L. Brewer (eds), *The Oxford Handbook of International Business* (Oxford: OUP).

Birkinshaw, J., O. Toulan and D. Arnold (2001) 'Global Account Management in Multinational Corporations: Theory and Evidence', *Journal of International Business Studies*, 32 (2), 231–48.

Chang, T., C. Chuang and W. Jan (1998) 'International Collaboration of Law Firms: Modes, Motives and Advantages', *Journal of World Business*, 33 (3), 241–55.

Cooper, D., C.R. Hinings, R. Greenwood and J. Brown (1996) 'Sedimentation and Transformation in Organizational Change: the Case of Canadian Law Firms', *Organization Studies*, 17 (4), 623–47.

Daniels, P., N. Thrift and A. Leyshon (1989) 'Internationalization of Professional Producer Services: Accountancy Conglomerates', in P. Enderwick (ed.), *Multinational Service Firms* (London: Routledge).

Fosstenløkken, S., B. Løwendahl and O. Revang (2003) 'Knowledge Development through Client Interaction: a Comparative Study', *Organization Studies*, 24 (6), 859–80.

Ghemawat, P. (2003) 'Semiglobalization and International Business Strategy', *Journal of International Business Studies*, 34 (2), 138–52.

Ghoshal, S. and C.A. Bartlett (1990) 'The Multinational Corporation as an Interorganizational Network', *Academy of Management Review*, 10 (4), 323–37.

Ghoshal, S. and N. Nohria (1993) 'Horses for Courses: Organizational Forms for Multinational Corporations', *Sloan Management Review*, Winter, 23–35.

Greenwood, R. and L. Empson (2003) 'The Professional Partnership: Relic or Exemplary Form of Governance?', *Organization Studies*, 24 (6), 909–34.

Greenwood, R. and C.R. Hinings (1993) 'Understanding Strategic Change: the Contribution of Archetypes', *Academy of Management Journal*, 36 (5), 1052–81.

Greenwood, R. and C.R. Hinings (1996) 'Understanding Radical Organizational Change: Bringing Together the Old and the New Institutionalism', *Academy of Management Review*, 21 (4), 1022–54.

Grosse, R. (2000) 'Knowledge Creation and Transfer in Global Service Firms' in Y. Aharoni and L. Nachum (eds), *The Globalization of Services: Some Implications for Theory and Practice* (London: Routledge).

Hedlund, G. (1994) 'A Model of Knowledge Management and the N-form Corporation', *Strategic Management Journal*, 15 Special Issue, Summer, 73–90.

Jones, S. (1985) 'Depth Interviewing', in R. Walker (ed.), *Applied Qualitative Research* (Aldershot: Gower).

Kipping, M. (2002) 'Trapped in Their Wave: the Evolution of Management Consultancies', in T. Clark and R. Fincham (eds), *Critical Consulting: New Perspectives on the Management Advice Industry* (Oxford: Blackwell).

Krippendorff, K. (1980) *Content Analysis: an Introduction to its Methodology* (Beverly Hills, Calif.: Sage).

Lee, T. (1999) *Using Qualitative Methods in Organizational Research* (London: Sage).

Legal Business at http://www.icclaw.com, accessed 06/06/05.

Legal500.com at http://www.legal500.com, accessed 09/10/2002 and 06/06/2005.

Lorsch, J.W. and P.F. Mathias (2001) 'When Professionals Have to Manage', *Harvard Business Review*, July–August, 78–83.

Løwendahl, B. (2000) 'The Globalization of Professional Service Firms – Fad or Genuine Source of Competitive Advantage?', in Y. Aharoni and L. Nachum (eds), *The Globalization of Services: Some Implications for Theory and Practice* (London: Routledge).

Løwendahl, B., O. Revang and S.M. Fosstenløkken (2001) 'Knowledge and Value Creation in Professional Service Firms: a Framework for Analysis', *Human Relations*, 54 (7), 911–31.

McLaughlin, C.P. and J.A. Fitzsimmons (1996) 'Strategies for Globalizing Service Operations', *International Journal of Service Industry Management*, 7 (4), 43–57.

Maister, D. (1993) *Managing the Professional Service Firm* (New York: Free Press).

Malnight, T.W. (1996) 'The Transition from Decentralised to Network-based MNC Structures: an Evolutionary Perspective', *Journal of International Business Studies*, 27 (1), 43–65.

Miles, M. and M.A. Huberman (1994), *Qualitative Data Analysis*, 2nd edn (London: Sage).

Morris, T. and A. Pinnington (1998) 'Patterns of Profit-sharing in Professional Firms', *British Journal of Management*, 9 (1), 23–39.

Morris, T.J. and Pinnington, A.H. (1999) 'Continuity and Change in the Professional Firm', in D. Brock, M. Powell and C.R. Hinings (eds), *Restructuring the Professional Organization: Accounting, Health Care and Law* (London: Routledge).

Nachum, L. (1998) 'Danish Professional Service Firms: Why Are They Not Competitive Internationally?', *Scandinavian Journal of Management*, 14 (1/2), 37–51.

Nachum, L. (1999) *The Origins of the International Competitiveness of Firms: the Impact of Location and Ownership in Professional Service Industries* (Cheltenham: Edward Elgar).

Pinnington, A.H. and T.J. Morris (2002) 'Transforming the Architect: Ownership Form and Archetype Change', *Organization Studies*, 23 (2), 189–211.

Pinnington, A.H. and T.J. Morris (2003) 'Archetype Change in Professional Organizations: Survey Evidence from Large Law Firms', *British Journal of Management*, 14 (1), 85–99.

Ramcharran, H. (1999) 'Trade Liberalization in Services: an Analysis of the Obstacles and the Opportunities for Trade Expansion by US Law Firms', *Multinational Business Review*, Spring, 27–36.

Robertson, M., H. Scarbrough and J. Swan (2003) 'Knowledge Creation in Professional Service Firms: Institutional Effects', *Organization Studies*, 24 (6), 831–58.

Segal-Horn, S. (1993) 'The Internationalization of Service Firms', *Advances in Strategic Management*, 9, 31–55.

Segal-Horn, S. (2005) 'Globalization of Service Industries', in J. McGee (ed.), *Encyclopaedic Dictionary of Strategic Management* (Oxford: Blackwell).

Shapiro, M. (1993) 'The Globalization of Law', *Global Legal Studies Journal*, 1 (1), 1–33.

Silver, C. (2000) 'Globalization and the US Market in Legal Services – Shifting Identities', *Law and Policy in International Business*, 31, 1093–150.

Spar, D. (1997) 'Lawyers Abroad: the Internationalization of Legal Practice', *California Management Review*, 39 (3), 8–28.

Szulanski, G. (2003) *Sticky Knowledge: Barriers to Knowing in the Firm* (London: Sage).

Teece, D.J. (2000) *Managing Intellectual Capital* (Oxford: Oxford University Press).

Terpstra, V. and C. Yu (1998) 'Determinants of Foreign Investment of US Advertising Agencies', *Journal of International Business Studies*, 19 (1), 33–46.

Van Maanen, J. and A. Laurent (1993) 'The Flow of Culture: Some Notes on Globalization and the Multinational Corporation', in S. Ghoshal and D. Westney (eds), *Organization Theory and the Multinational Corporation* (New York: St Martin's Press).

Yin, R.K. (1984) *Case Study Research: Design and Methods* (Newbury Park, Calif.: Sage).

Yip, G.S. (1996) *Total Global Strategy*, 2nd edn (Englewood-Cliffs, NJ.: Prentice-Hall).

Yip, G.S. (2005) 'New Directions in International Business: the State of Global Strategy', keynote address, Academy of International Business UK Conference, Bath.

9
The Performance Management–Training Interface in Australian Firms in China

Susan McGrath-Champ and Xiaohua Yang

Introduction

Performance management in the context of overseas assignments has attracted increasing attention recently. There have been a number of studies examining various aspects of performance management. Lindholm (2000) studied three aspects of performance management – goal setting, evaluation and feedback and development – identifying their impact on job satisfaction. Suutari and Tahvanainen (2002) explored goal setting and evaluation aspects of performance management. Woods (2003) studied staff perception of performance management. So far, little has been said about the training aspect of performance management in international and global settings.

While it is understood that employee training and career development correlates with job satisfaction and performance (for example Flynn, 1995), there is little understanding of how training and career development in overseas assignments is integrated into performance management systems in foreign ventures. Such an understanding can be a valuable contribution to the existing international human resource management (IHRM) literature. In particular, this study seeks to understand how cross-cultural training and career development for expatriates is integrated into performance management in Australian ventures in China.

The focus on Australian firms is justified here for the following reasons. Australian firms have been internationalizing their operations for a shorter time than their North American and Western European counterparts, and therefore they may have been lagging behind other Western countries in developing effective performance management systems in their overseas ventures and have less developed preparation programmes for expatriates. In particular, the cross-cultural performance management problem of Australian expatriates in Asia has been examined in a number of studies with consistent findings that high-light cross-cultural capabilities as questionable or deficient (Dawkins et al., 1995; Rosen et al., 2000; Woods, 2003). However, the level of outward foreign investment originating from Australia has reached a historical high following the abolition of Australian restrictions on such investment (Parliament of Australia, 1995/6). In 2003, outward foreign direct investment from Australia was $A117,091 m ($US90,312 m), up from $A30,507 m ($US23,530 m) in 1990. Of this, the Australian FDI in China was $A37,006 m ($US28,542 m), 31 per cent of the total, up from $A2489 m ($US1917 m) over the same period (UNCTAD, 2004). The time is ripe for a closer look at performance management systems in Australian foreign ventures from both theoretical and practical perspectives, in particular the role of cross-cultural training and development in performance management.

The next section of the chapter reviews the relevant literature and provides a theoretical foundation concerning performance management and training. The third and fourth sections outline the methods used in the study, and set out the initial empirical findings, respectively. The fifth section discusses the findings and the final section draws conclusions regarding performance management and its connection with training systems.

Literature and theory

Performance management has been identified as 'a strategic and integrated approach to delivering sustained success to organizations by improving the performance of the people who work in them and by developing the capabilities of teams and individual contributors' (Armstrong, 1998). Within the realm of IHRM, performance management can be used as a mechanism to establish alignment between the goals of the parent company (or headquarters) and the subsidiary (Tahvanainen and Suutari, 2005) that acts as a 'pipeline' to the local market (Evans et al., 2002, p. 110). Thus, performance management is now regarded as a critical element of strategic global human resource management. Performance management provides managers with both a coherent manage-ment philosophy and a system for maintaining and enhancing staff perform-ance. Furthermore, it allows employees to focus on career and personal development that could lead to continuous improvement in performance (Rubienska and Bovaird, 1999).

Performance management has been identified as the process of transforming strategic corporate objectives into action, monitoring progress and rewarding results. The key elements of performance management include formulating individual performance goals and indicators, conducting performance appraisal and providing feedback and opportunities for improvement through training and development. It also involves links between results and reward systems, and with overall organizational strategy (Fenwick et al., 1999). Within performance management systems, individual goal setting takes place with extensive individual employee involvement and in the context of the job and the organization.

Conducting performance appraisal and providing feedback serve a developmental purpose aimed at continuous improvement and socialization to work settings when it is incorporated with training and development. Linking results and reward systems and linking overall organization strategy with the components of performance management mentioned above allow for a continuous process that connects people and jobs to the strategy and objectives of the organization to achieve its maximum benefits and optimum results (Fenwick et al., 1999; Mwita, 2000; Tahvanainen and Suutari, 2005).

Within multinational corporations, performance management is broader and more complicated than in domestic companies, where primarily local employees are managed within the local political, legal and cultural environment (Tahvanainen and Suutari, 2005). In a domestic context, performance goals are usually agreed jointly between individuals and their closest first-level manager. In contrast, the primary manager with whom an expatriate agrees his or her goals can be in the home or host location, or even some other third country unit (Tahvanainen and Suutari, 2005).

As performance management is an ongoing process aimed at increasing expatriates' effectiveness in foreign ventures and improving venture performance, identifying training and development needs and using the knowledge gained through training to improve performance of expatriates become critical to achieving corporate goals and objectives (Mwita, 2000). In overseas assignments, expatriates are faced with a new set of cultural imperatives and environments. Cross-cultural training is called for to adjust to the new settings.

Cross-cultural training provides expatriates with an opportunity to acquire knowledge and skills that will help them manage 'culture shock', prepare them for the initial and continuous challenges they will face, and reduce the likelihood of premature return (Shay and Tracey, 1997). It can also provide expatriates with an understanding of the very different ways of doing business in the host country. Some research findings reveal a positive relationship between cross-cultural training and adjusting to the new environment (Brewster and Pickard, 1994; Waxin and Panaccio, 2005). Successful adjustment and the resulting feeling of comfort can have a positive impact on the expatriate's performance. However, not all research concerning the effects of training is consistent. A recent study by Selmer (2005a) indicates that cross-cultural training does not necessarily lead to effective expatriate performance. Indeed, the effectiveness of expatriate performance is contingent on the specific context of the overseas assignment. This is consistent with Waxin and Panaccio's (2005) findings that the effectiveness of cross-cultural training depends on a number of factors, including the expatriate's prior international experience and cultural distance.

Black and Mendenhall (1990) reviewed 29 cross-cultural training studies. Fifteen examined the relationship between cross-cultural training and individual job/task performance. Black and Mendenhall summarized these studies by noting that 11 found a significant relationship between cross-cultural training and performance, two found mixed results, and two found non-significant relationships. The four studies with mixed or non-significant results were published before 1976, and three were laboratory studies using students as subjects. Studies that showed significant relationships between cross-cultural training and performance were more likely to use independent measures of performance, field study designs, and/or use of control groups. Thus, there is some support for the view that cross-cultural training will positively affect individual performance in the new work settings. As expatriates normally face a different environment from the one that they are used to at home, cross-cultural training appears to be a beneficial ingredient in expatriate management and needs to be integrated into the whole performance management system to ensure that expatriates achieve desirable performance outcomes in culturally different work settings.

IHRM literature suggests that as firms progress towards cross-border strategies, the skills needed by expatriate management change. If expatriates are unable to maximize opportunities because of their limited cross-cultural skills, they are not only unable to achieve their individual task goals, they will also prevent multinational corporations from successfully fulfilling their strategic goals. This calls for relevant cross-cultural training even prior to the manager's departure for the overseas assignment (Adler and Bartholomew, 1992; Dowling and Schuler, 1990; Schuler et al., 1993). Such training enhances the likelihood that expatriates' cross-cultural skills will match their task goals and eventually organizational strategic goals, but cannot ensure the achievement of goals.

However, the need for cross-cultural training is not routinely identified in expatriate assignments in either literature or business practice. There is a clear lack of understanding of the importance of cross-cultural training in developing expatriate capabilities for achieving desirable performance and venture success. Lack of an organizational structure for preparing expatriates can erode their confidence and motivation in the new cultural environment. Previous studies demonstrate that training associated with improved individual capabilities is correlated with performance (Lindholm, 2000). For performance management to be effective, a training component needs to be included to enhance expatriate capabilities and skills and so facilitate the adaptation of expatriates to a foreign cultural environment. In turn, successful adaptation to a new cultural environment will lead to effective performance and more desirable results.

The most usual time for training is before the expatriates' departure, but various writers (see Tahvanainen and Suutari, 2005, p. 98) have pointed out that training and development also need to continue throughout the assignment.

Close linking of performance management with training and development is particularly important since it is throughout the process of ongoing evaluation relative to goals that the training needs for expatriates can be identified beyond the need for initial cultural or language training.

Whether in the global setting or within the national/domestic domain, performance management is not unproblematic. While some 'high performing' companies have developed sophisticated approaches (Jesuthasan, 2003), performance appraisal – a core component of performance management – is commonly undertaken as a formality, an annual 'ritual' whereby managers/supervisors and employees can 'tick the box' to show that they have conformed (Nador, 1999; Wilson and Western, 2000). The emphasis on performance appraisal, often entailing numerical assessment scales, can render employees defensive (Nador, 1999). An organizational disposition of development and support deploying more frequent (than annual) assessments is needed to derive real benefits from performance reviews. There is no 'one-size-fits-all' solution. Rather, developing a performance management system that works well for an organization is costly and usually needs to be done specifically for that organization (Weatherly, 2004). There can be a tendency, where performance deficiencies are identified, for these to be directly referred to the training manager or department for correction. Training may be an appropriate corrective, but as Wilson and Western (2000) and Vesper (2001) caution, training cannot be assumed to be the appropriate performance 'solution'. Employees/managers may be well trained and performance deficiencies may arise from other influences. Training that is identified from performance appraisal can be hard to target and achieve. Training will be effective only if it is the real cause of the performance problem and discerning what the cause really is can be difficult. Wright and Geroy (2001, p. 587) comment that 'training activity, by itself, may have little direct relationship to results'. Though a powerful tool to achieve performance, training can be successful only if all other performance issues are also addressed (Vesper, 2001). This is particularly challenging in the complexity of international assignments.

Performance management systems can potentially have an important role in the performance-related pay (bonuses, incentives) component of expatriates' compensation packages. If performance goals are linked to outcomes that are significant to the employee and his/her manager, then these can motivate the employee to work hard to achieve the goals and the manager to facilitate this result. While there has been much discussion about some aspects of expatriate compensation, there is very little literature indicating how the components of performance-related pay are determined on the basis of performance (Tahvanainen and Suutari, 2005, p. 100).

The performance appraisal and feedback mechanism of a performance management system aims to optimize individual performance and enable individuals to achieve organizational goals. In a dynamic and changing global market, a firm's goals may be changing and thus the task nature of the expatriate may be changing. Organizational life cycle models also suggest that corporate strategic goals will change as organizations progress through birth, growth, maturity and revival or decline stages. Thus, performance management systems should be able to maximize the fit between human resource capabilities and strategic goals through continuous on-the-job training and career development. It is argued that expatriates' expectancy of the assignment for training and career development will impact job performance during the assignment (Yan et al., 2002). While the effectiveness of the assignment can be increased by selecting expatriates who possess cultural skills matching their task goals and organizational strategic goals, post-departure training and support are crucial for ensuring that the match continues to exist in conjunction with the changing nature of the business environment and business strategic goals (Hutchings, 2002; Katz and Seifer, 1996). Hence, training and career development should be built into the performance appraisal and feedback loop and reward infrastructure to motivate expatriates to achieve organizational goals and objectives in a changing global market environment. Based on the above analysis, a framework has been developed here to depict the performance management and cross-cultural training loop (see Figure 9.1).

The figure shows that performance appraisal, training, goals and rewards all interrelate. Further, the two-way line between training and performance indicates that these, ideally, are directly linked and interrelated. The performance of an individual can affect the goals and rewards associated with an assignment and vice versa, as indicated by the dual-pointing arrows in the diagram. Together, this set of interacting human resource management elements have an influence on the expatriate's performance outcomes and the success or otherwise of a foreign venture, as represented by the box and thick arrow at the bottom of the diagram.

A variety of contextual factors (summarized by Tahvanainen and Suutari, 2005, pp. 101–6) can influence expatriate performance management. A link has been discerned between the size of a company and expatriate performance management, with bigger companies having more formal performance management practices such as written goals, performance more officially evaluated and more frequent evaluations that include host country supervisors and which may entail team goals. The position of the expatriate within the organization and the type of tasks performed affect expatriate performance management. Written performance management goals are more common in management and in top management levels than in other positions. As for customer-oriented, project-based international assignments, formal goal setting and evaluation are commonly non-existent, with insufficient feedback on performance and no time to engage in training while on the assignment.

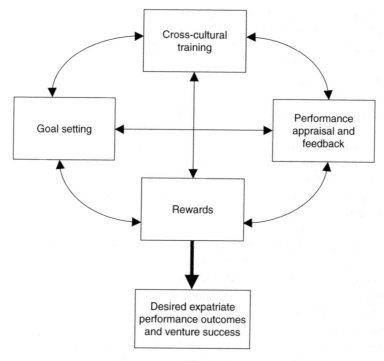

Figure 9.1   Model of cross-cultural training and performance management

Evaluations appear to take place more often after repatriation (Tahvanainen and Suutari, 2005, pp. 103–5).

The methods

Face-to-face interviews were deemed to be most effective for this exploratory study as they give the opportunity to explore and tease out issues as interviews go along. Data were collected through in-depth, semi-structured face-to-face interviews in four Australian ventures operating in China in June 2004. Background information on the nature of the organizations, drawn primarily from websites and company documents, was collected prior to and after the interviews, and was also gathered from interviewees.

The specific criteria for selecting organizations and interviewees include (1) organizations are registered Australian firms that (2) have been operating in China for a period of six months or more, (3) have offices or plants in Beijing, and (4) they have expatriates available for interview. The identification of such organizations was a significant challenge. The authors limited the field study to Beijing because of funding and logistics and approached the Australian Chamber of Commerce and Austrade (a government trade promotion agency) for lists of organizations operating in Beijing. With assistance from the Australian Chamber of Commerce, the authors identified approximately two dozen organizations that met the first two criteria. The initial contacts were made by phone to identify the appropriate informants and confirm their participation in the study. This resulted in five expatriates from Australian organizations being included in the study (one company offered two expatriates who were available on the interview day, but in most cases, one expatriate was available for interview (see Table 9.1). The limited number of respondents means the outcomes of this early stage of the research are provisional. It was necessary to relax the second criterion to include one company with only four months' operation in China rather than the six months originally specified. This provided a contrast with the other somewhat longer-established organizations in the sample.

Interviewees were selected ensuring that the expatriate assignments were for a minimum duration of six months and that expatriates were able to report on the performance management process. In terms of expatriate profile, all interviewees were male, middle- and upper-level managers (see Table 9.2). Three international assignees were Australian (home-country) nationals, and two were third-country nationals ('TCN') from neither home nor host countries.

The semi-structured interviews used a list of prepared questions that were designed to unfold and expand relevant issues. The questions were also informed by a pilot study conducted previously (McGrath-Champ and Yang, 2002). A third researcher based in China attended the interviews and facilitated scheduling and access to companies. The companies and individuals are disguised in order to maintain confidentiality. Each interview lasted an average of 90 minutes. Interviews were tape recorded to capture the richness of responses and two interviewers also took notes. Data were coded using manual content analysis procedures and tabulated into relevant categories.

The expatriate interviewees demonstrated a knowledge of general policy and practice within their company based on home country and expatriated experience and in most instances were able to relate their expatriate experience in China to that of the company overall. While this does not overcome the limited extent of corroboration possible at this early stage of research, it goes some way to furnishing an organization-wide depiction of performance management practice.

Key parameters from the interviews and related materials were documented in spreadsheet format amenable to analysis using computer software (Statistical Package for the Social Sciences, SPSS). Available resources allowed partial transcription of the interviews. A second stage of the study is extending the number of interviews and it is intended these will be augmented by a subsequent mail survey and analysis using both qualitative and quantitative methods.

Table 9.1 Company profiles

Company name	Company size (number of employees)	Duration of operation in China	Regions in which the company has expatriates presently	Stage of life cycle for the venture	Organizational form	Industry sector
Company A	28,000	18 years	Asia Pacific	Growth	International	Financial services
Company B	35,000	20 years	Africa, North America, Central America, South America	Growth	Global	Resources
Company C	5	8 years	China	Growth	International	Service
Company D	40	4 months	South-East Asia	Entry	International	Construction

Table 9.2 Expatriate profiles

Company	Origin	Age group	Marital status	Function	Gender	Time lived abroad for work purposes	Time employed with current company	Time lived abroad with current company
Company A	Australia	18–24	Single	Upper/middle management: team of 6	Male	0 years*	2.5 years	4 months
Company A	Taiwan	35–44	Married with family accompanying on assignment	Upper/middle management: branch manager	Male	0 years	5 years	2 years
Company B	United Kingdom	45–54	Married with family accompanying on assignment	Upper/middle management	Male	25 years	4.5 years	4.5 years
Company C	Australian born	25–34	Single	Top management	Male	7 years	2 years	2 years
Company D	Australia	25–34	Single	Project manager	Male	1.5 years	4.5 years	4 months

* No prior work abroad but lived as a student for 4 years in China.

The study findings

Of the four companies examined, company A is a medium-sized international firm in the financial services sector, Company B is a global conglomerate in the resource sector, Company C is a small non-profit organization providing commercial services to Australian firms in China, and Company D is a small international firm in the construction sector. Company A operates in three continents and has been in China for 18 years. Company B operates around the globe and has been in China for 20 years. Company C has had a presence in China for eight years. Company D has operations in Malaysia and entered the Chinese market only four months prior to the interview (see Table 9.1). The following is a report and analysis of each organization in terms of the company's adoption of performance management in relation to the framework developed here.

Company A

The two expatriates interviewed were selected internally. The company, a medium size, international, firm in the financial sector, normally selects expatriates both internally and externally after advertising within and outside the company. One expatriate was a mid to upper-level bank branch manager from Taiwan (a TCN) with a family. The other was a single, unmarried, middle-level commodity and trade finance manager from Australia.

It was reported that the headquarters establish the overall corporate goals. The main written goals and values include: (1) put the customer first, (2) lead and inspire people, (3) grow and create value for the shareholder, (4) branch out and be different from competitors, and (5) generate trust of the company. All expatriates have a set of key performance indicators (known as 'key result areas'). Individual performance plans are established for six months and can be adjusted by the supervisor half-yearly. Original targets are used as a benchmark. Individual performance goals are documented in the performance appraisal ('performance management review') document. The company uses a combination of both behavioural and outcome criteria for measuring performance. Growth in sales and revenue, and customer satisfaction are included in the criteria.

The performance appraisal process includes input from the expatriate. Every six months, employees submit their own rating that is confirmed by their supervisor. In the Australian environment, the company uses 360-degree performance evaluation whereby feedback about an employee is solicited from multiple sources including the employee, the supervisor, other managers and customers. For expatriates in Beijing, multiple evaluators contributed to the evaluation process, but were typically less wide-ranging than in Australia.

The reward component includes salary, housing allowances, education for children, medical insurance, and one return home trip per year. This is in accordance with the firm's standard overseas business policy. The expatriates have found the package adequate, although they are aware that the expatriate package has been trimmed recently in an effort to cut costs.

The expatriate training component in the performance management appeared to be lacking in this company. It did not provide any training for the expatriate from Taiwan probably because he could speak Mandarin and understands the culture in China. Neither did the company provide any cross-cultural training for the expatriate from Australia and only some brief technical training prior to departure. Although career development programmes were provided for employees in Australia, this was not apparent in the Chinese operations. Mentoring, one element of employee development and support, was entirely informal in the overseas subsidiary. The Australian commodity and trade finance manager who considered that appropriate recruitment obviated the need for formalized mentoring arrangements perceived this as acceptable:

> In Australia, the company does have one [a mentoring programme] and [prior to taking up the international assignment] I had a mentor. Here, it's informal. They choose people who are able to adjust already. I could tell you that mentoring has not helped me adjust to my overseas assignment but that is because I haven't needed any help. I have four or five friends who are based in Australia and I still call them and ask for advice – they don't need to be here [in Beijing].

The Taiwanese branch manager, however, reported a need for mentoring and related developmental programmes: 'For mentoring you rely on your line managers and colleagues in the same field, but it is very informal. The company needs to have some [expatriate development] programmes and some mentoring system.'

At the time of the interviews, no provision had been made for the employees' repatriation or development beyond the assignment. Again, there were contrasts in how this was perceived by the expatriates. The Australian considered it 'unrealistic to expect a job waiting for him in two years'. However, the Taiwanese branch manager contrasted this with the guaranteed 'job-on-return-home' policy of his previous finance-sector employer, indicating a preference for the latter arrangement.

Company B

Compared to other firms in the study, Company B is bigger and has much more extensive experience overseas. It is a global resources company with production and sales facilities in many countries. The sales function of this company has been established since the 1970s but the firm is at an 'entry' phase in terms of production in China. The interviewee is a 'career expatriate', with ten previous international assignments with several companies spanning 25 years. This is his first assignment in China – as a specialist upper-middle level manager. He is from the United Kingdom and was selected internally to develop new production business in China. This company sets the following three goals for its employees worldwide: first, to establish a win–win relationship with customers, second, to maintain high safety standards and, third, to invest in the environment.

Details about performance management are set out in the expatriate's contract. Performance management processes are generally similar throughout the company, with adaptation to suit different business units. Specifically, the firm uses a balanced scorecard system; goals are set out at the beginning of the year by expatriates' supervisors, accepted by expatriates, and assessed at the end of the year, usually with an interim review. Performance goals are identified by expatriates' supervisors and accepted by the expatriates. The performance evaluation criteria include behavioural and outcome indicators. Financial indicators used depend 40 per cent on firm-level performance and 60 per cent on performance at an individual level. Other criteria include health and safety and personnel management. The reward package includes a locally taxed salary set according to European standards, a housing allowance with a given ceiling, education for children with a given ceiling, one return home trip per year, and a 25–30 per cent bonus based on performance.

The interviewee articulated the difficulty in applying numerical outcome criteria to his work, which is not well suited to this type of appraisal:

> In business development, the dilemma is that you can do a very good job all year and not develop any [new] business. So, if I was measured purely on my achievement in China I would have got zero bonus because I haven't got anything to show for it. But on the other hand, if the right outcome was not to invest in China, then I have done the right thing. So I'd save the company a lot of money. That is the problem. In my area it's a bit difficult to measure.

He proposed that this could be addressed '. . . by trying to give me some credit for what the company has done during the year. So if my division does really well I get some benefit, even though it is not within my control to influence that.' This bears out some of the inadequacies that exist in assessing performance.

The company did not provide any form of training to the expatriate. The extent of his prior international experience obviated the need for some potential areas of training. He spoke no Chinese language on arriving in China and began to take Chinese language lessons on his own initiative after arrival.

There is a self-initiated informal mentoring relationship but no formal mentoring. No formalized repatriation arrangements existed.

Company C

This is a non-profit organization serving Australian firms in China through business support, government liaison and so forth. The expatriate, an unmarried Australian, was hired in China and had five years' prior international working experience. As the general and most senior manager of the organization, he answers to a board of directors. The unwritten organizational goals include to: (1) ensure organizational survival; (2) establish a stronger financial base; (3) create a sustainable business, and (4) attract new members/clients. Of these goals, the task of making the organization survive, primarily by strengthening its financial situation, and improving board accountability, were the most important. There are no specific criteria or quantifiable indicators for evaluating the organization's performance nor any specific goals or performance management processes in place for the expatriate. The reward component includes salary, paid and taxed locally, and one return home trip per year but no bonus. No training was provided to the expatriate and mentoring was informal – the incumbent would seek advice from members of its subcommittees or the organization's directors as needed. The expatriate expressed a desire for more structured goal setting and performance:

> I'm hoping that in the future, for whoever, has this role, there will be a bit more structure for them to be managed. At the moment, the community [organization's members] looks at what I've done and [it would be better] if performance was managed more on a calculated basis.

Company D

Company D is a small, project-based construction company with limited international business. The company was at an entry stage of business in China, this project being the company's first in that country. It had not formalized its performance goals; instead informally established goals include finishing the nine-month project and developing new business, without specifying any targets. This was the first expatriate assignment for the young, unmarried Australian who was deployed as a project manager for the purpose of managing a construction project. He had worked with the company previously in Australia and also had overseas (UK) work experience outside this firm.

There is no formal performance appraisal process specified. The evaluation criteria were rather vague: simply an implicit expectation that the project would be completed on time and new business established. Compensation included a salary and daily living allowance, a housing allowance and one return home trip during the nine-month project. The expatriate did not receive any training prior to departure nor during the project in China. He could not speak Chinese upon arrival and expressed a desire for assistance of an interpreter to enhance communication. Four months into his assignment, it was evident that cultural adjustment was still challenging. There was no formal mentoring. Instead the expatriate sought advice informally from two Australian-based mentors in light of a lack of rapport with his immediate (also Australian-based) superior 'who expected deliverables should be the same as in Australia [when] they just can't be'. No provision had been made for repatriation.

Discussion

Table 9.3 summarizes these findings and shows that there was enormous variation in the performance management systems across the four organizations studied. The research showed that Companies A and B have adopted a more formal and standard performance management system for expatriate assignments. Both are very specific about goal setting and appraisal and reward systems, whereas performance management is almost non-existent in Companies C and D. The findings show polarized approaches to performance management among the different companies with larger firms adopting more formal performance management systems and smaller firms with informal procedures. This is consistent with other findings concerning the influence of company size as reported by Tahvanainen and Suutari (2005). In Companies A and B, performance management inclined towards a developmental-style system, though the disposition was still one of fulfilling a mandatory organizational 'obligation'.

Generally, the higher the level of management positions, the more likely it is that there will be written performance management goals (Tahvanainen and Suutari, 2005, p. 103). There appears to be some deviation among this small group of companies compared with broader research. In Company C, the top manager has no formal performance arrangements at all. However, this was a small organization and, as a non-profit organization, it was atypical in terms of organizational form. In this instance, organization size and form may override status/level of management and suggest that the mixture of influences affecting performance appraisal is complex. The absence of performance assessment for the expatriate in Company D, a project construction company, is consistent with wider research (Tahvanainen and Suutari, 2005, p. 105) that performance management and training are commonly non-existent in project organizations.

None of the companies studied has integrated training and development in performance management except for Company A which provided six weeks of technical training for one of the expatriates. This was carried out pre-departure as a preparatory step and there was no evidence of any follow-up to evaluate whether this training had been of benefit to the individual or whether it

Table 9.3 Performance management (PM) components

Performance management components	Company A	Company B	Company C	Company D
Goal setting	Specific goals are set in line with corporate goals: (1) growth in sales and revenue; (2) achieve customer satisfaction	Specific goals are set by expatriate and supervisor at the beginning of the year: (1) financial indicators; (2) health and safety; (3) personnel management. 60 per cent of goals are set at individual level and 40 per cent are set at firm/unit level	Goals: (1) make organization survive; (2) get financial base; (3) have sustainable business; (4) attract new members/clients	Goals not specified in the contract: finish the project and develop new business in China
Performance appraisal	Appraisal carried out every 6 months using KPIs originally identified; individual submits own rating and confirmed by his/her boss. 15 per cent of performance is on customer satisfaction Standard appraisal form is used throughout the company	Appraisal carried out at the end of the year and interim check points are arranged with the manager. Appraisal is done by supervisor Standard appraisal form is used throughout the company, but tailored to the specific tasks for expatriates	No specific appraisal process and no quantitative assessment	No specific appraisal process

Rewards	Normal expatriate packages: salary, housing, education, medical, insurance and one return home trip per year	Normal expatriate package: salary, housing (with ceiling), education (with ceiling), one return home trip per year	Salary paid and taxed locally; one return home trip per year	Salary plus daily allowance net of tax; housing, one return home trip during the 9-month project term
	No specific bonus	Bonus is performance based: 25–30 per cent of salary	No bonus	No bonus
Training	6 weeks' technical training was provided, but no cross-cultural training	No training was provided	No training was provided	No training was provided
Development	No formal mentor	No formal mentor	No formal mentor	No formal mentor
	No repatriation arrangement	No repatriation arrangement	No repatriation arrangement	No repatriation arrangement

contributed to his achievement of the organization's goals. While training is not an automatic panacea, as discussed above, the almost entire lack of connection between performance management and training indicates an underdevelopment of the interface between these human resource functions. Performance management as a means of support for employee development in an ongoing manner is missing.

There also appears to be relatively little connection between performance management arrangements and rewards in terms of the expatriate's remuneration and benefits package. As is common with expatriate packages, some elements of the interviewees' rewards packages are based on needs – the need to visit home (the annual airfare), the need for affordable housing and child education (the housing allowance and schooling allowance or fees payment). Such benefits are commonly incentives that attract employees to take up a package or to 'equalize' the differences with rewards at home, rather than acting as an incentive and reward connected with the organization's desired levels of performance. In only one instance (Company B) was performance-related pay a substantial component of the compensation package. Increasingly, the redesign of performance and reward systems is directed at tightening the connection between these in a manner that 'help[s] companies to bring strategy to employees, and turn employees' potential into the desired results' (Delery and Doty, 1996, cited in Tahvanainen and Suutari, 2005, p. 92). There appears to be some way to go to achieving this among Australian companies in China.

Conclusion

This chapter has examined performance management practices in four contrasting western (Australian) companies operating in the world's largest (and arguably most 'foreign' – Selmer, 2005b) developing economy, China. The exploratory study provides some evidence supporting the discrepancies in organizational performance management practices in the global realm. Though the scale of the initial phase of this project means that the findings must be interpreted with caution, it was evident that the companies which were more established and experienced in international business deployed more developed performance management arrangements. Those that were newly internationalized and smaller had not developed performance management systems for their international operations. Consequently, the achievement of strategic goals in the latter companies would occur more through chance than through linking with employee performance. It is possible that the human resource function generally in the international operations of the two larger organizations was also more fully established than in the smaller, less internationally established firms, though a wider evaluation was outside the scope of this study. Generally, the contrasts captured in these findings accord with the effect of key contextual variables of company size, level of internationalization, organizational structure and position of the expatriate in the organizational hierarchy.

Tahvanainen and Suutari (2005) comment that the performance management process can provide frequent information about the training and development needs of expatriates, over and above needs related to cultural training, and help organizations to support and train their expatriates. They also observe that there is 'fairly little evidence' on how well the existing performance management systems succeed in this task and that the involvement of training in performance management differs with the type of expatriate, as does the expatriate's satisfaction with performance management. The evidence from this study reflects a disconnection between performance management and training. It also indicated less usage of performance management systems for performance-related pay than found in other studies (Suutari and Tahvanainen, 2001 cited in Tahvanainen and Suutari, 2005).

It appears that the lack of theoretical development and empirical studies is reflected in the inadequate consideration of training and development in expatriate performance management systems. The small scale of this study notwithstanding, it seems this is a deficiency in international business practice. It suggests that theoretical models of expatriate performance management systems should connect with training and development to provide comprehensiveness and relevance, and to enhance the adequacy of the both the HRM literature and global business practice.

Acknowledgements

The authors acknowledge assistance from the Australian Academy of Social Sciences and the Chinese Academy of Social Sciences that has made the field study in Beijing possible. The advice and assistance of Rongping Kang are also gratefully acknowledged.

References

Adler, N.J. and S. Bartholomew (1992) 'Managing Globally Competent People', *Academy of Management Executive*, 6 (3), 52–65.

Armstrong, M. (1998) *Performance Management: the New Realities* (London: Institute of Personnel and Development).

Black, S. and M. Mendenhall (1990) 'Cross-cultural Training Effectiveness: a Review and a Theoretical Framework for Future Research', *Academy of Management Review*, 15, 113–36.

Brewster, C. and J. Pickard (1994) 'Evaluating Expatriate Training', *International Studies of Management and Organization*, 24 (3), 18–35.

Dawkins, P., L. Saveray and T. Mazzarol (1995) 'Enterprising Nation: Renewing Australia's Managers to Meet the Challenges of the Asia-Pacific Century – Customer

Views of Australian Management', *Asian-Pacific Viewpoints* (Canberra: Australian Government Publishing Service).

Dowling, P. and R. Schuler (1990) *International Dimensions of Human Resource Management* (Boston: PWS-Kent Publishing).

Evans, P., V. Puckik and J. Barsoux (2002) *The Global Challenge: Frameworks for International Human Resource Management* (New York: McGraw-Hill Irwin).

Fenwick, M.S., H.L. De Cieri and D.E. Welch (1999) 'Cultural and Bureaucratic Control in MNCs: the Role of Expatriate Performance Management', *Management International Review*, 3, 107–24.

Flynn, G. (1995) 'Training is the Key to Successful Performance Management', *Personnel Journal*, 74 (2), 26.

Hutchings, K. (2002) 'Improving Selection Processes but Providing Marginal Support: a Review of Cross-cultural Differences for Expatriates in Australian Organisations in China', *Cross-Cultural Management*, 9, 32–57.

Jesuthasan, R. (2003) 'Business Performance Management: Improving Return on Rewards Investments', *WorldatWork Journal*, 12 (4), 55–64.

Katz, J.P. and D.M. Seifer (1996) 'It's a Different World Out There: Planning for Expatriate Success through Selection, Pre-departure Training and On-site Socialization', *Human Resource Planning*, 19, 32–47.

Lindholm, N. (2000) 'National Cultural and Performance Management in MNC Subsidiaries', *International Studies of Management and Organizations*, 29 (4), 45–66.

McGrath-Champ, S. and X. Yang (2002) 'Expatriate Management, Venture Performance and the "New Economy": Insights from Exploratory Australia–China Research', *Proceedings of the Fourth Conference on Multinational Business Economy*, Nanjing, China, 18–21 May.

Mwita, J.I. (2000) 'Performance Management Model: a System-based Approach to Public Service Quality', *The International Journal of Public Sector Management*, 13 (1), 19–37.

Nador, S. (1999) 'A Properly Crafted Performance-management Program Aids Professional Development', *Canadian HR Reporter*, 12, 10.

Parliament of Australia (1995–6) *Inward Direct Foreign Investment in Australia: Policy Controls and Economic Outcomes*, Prepared by P. Hanratty, Parliamentary Library, Research Report 32 (http://www.aph.gov.au/library/pubs/rp/1995–96/96rp32.htm; accessed on 19 January 2005).

Rosen, R., P. Digh, M. Singer and C. Philips (2000) *Global Literacies – Lessons on Business Leadership and National Cultures* (New York: Simon and Schuster).

Rubienska, A. and T. Bovaird (1999) 'Performance Management and Organizational Learning: Matching Processes to Cultures in the UK and Chinese Services', *International Review of Administrative Sciences*, 65, 251–68.

Schuler, R.S., P.J. Dowling and H. De Cieri (1993) 'An Integrative Framework of Strategic International Human Resource Management', *Journal of Management*, 19 (2), 419–59.

Selmer, J. (2005a) 'Cross-cultural Training and Expatriate Adjustment in China: Western Joint Venture Managers', *Personnel Review*, 34, 68–84.

Selmer, J. (2005b) 'Western Business Expatriates in China: Adjusting to the Most Foreign of All Foreign Places', in H. Scullion and M. Linehan (eds), *International Human Resource Management: a Critical Text* (New York: Palgrave Macmillan).

Shay, J. and J. B. Tracey (1997) 'Expatriate Managers', *Cornell Hotel and Restaurant Administration Quarterly*, 38 (1), 30–5.

Suutari, V. and M. Tahvanainen (2002) 'The Antecedents of Performance Management among Finnish Expatriates', *International Journal of Human Resource Management*, 13 (1), 55–75.

Tahvanainen, M. and V. Suutari (2005) 'Expatriate Performance Management in MNCs', in H. Scullion and M. Linehan (eds), *International Human Resource Management: a Critical Text* (New York: Palgrave Macmillan).

UNCTAD (2004) *Country Fact Sheet: Australia*, prepared by United National Conference on Trade and Development, World Investment Report 2004: The Shift Towards Services (www.unctad.org/fdistatistics; accessed on 16 June 2005).

Vesper, J. L. (2001) 'Performance: the Goal of Training or Why Training Is Not Always the Answer', *Biopharm*, 14 (2), 44–6.

Waxin, M-F. and A. Panaccio (2005) 'Cross-cultural Training to Facilitate Expatriate Adjustment: It Works!', *Personnel Review*, 34, 51–67.

Weatherly, L.A. (2004) 'Performance Management: Getting It Right from the Start', *HR Magazine*, 49 (3), 1–11.

Wilson, J.P. and S. Western (2000) 'Performance Appraisal: an Obstacle to Training and Development?', *Journal of European Industrial Training*, 24 (7), 384–90.

Woods, P. (2003) 'Performance Management of Australian and Singaporean Expatriates', *International Journal of Manpower*, 24 (5), 517–36.

Wright, P.C. and G.D. Geroy (2001) 'Changing the Mindset: the Training Myth and the Need for World-class Performance', *International Journal of Human Resource Management*, 12 (4), 586–600.

Yan, A., G. Zhu and D.T. Hall (2002) 'International Assignments for Career Building: a Model of Agency Relationship and Psychological Contracts', *Academy of Management Review*, 27 (3), 373–91.

10

Country of Origin Effects on Knowledge Transfers from MNEs to their Chinese Suppliers: an Exploratory Investigation

Jing-Lin Duanmu

Introduction

This chapter is derived from a broader study (Duanmu, 2005) that investigates the process and content of vertical knowledge transfers from multinational enterprises (MNEs) to Chinese supplier firms in the electrical and electronics industry. Although there is much work on the role of spillover effects from foreign direct investment (FDI) on the host economy, our understanding about how they occur at a micro-level is limited. The broader study is a response to Meyer's (2004) call for work on spillover effects through forward and backward linkages based on convincing theoretical arguments. It attempts to reveal the varied and complicated micro-level considerations in the process of vertical knowledge transfer. One such influential factor is the country of origin (COO) of the inward-investing MNE; this is the focus of the present chapter. It draws upon data gathered from interviews with US, EU and Japanese MNEs with operations in China and their respective Chinese component suppliers. It demonstrates that COO effects are quite distinct between East and West, with different implications for the types of knowledge transferred to suppliers and the timing of such activities in the duration of a supply relationship.

The chapter is structured as follows. Having introduced the topic, the second section briefly reviews the international business (IB) literature regarding the spillover effects of FDI and COO effects. The next section presents the research methodology and outlines the data collection process. The research findings are then discussed and the chapter concludes with practical recommendations for the local indigenous suppliers about how they might encourage the development of desirable supply relationships with MNEs.

Literature review

MNEs play a pivotal role in linking rich and poor economies by transmitting capital, knowledge, ideas and value systems across borders (Meyer, 2004). The expectation that FDI will benefit the local economy has motivated many governments to offer attractive incentive packages to entice MNEs, but despite the policy relevance, the research on impact of MNEs on host economies fails to draw reliable conclusions (Caves, 1996) and the hard evidence on the extravagant claims about positive spillovers from FDI is sobering (Rodrik, 1999).

Received theory has shown that FDI can exert multiple impacts on host economies via discrete channels. On the negative side, FDI can have potentially damaging effects on the local economy. Firstly, by taking market share from domestic firms, MNE competition may have a negative impact on indigenous firms, especially in the short term (Aitken and Harrison, 1999). Secondly, due to possible positive wage differentials, local firms may find it difficult to attract and retain their most experienced and valuable personnel. It is more likely that human capital will move from domestic firms to the inward invested MNEs than the reverse. Indeed, the effects of labour migration could turn out to be negative when experienced personnel move from the domestic sector to MNEs and take with them the local knowledge and information that MNEs often lack (a form of 'brain drain' from indigenous enterprises to MNE subsidiaries).

Apart from these undesirable effects, however, a number of positive effects may arise. Firstly, demonstration effects allow local firms to learn by observing MNEs operating with higher levels of technology. After noticing a product innovation or a new form of organization adapted for local conditions, local entrepreneurs may strive to imitate the innovation (Sinani and Meyer, 2003). As local business interacts with the technology used/produced by the MNE, information is diffused; uncertainty is reduced and imitation levels increase (Blomstrom and Kokko, 1998). Secondly, domestic firms may react to foreign competition by using their existing technology more efficiently or by investing in new technology in order to maintain their market share. Thirdly, local employees trained by MNEs may gradually move to jobs in domestic firms either through an independent entrepreneurial spirit and/or a sense of sovereignty and patriotism, taking the upgraded human capital with them. Fourthly, positive spillovers could also take place through MNEs' backward and forward linkages through business transactions with their local suppliers and customers. To sum up, FDI can generate a complicated set of impacts on a host economy with the net outcome being uncertain.

Most prior studies (Kueh, 1992; Zhan, 1993; Wang; 1995; Lan, 1996; Wu, 1999; Zhu and Tan, 2000; Buckley et al., 2002; Zhou et al., 2002) investigate the impact of FDI on the host's economic development at aggregated economic levels without distinguishing between the different channels and mechanisms through which the influence of FDI is delivered. Similarly, few authors explore the conditions under which positive spillovers occur (Sinani and Meyer, 2003). This not only means that the results of studies investigating the effects of FDI on local industry are mixed for both developed countries and for transition economies (for a summary see Sinani and Meyer, 2003), but also makes it difficult to propose positive and rational intervention at the microeconomic level for both firms and policy-makers (Meyer, 2004).

This previous lack of coverage triggered the present body of research to focus on the exact mechanisms and process of knowledge transfer from MNEs to the local economy. In particular, this study focuses on MNEs' backward linkages to their indigenous Chinese supplier firms.

Foreign firms may purchase intermediate goods from domestic suppliers to economize on transportation costs or to accommodate local content requirements. A review of the literature shows that MNEs' backward linkages to suppliers represent one of the most distinctive and direct channels through which MNEs can have a positive impact on the local economy. Development economics has emphasized the creation of what Hirschman (1958) termed 'backward and forward linkages' identifying the relationships that multinationals can activate with local suppliers and customers respectively. Hirschman (1958) suggested that FDI could create strong external economies in sectors that supply or buy from MNEs if new investments are undertaken to exploit them. Lall (1978) suggests that MNEs improve the productivity of indigenous firms by providing technical assistance and training, by assisting them in the purchase of raw materials, and by pressuring suppliers to meet standards of reliability and speed of delivery. However, actual evidence about the real impact of FDI on linkage creation and on host countries' development is scarce and that which exists is contradictory, as reported by Dunning (1993), Barkley and MacNamara (1994), Turok (1994) and Blomstrom and Kokko (1998) among others. To quote Blomstrom et al. (1999, p. 29), the degree to which international linkages generate appropriable positive spillover benefits for the host country 'is an extremely important policy issue for which there is a disappointing amount of evidence'.

As China is becoming one of the most important countries to which MNEs outsource or locate their manufacturing activities, it provides us with a good opportunity to observe the direct linkages between MNEs and local Chinese firms and how these relationships influence the indigenous Chinese firms' development. It is believed that foreign MNEs potentially contribute to a more viable economic climate by associating closely with local enterprises and assisting local entrepreneurs by upgrading their technology and improving their organizational skills (Lin et al., 1999). As local enterprises face continual reform and market rationalization, productive foreign multinational–local linkages offer them a unique, yet important, development path. Such linkages could potentially provide employment, tax revenue and, crucially, the expertise needed to build market-based, competitive firms with advanced technology and modern organizational techniques. In particular, due to the inherent competitive strengths of MNEs, their linkages with local indigenous supplier firms have been empirically proven to be significant mechanisms for promoting local firms' technological development, competitiveness and growth (Wong, 1992; Foray and Lundvall, 1996; Matthews, 1996).

Given this research focus, some studies have argued that COO should be an important construct in examining knowledge transfer (for example Young and Lan, 1997; Giroud, 2000), so a further question is posed: does the COO of MNEs influence these vertical knowledge spillovers and transfers? In the international business field, the COO effect has been found to affect MNEs' location decisions (He, 2003), entry mode choice (see Zhao et al., 2004), business performance (for example Kessapidou and Varsakelis, 2002) and human resources management (Ferner et al., 2001). Other studies, however, found limited COO effects. For example, Child and Yan (2001) discovered very limited COO effects on MNEs' strategic orientation, training, management controls and other management dimensions among the multiple countries from which the foreign partners in Chinese JVs originate. Yet in each of these studies, the MNE is the primary focal concern; few studies consider the impact of the MNE's COO on the host country's firms that have relationships with them.

One such study is Giroud (2000) who provides one of the first systematic investigations of foreign MNEs' linkages with local firms with a specific emphasis on the COO effect. The COO is found to be significant in explaining the *existence* of vertical knowledge transfer, but less so in the explanation of the *degree* of transfer. Transfers by Japanese firms are reported to be scarce compared to European and US MNEs; Western MNEs are more likely to transfer knowledge to the local economy compared to their Asian counterparts. His research concludes that overall, the knowledge transfer from the foreign investors to their local suppliers is quite limited. Similarly, a study by Banga (2003) considered the impact of COO on the host economy in India and found that the impact of inward FDI on export intensity varies with respect to the source country of FDI. The impact of US FDI in the non-traditional exports industries was found to be significantly positive but the impact of Japanese FDI in these industries was not significant.

Consequently, present understanding of the COO effect on the knowledge transfer issue is not satisfactory. The COO effect could be interpreted differently depending on the perspective taken. It is not clear whether the COO effect is indicative of managerial preferences arising from the different cultural traits of decision-makers in the MNEs, whether it is more a reflection of MNEs' business strategy in a host country, or whether there are other reasons. Is it that cultural distance makes effective communication in knowledge transfers difficult or is it the MNEs' attitude in protecting or exposing relevant information and knowledge to their suppliers, or a combination of both? As such, a micro-level examination is needed to reveal the actual mechanisms associated with MNEs' knowledge transfer to their local suppliers and then, in turn, we can see whether and how the COO exerts influence upon the process.

Research methodology and data collection

To reveal whether and how the COO influences inter-firm knowledge transfer, an interview-based, qualitative methodology was adapted to facilitate a process-oriented understanding of the research question. Specifically, the processual case study approach from the area of organizational behaviour (Pettigrew, 1997; Pentland, 1999) was adopted because it was capable of generating knowledge not only of processes and outcomes but also of why and how different outcomes were shaped by different processes (Van de Ven, 1992; Pettigrew, 1997). It is especially useful when the research focus is on the 'process' of inter-firm know-ledge transfer instead of the 'input–output' correlations (Autio and Laamanen, 1995). The other advantage of the methodology was that by interviewing both MNEs and their suppliers, a balanced view could be obtained to provide a more comprehensive understanding of the inter-firm knowledge transfer. As such, it breaks the conventional mould of international business research, which has been largely to look inwardly at the MNE, rather than looking out from MNEs to the societies in which they are operating (Meyer, 2004).

The data collection proceeded in three stages. First, in April 2003, with assistance from Wuxi New District Committee, a questionnaire survey was distributed by fax in Wuxi Industrial Zone to identify the foreign electrical and electronics multinationals with local procurement.[1] Altogether 52 electrical and electronics foreign multinationals were identified and contacted, 50 responded and 28 of them were found to have local purchasing arrangements with 93 suppliers in China. Of these 93 local suppliers, however, only 22 were indigenous Chinese firms.[2] Thus those MNEs with relationships with the 22 indigenous suppliers were selected for the study. As only MNEs with ongoing supply relationships with indigenous Chinese suppliers were identified, this introduced selection bias into the sample in the form of its inability to report on failures.

In the second stage, the research framework and interview questions gener-ated from the literature review were refined through four pilot interviews that were conducted in May 2003. Finally, extensive fieldwork was conducted from November 2003 to March 2004 where semi-structured interviews were used to gather retrospective information for the case study analyses. Interviews were conducted in Mandarin and recorded; all interviews were then simultaneously transcribed and translated into English. Access was gained to 17 of the 22 indigenous Chinese suppliers identified (five state-owned enterprises (SOEs), two collectively owned enterprises (COEs) and ten privately owned enterprises (POEs)) and to 18 foreign MNEs (13 Japanese, three European and two American firms). Table 10.1 provides a list of interviewed companies where companies' names are kept anonymous for reasons of confidentiality.

There are 16 'complete' sets of data where access was gained to both the customer and supplier side of a dyadic relationship. In other instances, data are 'incomplete' as access was only gained to either the customer side or the supplier side. These are treated as an additional source of evidence when considering the side of the relationship for which data were available. This information is also included in Table 10.1. Each set of complete data contained between two and six interviews depending upon access to personnel. Purchasing and general managers of the customer firms and supplier managers were the key interviewees, and relevant members of staff, such as technology supervisors and middle-level management, were interviewed when possible. Altogether 49 interviews were conducted giving 67 hours of interviews. NVivo (Bazeley and Richards, 2000) was used as the supporting software package to categorize, code and analyse data. The empirical findings are presented in the next section.

Empirical findings

From earlier research (Duanmu and Fai, 2004), a three-stage process of relationship development between the MNE customer and Chinese supplier was identified. The first stage is the 'initiating stage', where the main activities that engaged both sides were factory evaluations and product sample tests. This stage allowed the customer firm to comprehensively inspect facilities and test the supplier's production capability prior to the formal approval of the relationship initiation. The second stage is the 'developing stage'. At this point, the relationship focus changes from being simply concentrated on the factory facilities and quality of samples to ensuring that the supplier is able to deliver mass-produced output of satisfactory quality. The customer requires suppliers to systematically upgrade their firms in terms of technical facilities and management practices to ensure quality output, consistent delivery performance and efficient cost control. All the dyadic relationships in the study entered this stage. The third stage is the 'intensifying stage'. Experience in the relationship can lead to recognition of the indigenous firm's capabilities, the establishment of greater degrees of trust, and convergence in managerial ideologies can move the cooperation forward. The relationship between the MNE and the local supplier shifts from being merely manufacturing cooperation to more technological cooperation with greater original, cognitive inputs from the supplier. However, in the sample only three of the 16 local supplier firms had entered this stage at the time of interviewing.

Table 10.1 Composition of firms interviewed

Dataset number	Foreign multinational			Products exchanged	Chinese supplier firm	
	Nationality	Ownership	Number of interviews		Ownership	Number of interviews
Complete data						
1	Sino-Japanese	JV	2	Seal-up component	Private	1
2	Sino-Japanese	JV	1	Surface-mounted technology	SOE	1
3	Sino-Japanese	JV	1	Chassis	Private	2
4	Japanese	WOE	1	Plastic parts	Private	1
5	Italian	WOE	3	PC controller	Private	2
6	Japanese	WOE	1	Porcelain shell	Private	1
7	Japanese	JV	1	Outer bucket	Private	1
8	Japanese	JV	1	Pressing parts	Private	2
9	Japanese	JV	3	PC controller	SOE	3
10	Japanese	JV	1	Radiator	Private	1
11	Japanese	JV	1	Component of defroster	Private	1
12	Japanese	WOE	1	Nickel foam	SOE	1
13	Swedish	WOE	1	Metal parts	Collective	2
14	Japanese	WOE	1	Manganese	SOE	2
15	US	JV	1	Electrical starter	Collective	1
16	Japanese	WOE	1	Electrical parts	Private	1
Incomplete data						
1	US	WOE	1	Electrical parts	No access	NA
2	German	WOE	2	Electrical parts	No access	NA
3	South Korea	No access	NA	Electronics parts	SOE	2

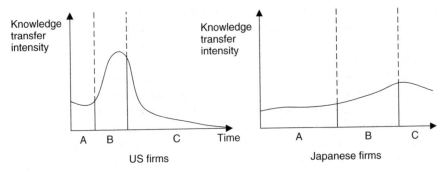

Figure 10.1 Knowledge transfer intensity and relationship development

It appears that the behaviour of Japanese and Western firms is quite different in each of these stages, with Japanese and US behaviour presenting the two extremes and the EU firms falling somewhere in-between. A tentative discussion of the differences in the two extremes is advanced below. However, the findings must be interpreted with care because only 16 dyadic relationships are sampled in this qualitative investigation. Also, the sample is biased towards Japanese MNEs (Table 10.1), although this reflects the general composition of the population of MNE nationalities in Wuxi's electrical and electronics industry. A further caveat is that while only two US firms are in the sample of dyadic relationships, their different management style was frequently mentioned by other Chinese firms who have had cooperation experience with them even if the specific relationship that was being discussed in the interview was not with an American MNE. Thus it is perceived to be worthwhile to discuss such comparison.

The horizontal axis of Figure 10.1 shows the developing relationships and knowledge benefits associated with the initiating, developing and intensifying stages (A, B and C respectively). The vertical axis represents the intensity of the knowledge transfer from the MNE customer firms to the Chinese supplier.[3]

The interviews suggest that, comparatively speaking, US firms prefer local firms with higher levels of initial technological capability as this allows them to quickly set up a vertical relationship. Therefore as Figure 10.1 shows, in the initiating stage A, US firms feel they can transfer quite high levels of knowledge to their supplier relative to the Japanese firms (see the intersections of the curves on the vertical axes in each case). The initiating stage for US firms is often very brief, and the relationship will soon move to the developing stage (B) where both the quantity and quality of purchasing volume rapidly increase. To ensure stability in the quality of the supplied components, US firms are very willing to provide assistance to nurture the supplier firms through intensive and systematic training. Such training does not simply focus on the technical details; instead managerial training is surprisingly abundant with the aim of infusing their management culture into the suppliers. As a result, the developing stage B is very knowledge intensive and the occurrence of knowledge transfer appears to cluster in this relatively short time span.

It can be demanding for Chinese suppliers to sustain long-term cooperation with US firms, however, because the latter are particularly focused on cost reduction measures. So even if the cooperation does go well with US firms, the relationship can be terminated when the customer firm finds a 'better' candidate – a new supplier that can provide similar products at lower prices. Consequently, the stability of vertical relations is relatively low. For example, one US firm's purchasing manager reported that: 'Yes we keep searching better suppliers. We often switch to better ones' (Incomplete dataset 1, US customer firm).

As a result, fewer relationships evolve to the intensifying stage (C), and knowledge transfer intensity can drop dramatically once the relationship stabilizes or the incumbent supplier is simply replaced by new suppliers. While the earlier caveat on the bias in the composition of the COO of MNEs is recognized, this evidence is fully in line with other investigations about US firms' attitudes to cost and capabilities. For example, Helper and Kiehl (2004) found that financing is a constant pressure for US supplier firms which often leads them to 'fight fires' instead of building capabilities for the long run. Sako has also expressed similar views and she quoted Hajim Ohba, director of the Toyota Supplier Support Centre in the US:

> My experience is that much of American's revitalization has been focused on short-term cost reductions to improve profitability. This has resulted in an emphasis on 'quick fix' programs and applying technical tools on the shop floor. While these technical tools are part of TPS (Toyota Production System), taken alone they are isolated islands. (Ohba, 1997, cited in Sako, 2002, quoted from Helper and Kiehl, 2004, p. 104)

In contrast, Japanese firms are willing to engage with indigenous firms which do not possess such strong a priori competence (see Figure 10.1). What matters is whether the supplier firms can pass the product sample assessment and demonstrate potential. Supplier firms normally had to endure a longer and stricter assessment process in the initial phase. Japanese firms were described by Chinese suppliers as very 'passive' in providing technical information and assistance in stage A. It seems that the Japanese firms interviewed took the attitude that if the Chinese supplier firm wanted to build up the relationship, it needed to take on some responsibility to prove itself. The Japanese companies generally provided technical information when they perceived that they had received a 'relevant' request from the supplier firm.

We were kind of passive at the beginning; they were supposed to be active if they want to be our supplier. (Dataset 6, customer firm)

We are happy to provide assistance. But in the beginning, we would like to see the supplier firm put much effort in achieving our standards. So initially it is their job to get things done. Once they passed the sample test, we would have more confidence in both their motivation and capability and we are happy to provide more assistance. (Dataset 9, customer firm)

Such a passive 'teaching' attitude is one of the reasons why the initiating stage for supplier relations with Japanese customer firms is lengthy (compared to that with US firms) and for this reason, the initial stage is a critical period in which the supplier firms upgrade their skills and capabilities and learn. The evidence shows very high learning commitments from local indigenous firms, especially those from the private sector.

Despite these difficulties, not a single Chinese supplier firm gave up the opportunity of becoming a supplier to these Japanese firms.[4] All the supplier firms were actually reported to be willing to undertake the cost involved with the initial assessment and sample products despite the lack of help. In fact, a strong awareness of their own 'backwardness' permeates Chinese firms, and their eagerness to build up relationships with, and learn from, foreign multinationals cannot be more obvious. Indeed, this attitude towards Japanese firms has a good pay-off. Chinese firms reported that once they were involved in the Japanese firms' value chain system, relationships tend to be more dependable and stable compared to those with US firms.

During the cooperation process, Japanese customer firms, like the American ones, raise their expectations and requirements but they are less intensely cost driven and appear to be more concerned with overall system's quality. They are more likely patiently to assist the supplier firm to achieve the improvement that they require. Numerous Chinese firms have sensed such differences and reported as follows:

This Japanese firm monitors all our manufacturing processes from material purchase, self assessment books, to quality systems etc. They are different from Western firms. We could not understand why they cared about so many details, but we now know it is so important. (Dataset 8, supplier firm)

Western firms have shorter assessment processes once they get satisfactory samples, that is all. But Japanese firms are fussy; they tend to be more conservative. They not only check the sample products, but also the whole processes that delivered the products. But once you become their partner it is difficult to break up. But western firms tend to be more changeable. They are always seeking cheaper or more capable suppliers. But if the same situation occurs to Japanese customers they will help extant suppliers to reduce price but not change the suppliers. (Dataset 9, supplier firm)

Japanese firms are more bureaucratic and conservative; but once we become their supplier, the relationship will not easily break up. They care about long-term cooperation. When they get (market) information that there are other firms that can provide cheaper (same) components or with higher quality standard, they won't easily dump us. What they do is set those standards as the new requirements and help us to improve. (Dataset 11, supplier firm)

This evidence is similar to that of Chung et al. (2003) who found that Japanese assemblers often purchased components from local suppliers that had lower initial productivity levels and, in turn, the relationship with Japanese transplants extended the survival of the suppliers.

The evidence and analysis above help to bring together two previous pieces of work on the relationships of American and Japanese firms with their suppliers. From Giroud (2000), Japanese firms were found to have little technology transfer to their indigenous Malaysian suppliers compared to American firms. In the supply chain literature, Japanese firms have a reputation for their long-term commitment to suppliers (Sako, 1992, 2004). Context-free studies derived from cross-sectional data might have difficulty revealing the context-bounded understanding. The findings given here can reconcile these two studies. In the short term, very able indigenous Chinese suppliers can get a good deal of knowledge from their American partners. The problem is that US firms are not committed to long-term relationship building, but are driven strongly by lowering costs. As a result, progress and development for the Chinese supplier are limited and leave them feeling vulnerable. As one Chinese firm's managers expressed it: 'We feel uncertain. We do not know when they may find better ones' (Dataset 15, supplier firm).

In contrast, Japanese firms are willing to engage some relatively 'weak' local firms to be their suppliers and appear initially relatively less proactive about transferring information and knowledge to them. However, once these suppliers can prove their worth and achieve the Japanese firms' initial sample product requirements, passive 'teaching' attitudes become more proactive and deliberate over time. Such practice appears to be more beneficial to the local Chinese economy in that it actually gives ordinary firms the opportunity to upgrade their production capabilities systematically rather than being primarily focused on cost reduction mechanisms. Given that the majority of indigenous Chinese firms are small and medium-sized with relatively weak capabilities, the practices of the Japanese MNEs are more desirable in the Chinese context. After all, the reason for MNEs outsourcing to, and purchasing from, China is often related to cost-based measures. Consequently, the time dimension needs to be appropriately considered when assessing the extent of knowledge transfer by MNEs of different nationalities in a host country.

In the fieldwork, questions were also asked about whether language difficulties and cultural differences made knowledge transfer difficult. Since knowledge transfer requires communication between firms, these two aspects are perceived to be potentially relevant issues that might have an influence upon the process. The general response was negative. A few supplier firms acknowledged that they encountered difficulties in initiating the relationship with MNEs, but felt the difficulties were mainly due to their lack of experience in adapting to the management practices of the MNEs or their lack of knowledge to produce qualified samples in the initiating stage. However, they also report that the Chinese employees from the MNEs play an important role in mediating such difficulties. It is found that most Chinese personnel in MNEs have a certain degree of patriotism and are very willing to give assistance to the indigenous suppliers. They believe such vertical linkages will substantially benefit these indigenous Chinese firms in both a financial and technical sense, and currently indigenous Chinese firms are still a 'minority' within the supplier networks of these MNEs. At the same time, these Chinese employees in the MNEs also improve the MNE's ability to appropriately adapt to some local situations; they facilitate the MNE–local firm cooperation, make it more feasible and effective. In sum, these employees play a very important role in bridging the two sides by mediating the managerial and cultural differences between them. It is also found that most MNEs in China use Chinese as their official language which makes language a much less relevant issue in inter-firm communication than one might expect, although some of the higher-level, home or third country expatriate managers in the MNEs continue to use their native language and work through their interpreters.

One of the reasons for focusing on the extremes of the Japanese and US practices is that no distinguishable 'European' supply chain management practice was discernible among the firms in the sample. It seems practices differ by European nation: some of them attempt to imitate the Japanese model because of the great success that Japanese MNEs have achieved in the automobile and electronics industry since the 1980s; some of them keep a close affiliation with US practices due to cultural and language similarities, and some of them are found to be highly 'localized' to the context of the Chinese market. It is quite hard to generalize them as a highly unified group, as highlighted in the two interview extracts below:

> The Italian firm is much less rigid than, for example, our German customer. German firms barely change their design once they give you the components blueprints. It is helpful for us to produce. However, the Italian firm is much

less strict and often change their design. It makes our job difficult and some-times the sample products we produced become obsolete because they have changed their ideas!...They are different but at the same time, they all require good quality products. (Dataset 5, supplier firm)

I find the Swedish firm is so localized. Sometimes we joke they are becoming very Chinese. I feel US customer firms seem to deliberately keep their original style because they are big and very successful. But this Swedish firm is not big and seems to be willing to adapt to our culture. (Dataset 13, customer firm)

Generally, it seems European firms are less easily distinguishable in their development of relationships with suppliers than Japanese or US firms and therefore their behaviours and attitudes are assumed to lie somewhere between the Japanese and US positions presented here.

Conclusions and managerial implications

This chapter has concentrated on the influence of COO on the vertical know-ledge transfers from MNEs to their indigenous suppliers. Fieldwork data showed that Japanese MNEs are different from US MNEs in their attitude to assisting local indigenous supplier firms. The Japanese firms can be described as 'conser-vative' yet 'reliable' and US firms are relatively 'giving' but more 'footloose'. However, it was also found that factors such as the local firm's learning ability plays an important mediating role in reducing such different behaviours.

There are, as yet, no apparent COO effects with respect to how cultural differences might constrain knowledge transfers to Chinese supplier firms. Such cultural differences which exist and might act as barriers are largely reduced by Chinese managers in the foreign MNEs acting as mediators or bridges. As a result, the differences in COO effects appear to be indicative of managerial preferences rather than cultural traits although, of course, the two are complexly intertwined at a deeper level of analysis not attempted here. Nevertheless, the findings here fit with the broad stereotypes of Japanese and American managers emerging from other studies in international business and management that have been mentioned above. The former are concerned with long-term relationships, built on trust, are highly concerned with quality of the products, and the holistic nature of the systems that produce them. The latter are generally focused on the financial 'bottom line' and hence primarily focused on cost production and relatively short time horizons.

In terms of implications for managers, much more effort is required by managers of Chinese firms that are cooperating or want to step into such rela-tionships to ensure the efficient *implementation* of internal quality systems if they want to systematically upgrade their technological and managerial capabilities. More importantly, a clearly defined and consistent quality system, combined with appropriate training and guidance, can gradually shift the employee's attitude to maintaining or even raising quality standards over time. As Helper and Kiehl (2004) have pointed out, upgrading systematic production capabilities is a complex technical and behavioural task; it involves not just streamlining flows of work through the production process, but requires changes in embedded attitudes to facilitate the required employee involvement. Such effort is needed no matter from where the MNEs come.

Another lesson for Chinese managers is to be aware of the temporal differences between transfers from Japanese and American MNE partners. Recognition of the pattern of Japanese behaviour should mean that Chinese firms need not necessarily be fearful that they are about to lose a partnership with a Japanese firm if transfers are not forthcoming in the early stages of the relationship, but they should endeavour to prove themselves worthy of a long-term relationship. Similarly, by recognizing that transfer intensity drops off quite substantially in the developing stage of the relationship under the American pattern of behaviour, the Chinese firm can either try to encourage the US firm to transfer more to them, or establish a contingency strategy whereby the next stage of their learning might have to take place with another MNE partner if no more is to be gained from the US one.

Nevertheless, it is recommended that all indigenous firms develop good relationships with multiple customer firms, since single supply relationships are rare and this strategy can reduce the risks of overdependency on one firm. This may be more pertinent for those Chinese firms supplying primarily US firms than those who are supplying Japanese firms because of their focus on the short term. In addition, by supplying different MNEs, supplier firms obtain more chances to learn different competences from their customers (Bessant et al., 2003).

Managers of US firms with, or seeking to establish relationships with, indigenous Chinese suppliers should continue to select suppliers with relatively high levels of competency if they have this luxury but, as was pointed out, Chinese suppliers are more often than not starting with a very low base. In such instances the amount of information and knowledge that is passed on to Chinese firms is very welcome but perhaps a little overwhelming. It takes time to absorb all the information, to figure out how to adapt it from one cultural and business environment to another. It takes even more time to develop technical capabilities and managerial skills that enable firms to move down the average cost curve. It seems American managers need to allow more time for standards and procedures to become routinized; to pay more attention to the medium-term relational assets which might lead to alternative benefits apart from just cost reductions. It would perhaps be in the US manager's interest to develop relationships with a few Chinese suppliers at a time. They will have different phases of learning and improvement, so that slow periods of knowledge accumulation by one may be offset against a fast period of accumulation by another. This way, the sunk costs of finding, selecting and initiating supplier relationships are not completely lost when they switch between suppliers. Also it means the US firm will have a diversified portfolio of Chinese suppliers that can ensure a constant supply of components, which hopefully continually improve in quality as the suppliers enter a semi-competitive environment, in much the same way the Japanese as firms play off their multiple suppliers.

It appears useful for Japanese managers to 'test' the potential of Chinese suppliers. Perhaps a more proactive stance in providing assistance sooner could lead to a quicker establishment of a firm relationship so that progress to the 'developing stage' could occur earlier.

The above discussion provides an avenue for future empirical studies on the behaviour of MNEs of different country origins towards their host country suppliers. As illustrated above, the time dimension needs to be appropriately considered in any future empirical investigation since it has been revealed as an important moderating factor which, if excluded, might mean that the real differences between MNE behaviours are concealed.

The MNEs sampled in the study are all from developed economies, yet MNEs from emerging economies (for example, ASEAN, CEE, Brazil, India) are also drawn to China for market-seeking purposes. There is a high probability that the knowledge possessed by the latter will be different from that possessed by developed country MNEs. In this study, much of what is transferred appears to be managerial knowledge; the fact that it comes from an emerging nation does not necessarily make it less valuable than such knowledge coming from the developed MNEs examined here – just different. The difference between Western MNEs and those from less developed countries should be considered as a potentially important factor for investigation in future studies.

Notes

1. The data regarding the presence of MNEs in the electrical and electronics industry in Wuxi was accessed from the Wuxi Statistics Report (2003).
2. A deliberate distinction was made between local firms and indigenous firms because 'locals' included foreign suppliers who have located in China and who partner MNE customers. 'Indigenous' suppliers are firms with Chinese origins and ownership.
3. Note the concept of knowledge intensity in this respect is an ordinal measure interpreted from the interviewee's opinion rather than a cardinal measure based on discrete units of measurement.
4. Again it might reflect the unavoidable bias of the sampled research subjects, where failed relations simply slide away from possible access.

References

Aitken, B. and A. Harrison (1999) 'Do Domestic Firms Benefit from Direct Foreign Investment? Evidence from Venezuela', *American Economic Review*, 89 (3), 605–18.

Autio, E. and T. Laamanen (1995) 'Measurement and Evaluation of Technology Transfer: Review of Technology Transfer Mechanism and Indicators', *International Journal of Technology Management*, 10 (7/8), 643–64.

Banga, R. (2003) 'The Export-diversifying Impact of Japanese and US Foreign Direct Investments in India Manufacturing Sector', India Council for Research on International Economic Relations Working Paper 110 (New Delhi: India Habitat Centre).

Barkley, D.L. and K.T. McNamara (1994) 'Local Input Linkages: a Comparison of Foreign-owned and Domestic Manufacturers in Georgia and South California', *Regional Studies*, 28 (7), 725–37.

Bazeley, P. and L. Richards (2000) *The NVivo Qualitative Project Book* (London/Thousand Oaks/New Delhi: Sage).

Bessant, J., R. Kaplinskyu and R. Lamming (2003) 'Putting Supply Chain Learning into Practice', *International Journal of Operations and Production Management*, 23 (2), 167–84.

Blomstrom, M., S. Globerman and A. Kokko (1999) 'The Determinants of Host Country Spillovers from Foreign Direct Investments: Review and Synthesis of the Literature', *SSE/EFI Working Paper Series in Economics and Finance*, 239–72.

Blomstrom, M. and A. Kokko (1998) 'Multinational Corporations and Spillovers', *Journal of Economic Surveys*, 12, 247–77.

Buckley, P., J. Clegg and C. Wang (2002) 'The Impact of Inward FDI on the Performance of Chinese Manufacturing Firms', *Journal of International Business Studies*, 33 (4), 637–55.

Caves, R.E. (1996) *Multinational Enterprises and Economic Analysis*, 2nd edn (Cambridge University Press: Cambridge).

Child, J. and Y. Yan (2001) 'National and Transnational Effects in International Business: Indications from Sino-Foreign Joint Ventures', *Management International Review*, 411, 53–75.

Chung, W., W. Mitchell and B. Yeung (2003) 'Foreign Direct Investment and Host Country Productivity: the American Automobile Component Industry in the 1980s', *Journal of International Business Studies*, 34, 199–218.

Duanmu, J.L. (2005 forthcoming) 'Vertical Knowledge Transfer from MNEs to their Indigenous Chinese Suppliers', PhD thesis, University of Bath.

Duanmu, J.L. and F.M. Fai (2004) 'MNE Knowledge Transfer to Chinese Suppliers: Context Nature and Extent as Influenced by MNE Nationality', Conference paper presented at the 30th European International Business Academy, Slovenia, 6–9 December.

Dunning, J.H. (1993) *Enterprises and the Global Economy* (Wokingham: Addison-Wesley).

Ferner, A., J. Quintanilla and M. Varul (2001) 'Country of Origin Effects, Host-country Effects and Management of HR in Multinationals: German Companies in Britain and Spain', *Journal of World Business*, 26 (2), 107–27.

Foray, D. and B. Lundvall (1996) 'The Knowledge-based Economy: from the Economics of Knowledge to the Learning Economy', in OECD (eds), *Employment and Growth in the Knowledge-based Economy* (Paris: OECD).

Giroud, A. (2000) 'Buyer–Supplier Transfers and Country of Origin: an Empirical Analysis of FDI in Malaysia', *Globalisation and the Uniqueness of Asia*, Euro-Asia Management Studies Association 2000 Conference, INSEAD, Singapore, 23–25 November 2000.

He, C. (2003) 'Location of Foreign Manufacturing in China: Agglomeration Economies and Country of Origin Effects', *Regional Studies*, 82, 351–72.

Helper, S. and J. Kiehl (2004) 'Developing Supplier Capabilities: Market and Non-market Approaches', *Industry and Innovation*, 11 (1/2), 89–107.

Hirschman, A.O. (1958) *The Strategy of Economic Development* (New Haven: Yale University Press).

Kessapidou, S. and N. Varsakelis (2002) 'The Impact of National Culture on International Business Performance: the Case of Foreign Firms in Greece', *European Business Review*, 14, 268–75.

Kueh, Y.Y. (1992) 'Foreign Investment and Economic Change in China', *China Quarterly*, 131, 637–90.

Lall, S. (1978) 'Transnationals, Domestic Enterprise and Industrial Structure in LDSs: a Survey', *Oxford Economic Papers*, 30, 217–48.

Lan, P. (1996) *Technology Transfer to China through Foreign Direct Investment* (Aldershot: Ashgate).

Lin, J., Y. Ping and D. Yong (1999) 'Economic Impact of the Coca-Cola System on China', *China Centre for Economic Research Working Paper Series*, 12–23.

Matthews, J. (1996) 'Organizational Foundation of the Knowledge-based Economy', in OECD (eds), *Employment and Growth in the Knowledge-based Economy* (Paris: OECD).

Meyer, K. (2004) 'Perspectives on Multinational Enterprise in Emerging Economies', *Journal of International Business Studies*, 35, 259–76.

Pentland, B. (1999) 'Building Process Theory with Narrative: from Description to Explanation', *Academy of Management Journal*, 24 (4), 711–24.

Pettigrew, A.W. (1997) 'What is a Processual Analysis?', *Scandinavian Journal of Management*, 13 (4), 337–48.

Rodrik, D. (1999) 'The New Global Economy and Developing Countries: Making Openness Work', *Overseas Development Council, Policy Essay*, 24 (Washington, DC: Johns Hopkins University Press).

Sako, M. (1992) *Prices, Quality, and Trust: Inter-firm Relations in Britain and Japan* (Cambridge: Cambridge University Press).

Sako, M. (2004) 'Supplier Development at Honda, Nissan and Toyota: Comparative Case Studies of Organizational Capability Enhancement', *Industrial Corporate Change*, 132, 281–308.

Sinani, E. and K. Meyer (2003) 'Spillovers of Technology Transfer from FDI: the Case of Estonia', *Journal of Comparative Economics*, 32, 445–66.

Turok, I. (1994) 'Inward Investment and Local Linkages: How Deeply Embedded is Silicon Glen?' *Regional Studies*, 287, 401–17.

Van de Ven, A.H. (1992) 'Suggestions for Studying Strategy Process: a Research Note', *Strategic Management Journal*, 132, 169–88.

Wang, Z.Q. (1995) *Foreign Investment and Economic Development in Hungary and China* (Aldershot: Avebury).

Wong, P. (1992) 'Technological Development through Subcontracting Linkages: Evidence from Singapore', *Scandinavian International Business Review*, 1 (3), 28–40.

Wu, Y. (1999) *Foreign Direct Investment and Economic Growth in China* (Cheltenham: Edward Elgar).

Wuxi Statistics Report (2003) Wuxi New District Municipal Government Publisher, (April), Wuxi, China.

Young, S. and P. Lan (1997) 'Technology Transfer to China through Foreign Direct Investment', *Regional Studies*, 31 (7), 669–79.

Zhan, X.J. (1993) 'The Role of Foreign Direct Investment in Market-oriented Reforms and Economic Development: the Case of China', *Transnational Corporations*, 2, 121–48.

Zhao, H. Y.Luo and T. Suh (2004) 'Transaction Cost Determinants and Ownership-based Entry Mode Choice: a Meta-analytical Review', *Journal of International Business Studies*, 35, 524–44.

Zhou, D., S. Li and D. Tse (2002) 'The Impact of FDI on the Productivity of Domestic Firms: the Case of China', *International Business Review*, 11, 465–84.

Zhu, G. and K. Tan (2000) 'Foreign Direct Investment and Labor Productivity: New Evidence from China as the Host', *Thunderbird International Business Review*, 42 (5), 507–28.

11

Foreign Direct Investment Flows into an Integrating Europe: MNE Strategy and Location Decisions, 1981–2001

Dimitra Dimitropoulou and Robert Pearce

Introduction

The extensive availability of officially compiled series of data on flows and stocks of foreign direct investment (FDI) has stimulated a very considerable literature on the determinants of such FDI.[1] In the main, this has been positioned within the theoretical precepts of mainstream economics, using its established techniques to contribute to its existing subject areas. The motive behind the FDI decision tends to be modelled as a uniform one, reflecting the direct profit maximization of a neoclassical framework, the efficiency concerns of an established production function or some variant of an investment-stock adjustment process. Although many of these studies have enriched their perspectives through the selective interjection of some of the insights and conceptualizations of the theories of international business, few have placed these at the centre of analysis (Filippaios et al., 2004). The present chapter seeks to address this by suggesting that each FDI decision taken by managers aims in some way to further the competitive performance and development of the MNE group as a whole. By doing so, the key emphasis is placed on various dimensions of heterogeneity, with the MNE essentially modelled as a heterarchy (Hedlund, 1986, 1993; Birkinshaw, 1994), operating through variegated networks that respond to different needs and potential in different parts of the global economy. Against this background, new FDI flows would be seen as reflecting new investments or the expansion of existing ones that are made in a particular location because some characteristic of that location provides the potential to make a distinctive contribution towards one of the strategic priorities of an MNE (Buckley et al., 2003).

The FDI location tested in this chapter is Europe (in terms of the separate individual member economies of the EU); the sources of FDI, whether US,

Japan or intra-EU (Clegg and Scott-Green, 1999), and three types of broadly defined strategic objectives that may impel new investment are the other dimensions of differentiation. One would expect MNE strategy to react to the differences between European economies in increasingly more proactive ways, leveraging different input capacities into efficiency-seeking supply programmes and technological and skill competences into their emerging network approaches to innovation and R&D.

Two issues will be highlighted. Firstly, in terms of managerial perspectives, the strategic development of MNEs will be seen to rely increasingly upon the international networking of both their supply and creative programmes. Secondly, it will be recognized that the positioning of these strategic aims has to be considered in a specific facilitating context, in this case, that of European economic integration.

The next section introduces the basic conceptualization of the strategic heterogeneity of the contemporary MNE and outlines the three different priorities reflected in the subsequent analysis. The third section describes the sources and format of the dependent variable (FDI flows) and reviews the choices of analytical techniques used. Following that, the fourth section introduces the independent variables adopted and indicates their intended purpose in terms of differentiating between the broadly defined strategic aims. Regression results are reported and discussed in the penultimate section and conclusions are drawn in the final part.

FDI and competitive development in the modern MNE

Acts of FDI, whether to establish new subsidiaries or to expand or reposition existing ones, are components of a perpetual evolution in the competitive networks of globally oriented MNEs. Thus the following tests can *inter alia* show whether decisions to invest in Europe by managers of US, Japanese or European MNEs seem to be differently positioned within the wider strategic aims of these companies. Two dimensions that may affect this positioning are whether or not the MNE's ultimate HQ is in Europe (that is, differentiating between intra-European FDI and that from outside) and the length of strategic commitment to European operations (probably differentiating between managers of US and European MNEs and those from Japan).

Two fundamental dimensions need to be acknowledged in an initial broad characterization of the strategic priorities of MNEs. Firstly, managers in these companies need to apply their existing sources of competitiveness in the most effective way possible. Here MNEs can be seen as possessing a fixed stock of ownership advantages (OAs) at a point in time (Dunning, 1977, 1993, 2000), with managers seeking to optimize the competitive use of these across a range of different economies. This, in turn, will require close attention to differences between potential locations, with location advantages (LAs in Dunning's terminology) acting as determinants of where, how extensively and, crucially, why MNEs carry out specific acts of FDI. Secondly, managers of MNEs need to be perpetually aware of the need to renew and reconfigure their firm-level sources of competitiveness as the basis of future profitability and survival (that is, in effect, to continually regenerate their OAs). One of the most important strands in the understanding of MNEs' development over recent decades has concerned their growing commitment to international programmes of innovation (Bartlett and Ghoshal, 1989; Papanastassiou and Pearce, 1999; Narula 2003; Archibugi et al., 1999) and R&D (Pearce, 1999; Pearce and Papanastassiou, 1999; Niosi, 1999; Taggart et al., 2000) as sources for the continual restructuring of their competitiveness. This has added new characteristics of national economies to the range of potentially relevant LAs in the form of dynamic inputs (such as technology, tacit knowledge and skills, research capacity and programmes) into creative activities.

Against this background, for the present analysis, a three-part typology of MNE strategic motivations can be adopted (Manea and Pearce, 2004a, b), that itself derives from earlier categorizations of Behrman (1984) and Dunning (1993). Firstly, 'market seeking' (MS) motivation. In its traditional formulation managers would locate an MS investment in a particular country specifically to supply the market of that country. The LA provoking such an MS operation would usually have been some form of trade restraint which prevented the MNE from supplying that market from a lower-cost location. From this it would follow that such MS behaviour served to defend profitability, rather than to enhance it in any way. The historical contexts for such MS activities of MNEs were the protectionist environments implemented by many industrial economies during the 1920s and 1930s (and persisting for some time after the Second World War) and the import substitution industrialization strategies adopted by developing countries in the 1950s and 1960s.

Though these contexts are now largely less relevant to MNE strategic motivations, two factors can be suggested that may account for the persistence of aspects of MS behaviour currently. Firstly, in the case of European integration, it has been suggested that though freer trade may have strongly affected strategic options taken within Europe, the fear of 'fortress' Europe (with de facto increases in the trade barriers around the Union) may have caused significant amounts of new investment by MNEs from outside the EU. Here, continued access to the European market per se would have been the primary strategic motivation. Secondly, it may be that currently MNEs establish production, as well as marketing, operations in a particular economy in order to tailor supply to meet distinctive local consumer tastes better. The fact that much of MNEs' early expansion into Central and Eastern European transition economies appears to have been strongly MS-oriented (Manea and Pearce, 2004a) suggests the initial prioritizing of responsive adaptation to their unfamiliar and distinctive characteristics.

The second strategic motivation considered is 'efficiency seeking' (ES). Here MNE managers set up production subsidiaries in a particular location because this will enhance (and ideally optimize) the cost efficiency with which goods can be supplied to price competitive markets. The aim is, then, to generate integrated global supply networks in which different goods are produced in different locations so that, to the greatest degree possible, the inputs specified by the technology are those which are most readily available (sources of static comparative advantage) in the country. The main factor that has made it necessary and feasible to move towards such integrated ES supply networks has been the general lowering of trade barriers (GATT/WTO) and the emergence of regional free trade areas (with the EEC/EU central to this analysis). Once again, the ES motivation (like MS) depends on the relocation/transfer of existing technologies of the MNE group, but this time the aim is to boost rather than defend profitability by improving the efficiency with which technologies are used.

Finally, 'knowledge seeking' (KS) motivations can be distinguished as a generic description of two, often interrelated, strategic developments in MNE behaviour in recent years: the decentralization of R&D and of innovation. This reflects a reformulation by managers of their approach to the second broad strategic imperative, in terms of the revitalization of their product range and reinforcement of the scientific bases of their firms' technological scope. In terms of innovation, senior management personnel have increasingly realized that it has become very myopic to rely entirely on home country operations to generate new goods. By contrast, it is increasingly accepted that subsidiaries in many locations have the potential to access (from original technology and/or market insights) the core ideas for new goods and the ability to pull together, from local resources, the strong functional capacities (R&D/technology, marketing, engineering and entrepreneurial management) needed to develop and operationalize them. The product mandate (PM) subsidiary is a frequently discussed manifestation of this.

Though dispersal of R&D can be part of the decentralization of innovation strategy in MNEs, it can also target high quality work in terms of pure/basic scientific research. Thus managers of MNEs seeking to secure priority access to important breakthroughs in scientific investigation may locate several basic research laboratories in different countries to reflect the different scientific specialists that have emerged there. Ultimately, the various facets of KS represent both the MNEs' wider perspective on the sourcing of renewed and strengthened OAs and the increasing ability of countries, as they develop, to manifest creative LAs in the form of technologies, research capacity, and intangible skills, insights and perceptions.

Data and methodology

The FDI data used for this chapter were obtained from the OECD International Direct Investment Statistics dataset and it includes FDI inflows of all countries in the EU before the latest accession of Eastern European countries. The data sample therefore includes Austria, Belgium, Denmark, Finland, France, Germany, Greece, Ireland, Italy, Luxembourg, the Netherlands, Portugal, Spain, Sweden and the United Kingdom, a total of 14 countries since Belgium and Luxembourg are reported as one region under the denomination BLEU. For each of these countries inward direct investment flows[2] data were collected for the time period 1980–2001. The data were furthermore broken down into four categories according to the origin of FDI: FDI inflows from the rest of the world (FW from now on), FDI from the USA (FUS), FDI from Europe[3] (FEU) and FDI from Japan (FJ). The series of FUS, FEU and FJ include a number of missing observations because some countries do not report any or sufficient information for the geographical origin of the investment. The problem is substantial for countries such as Austria and Greece for all three of these series, and far less serious, or non-existent, for the rest of the countries in the sample. However, as the data are used to create a panel of all recipient countries and all years for each of the geographical origins, the number of missing observations does not create serious problems for the regression analysis. The resulting panels from the collection of data are presented in Table 11.1.

Finally, the data were transformed into US dollars from euros using the end of year exchange rate of euro to the US dollar (OECD International Direct Investment Statistics) and was deflated using the GDP deflator (OECD online statistics: National Accounts of OECD Countries).

Each of the three series of inward FDI was estimated using pooled ordinary least squares (POLS) and one-way fixed effects (also called least squares dummy variables (LSDV) estimation). The choice of POLS implies that foreign investment into EU countries occurs homogeneously across all countries. However, it is reasonable to assume that inward FDI displays a certain level of heterogeneity

Table 11.1   FDI inflows by origin; number of observations in each panel

Series	No. of countries	No. of years	No. of missing observations[a]	No. of observations[b]
FW	14	22	None	308
FUS	14	21[c]	34	260
FEU	14	21[c]	49	245
FJ	14	21[c]	57	237

[a] Pertains to the total number of missing observations for all 14 countries.
[b] No. of observations = (No. of countries * No. of years) – No. of missing observations.
[c] From 1981 to 2001.

between countries. The fixed effects model (where $fdi_{it} = \alpha_i + \beta X_{it} + u_{it}$) appears therefore to be more appropriate for this analysis than the POLS model, where the intercepts are identical for each country ($fdi_{it} = \alpha + \beta X_{it} + u_{it}$) ($fdi_{it}$ here is the dependent variable and represents FDI inflows into country i in year t and X is the matrix of the explanatory variables). It is expected that more homogeneity will be apparent in smaller, specific subsamples of the data, or in other words, that the same macro-variables are similarly important for the attraction of FDI flows into more similar countries, for example 'core' or 'periphery' countries. Nevertheless, there are several econometric tests that can help to decipher the heterogeneity question and give an indication of the right choice of model.

The POLS and LSDV models were tested for their applicability to the data. A likelihood ratio test rejected the hypothesis that the intercepts are identical, thereby suggesting that the fixed effects model would be more appropriate compared to the POLS for three of the four series of regressions: FW, FUS and FEU. The results differ for the estimation done on FDI from Japan, where the likelihood ratio test accepted the POLS model as opposed to the fixed effects one.[4]

The results that are reported below are the LSDV regression results for FW, FUS and FEU and the POLS regression results for FJ, using White's heteroskedastic consistent standard errors in all cases.

Factors influencing FDI strategy

The first independent variable used is the GDP of each national economy for each year ($US million). This variable (GDP) aims to test the most traditional form of MS strategic behaviour in which the sheer size of a national economy serves as an indicator of the potential profits available from supply of the market (Culem, 1988; Veugelers, 1991; Wheeler and Mody, 1992; Braunerhjelm and Svensson, 1996). The logical hypothesis from this would be that MS-oriented MNEs would, at a point in time, invest more in larger economies and also, over time, increase their investment in a particular economy in line with its growth. This view of MS, however, is also dependent on the presence of quite extensive restraints on trade (Barrell and Pain, 1999a, b; Neven and Siotis, 1996), so that the attractive market cannot be supplied to a significant or reliable extent from, potentially more efficient, sources elsewhere in an MNE's supply network. In terms of the context of this investigation, the expectation is that firms competing in Europe had become fully attuned to a more or less free-trade environment during the period covered here. This would remove the need to locate supply facilities in a market only in reflection of its size and, thereby, diminish the relevance of GDP as a determining variable. GDP was, therefore, tested as a potentially relevant variable. It had considerable provenance in earlier investigations but may have become of little importance during the time period studied here.

A perhaps more contemporary version of MS behaviour may be proxied by GDP per capita (PERCAP) (Filippaios et al., 2004; Chakrabarti, 2001). If GDP focused on a quantitative view of a market, then PERCAP may reflect a more 'qualitative' evaluation by MNEs. The core of this argument would be that across as extensive a geographical space as Europe, and with its wide differences in average income levels, there is plenty of scope for significant taste differences. Thus even where the basic services offered by a firm's goods may be welcomed by consumers across the region there may be resistance to product standardization, with a range of influences (climate, culture and tradition) then providing for totally different preferences as regards particular details of the form in which the goods are offered. GDP per capita may then be an indicator of both the extent of these taste differences (increasing prosperity may give consumers the ability to manifest previously suppressed sources of demand individualization) and the willingness of MNEs to respond to them through subtle locally responsive product differentiation. Where such supply individualization is planned the logic would be to activate it within a subsidiary (possessing strong market research capabilities, along with technological and engineering competence) that is well rooted within the relevant location.[5]

This might well reflect a wider supply-side element to PERCAP in the sense that it may proxy attributes of an economy that may attract MNEs' operations that have moved beyond routine cost-efficiency. This could cover infrastructure, production-oriented or managerial skills and aspects of technological and other creative inputs.

An economy's degree of openness or trade orientation is likely to be related (with some two-way causation likely) to the strategic form of MNEs' FDI, as implied by the earlier discussion. Thus a variable (OPEN) is adopted, which is calculated as exports plus imports divided by GDP for each host country in each year. A very low value of OPEN implies an economy that is isolated from the international trade environment (due to presumably mainly policy-based forces) so that the MNEs might well be attracted to invest in it to supply the local market, but would be unlikely to do so as a base for export-oriented supply. Thus, if MS was the dominant strategic motivation in a group of MNEs (here those from a particular country/regional origin) then a negative relationship between OPEN and flows of FDI would be expected. As OPEN takes on higher values, however, it becomes less necessary (indeed probably less viable, in the face of increasing import competition from often lower-cost locations elsewhere) to produce in the country for the local market and, instead, it becomes easier to adopt the country as an export-oriented supply base. So if ES is the dominant strategic motivation then a positive relationship between OPEN and FDI would be expected. The aim of European integration, of course, has been to develop an institutional environment conducive to increases in OPEN and, therefore, in effect to facilitate a concomitant reformulation of

MNE strategic priorities from MS to ES. The results here may reflect differences in the balance of these motivations between source country MNEs and also the extent of completion of any moves to ES before, or early in, the period studied.

The group of independent variables includes two that reflect ES motivation with different degrees of directness. Firstly, unit labour costs (ULC) (Cushman, 1987; Culem, 1988; Veugelers, 1991; Wheeler and Mody, 1992; Barrell and Pain, 1996, 1999a, b) provide a measure of the cost per unit of output of perhaps the key input in influencing pure ES strategy and point directly to the potential competitiveness of an economy as a supply base for MNEs' more mature price-competitive goods. Secondly, a broader measure of an economy's competitiveness in trade (COMP) is used (Filippaios et al., 2004) in the form of exports divided by exports plus imports. The higher the value of this ratio, or the more pronounced or sustained its rise over time, the more likely it is to reflect the presence of sources of international competitiveness in an economy that may attract MNEs. Though labour costs are very likely to be one of the influences on this *ex post* indicator of competitiveness, an extensive range of other input costs and environmental factors may also have an impact. Many of these may fall within the decision framework of MNEs. Part of this may be that, in fact, increasing values of COMP do not reflect pure cost influences at all but, instead, represent trade performance that derives from improved quality and innovative characteristics of goods. A positive expectation of the relationship between COMP and FDI may, therefore, include a mix of possible ES and KS behaviour.

Finally, two variables are included that seek to provide indicators of the scientific and/or innovative capacity of host economies, of the type that could, therefore, attract KS FDI of MNEs. Firstly, total expenditure on R&D (business and government funded) as a proportion of GDP (RAD) (Wheeler and Mody, 1992; Braunerhjelm and Svensson, 1996; Barrell and Pain, 1999a). This can be seen as an input measure that would suggest forward looking technology based potential in an economy that MNEs should seek to involve themselves with through current FDI. Alternatively, the measure of number of patent applications to the European patent organization per million of population (PAT) is also used. This can be interpreted as an output measure of how effective a country's science base, and its industry-based creative activity, has been in generating patentable new knowledge. Again, high values of PAT could be taken as suggesting to MNEs that their own scientific (research) and innovation (development) needs could be supported by FDI in an economy.[6]

The regressions also include the values of FDI stock ($US) in each country lagged by one year (FST) partly as a control. At the simplest and most mechanistic level this would acknowledge that new investments may simply be made in countries that have already demonstrated the ability to attract and retain FDI. Part of this possibility could reflect reinvestment by existing subsidiaries from their own profits. This, of course, need not be a routine reflex, since such reinvestment would need to be validated as embodying a logical strategic need (responding to a motivation reflected in one of the other variables rather than the mere availability of in-house funds). FST could also be taken as an indicator of agglomeration possibilities of FDI, suggesting interactive or spillover benefits from collocation with longer-established operations of other MNEs.

Results

Table 11.2 provides the regression test results for FDI from all sources (world) and separately for FDI from US, Japanese and European MNEs. In these GDP is insignificant in all regressions and, in fact, takes a negative sign (quite close to significant at 10 per cent) for US FDI. These results suggest that if national markets have any effect on MNEs' European supply programmes this does not operate through levels of GDP and that this, in turn, reflects the absence of any trade restraint influences on their sourcing policies.

PERCAP emerges as significantly positive in the equations for all FDI and for that from the USA. This suggests that in looking at potential income-related influences on FDI, US and European MNEs perceive average income levels as indicative of degrees of market segmentation that can still influence the location patterns of their operations.

Table 11.2   Regression results, one-way FE and POLS

Explanatory variables	Dependent variable			
	LSDV			POLS
	FDI from world	*FDI from USA*	*FDI from EU*	*FDI from Japan*
1. GDP	0.005 (0.869)	−0.008 (0.137)	0.007 (0.837)	0.000 (0.388)
2. GDP per cap	1.995 (0.019)**	0.410 (0.006)***	0.806 (0.461)	−0.014 (0.114)
3. OPEN	−62 145 (0.028)**	1566 (0.600)	−47 363.4 (0.121)	536 (0.021)**
4. COMP	7097 (0.945)	−6850 (0.320)	6921 (0.955)	−1652 (0.149)
5. ULC	1838.6 (0.594)	1345.5 (0.202)	−3846.1 (0.483)	−499.1(0.003)***
6. R&D	−67.4 (0.993)	−4766 (0.035)**	−1051 (0.879)	214.4 (0.140)
7. Patents	18.1 (0.762)	23.4 (0.114)	58.615 (0.455)	−0.526 (0.708)
8. FDI stock t-1	0.138 (0.018)	0.025 (0.079)*	0.152 (0.092)*	0.002 (0.010)*
Model statistics	$n = 308$	$n = 261$	$n = 239$	$n = 230$
	$F = 15.15$ (0.000)	$F = 16.72$ (0.000)	$F = 7.8$ (0.000)	$F = 4.82$ (0.000)
	Adjusted $R^2 = 0.49$	Adjusted $R^2 = 0.56$	Adjusted $R^2 = 0.48$	Adjusted $R^2 = 0.12$

Notes: Probability values are in parentheses and are based on heteroskedastic consistent standard errors. *** Statistically significant at the 1% level; ** Statistically significant at the 5% level; *** Statistically significant at the 10% level.

Responding with this degree of subtlety to the implications of such differences in per capita income may reflect a relatively prolonged involvement in European production or, at least, extended experience of the emergence of European markets by US MNEs. An alternative experience-based argument for PERCAP in the US MNE case could then be a supply-side ability to perceive and internalize qualitative input potentials (such as skill, talent and tacit knowledge) that again reflect an economic maturity proxied by PERCAP. The fact that PERCAP is quite close to negative significance in the Japanese FDI equation may then indicate lack of time to assimilate or respond to such taste or input differences and, as shall be suggested, at least an initial emphasis on the ES desire to mainly build operations into a cost-based Europe-wide supply network.

The variable OPEN is significantly negative for all FDI but significantly positive for Japanese FDI. The former result can be interpreted as reflecting a relatively slow, and therefore far from complete (especially for the negatively signed intra-European FDI), restructuring of US and European MNEs away from MS focus on individual markets during the closed pre-liberalization period towards those more export-oriented networked strategies that would reflect the emergence of an open and integrated European economy. The positive result for Japanese MNEs is then entirely in line with their strongest entry into Europe having occurred well into the period of substantial realization of EU integration programmes, so that their strategic postures can immediately adopt a powerfully ES-type of response to countries' supply potentials.

For the two variables seeking to reflect the current efficiency or competitiveness characteristics of national economies the only significant result is the negative sign on ULC for Japanese FDI. Taken with the interpretation of the significant positive result for OPEN, this again suggests that Japanese MNEs enter Europe with a clear strategy to establish a region-wide cost-effective supply network. The absence of a negative sign for US FDI can then be seen as compatible with the supply-side facet of the interpretation of the positive result for PERCAP in this test. Thus a positive sign for ULC could be speculatively interpreted as the payment of relatively high wage rates for skilled or talented labour involved in the supply of goods that compete through quality or originality rather than cost-driven low prices.

The results for COMP are somewhat surprising, only being positively signed (very weakly) in the European and full sample regressions and with a negative sign (approaching 10 per cent significance) in the Japanese test. Generally, this suggests that, once cost-effective production of standardized goods is directly tested by ULC, other sources of export competitiveness of national economies (quality and/or originality) are not reflected in FDI patterns. The initial dominance of ES networking of Japanese MNEs is again underlined.

Overall, the tests provide little evidence of presence of the KS motivation as a positively discriminating factor in determining FDI location. Thus while R&D

approaches positive significance for Japanese FDI it achieves negative significance in the US regression. PAT, the 'output' proxy for KS, is equally indecisive, positively signed for European and US FDI (approaching significance in the latter case) but negative for Japanese FDI.

The FDI stock variable, FST, is strongly significantly positive in the regressions for each of the separate-source regressions, and almost so for the world test. With the lack of decisive evidence for any particular strategic orientation for US and intra-European FDI over the period tested, and given the long-standing participation of these sources of FDI in European economies, it is possible that this result simply indicates a routine reinvestment in locations of established commitment and, therefore, a satisficing or bounded rationality complacency about more aggressive reorientation of new investments. In the case of Japanese MNEs, it seems that these more recent investors are able to combine entry into locations that are distinguished by considerable FDI already being in place (positive result for FST) with a clear commitment to an ES supply network (OPEN and ULC) and, perhaps (through R&D), incipient signs of KS.

Conclusions

The aim of the investigation has been to test for associations between two of the key evolutionary forces of recent decades. Firstly, in terms of managerial perspectives, the strategic development of MNEs towards the international networking of both their supply and creative programmes was investigated. Secondly, the positioning of these strategic aims was studied in a specific facilitating context, namely European economic integration. The expectation was that MNEs' strategies would react to differences in European economies in increasingly more proactive ways, leveraging different input capacities into efficiency-seeking supply programmes and different technological and skill competences into their emerging network approaches to innovation and R&D.

A decline in traditional market-seeking behaviour may be indicated by the insignificance of GDP in all regressions. By contrast, the significance of per capita income for US FDI may indicate that American managers are increasingly responsive to distinctive needs and tastes that become more decidedly manifest (and therefore more rewarding to react to effectively) as income levels grow. The broad managerial message of such an interpretation is that it might be simplistic to correlate economic integration with market standardization and that locally responsive MS operations might, in some industries and some geographical spaces, still provide distinctive rewards.

The intended proxies for ES strategy (COMP and ULC) do not provide clear evidence of supply-network restructuring by US or European MNEs. However, ULC is significantly negative in the Japanese test, which may suggest that those relatively new entrants were able to address this aspect of European integration potential. More speculatively, it was suggested that the positive sign on ULC for US FDI, taken with a supply-side interpretation of the positive result for PERCAP, could reflect a managerial pursuit of more skilled and talented labour perhaps conducive to the types of locally responsive MS behaviour postulated above.

The tests that provide a degree of positive evidence for KS behaviour are the near significant results for RAD in the Japanese FDI regression and for PAT in the US regression. Perversely, US FDI seems to actively avoid locations with strong current levels of R&D expenditures. Given that competitiveness in the European market and potentials for new exports from Europe are likely to increasingly depend on product originality and quality rather than on the pure cost competitive supply of established goods, MNE management could apparently benefit from clearer perceptions of diverse learning and creative potentials available in Europe and develop the scope for making them components of integrated innovation and scientific programmes.

The existing stock of FDI (FST) is strongly positively significant in the three separate-source equations. Though this could reflect positive pursuit of agglomeration benefits, the lack of significant results elsewhere in the US and European regressions may, instead, indicate a strategic inertia involving further investment in established locations and neglecting the potentials of greater response to differences between economies. The positive result for FST for Japanese FDI suggests that these firms' initial entry into Europe also targets locations with well-established MNE presence. This could, again, reflect the pursuit of possible agglomeration benefits but, in any case, seems to be combined with more awareness of ES scopes (ULC significant) and KS potentials (at least as reflected in R&D). This would indicate a more complete understanding of the potentials of EU-wide operations from which longer-established US and European MNE management might need to learn.

A theme that runs through the broad conceptualizing, specific theorizing and interpretation of results in this chapter is of an evolutionary process, of which a key component is a progressive deepening of the institutions and scope of European integration. The investigation reported here was limited to the overall period 1981–2001 and this allowed broad conclusions about the comparative mix of strategic postures taken in intra-EU, US and Japanese MNEs' investments. This will be refined and changing strategic priorities will be addressed in more detail through subsequent analysis by subdividing the time period. Another dimension that can contribute to further elaboration of these perspectives will be the subdivision of the host European economies in terms of core and periphery. Developing analysis along these dimensions in the light of the results reported here should help us to understand the strategic dynamism of heterarchical MNEs in the context of economic integration and globalization.

Appendix 11.1 Explanatory variables; explanation and sources

Explanatory variables	Calculation and source
COMP	Exports with the world divided by exports plus imports with the world in US$: *UNCTAD Handbook of Statistics online*
FST	FDI stock of previous year in US$: OECD online statistics, *Direct Investment Data* Deflated using GDP deflator in US$: *UNCTAD Handbook of Statistics online*
GDP ($USm)	Gross domestic product at prices and exchange rates of 1995: OECD online statistics, *National Accounts of OECD Countries*, Vol. 1
GDP per capita ($USm)	GDP per capita at prices and exchange rates of 1995: OECD online statistics, *National Accounts of OECD Countries*, Vol. 1
OPEN	Exports plus imports with the world in US$: *UNCTAD Handbook of Statistics online* Divided by GDP in US$ at current prices and exchange rates: OECD online statistics, *National Accounts of OECD Countries*, Vol. 1
PAT	Number of patent applications to the European Patent Organization per million inhabitants: OECD online statistics, *Main Science and Technology Indicators*
RD (% of GDP)	Total expenditure on R&D as a percentage of GDP: OECD online statistics, *Main Science and Technology Indicators*
ULC	Index of unit labour cost, base year 1995

Notes

1. For a helpful recent overview of this literature see Chakrabarti (2001) and Seyf (2001).
2. Refers to direct investment in the reporting economy (here, each of the 14 EU countries), where a minus sign means disinvestments (OECD online statistics: *Glossary of Foreign Direct Investment Terms and Definitions*).
3. The geographical region EUROPE includes Austria, Belgium, Denmark, Finland, France, Germany, Greece, Ireland, Italy, Luxembourg, the Netherlands, Portugal, Spain, Sweden and United Kingdom for all years in the sample (OECD online statistics: *OECD International Direct Investment Statistics*).
4. A Hausman test for random effects was also conducted and its results were in favour of the fixed effects as opposed to the random effects model in all four cases.
5. National economies may, of course, only be an approximation for these 'regions of differential taste'.
6. PAT may have deficiencies as a proxy here for reasons that precisely reflect the international dimensions of KS behaviour by MNEs. Thus patenting by firms from a particular country may reflect knowledge partly created elsewhere in the firm's international operations. Then PAT would overstate the KS capacities of the country. By contrast, knowledge created in a country may become embodied in an innovation patented in another location, so that PAT could understate creative achievement in a country.

References

Archibugi, D., J. Howells and J. Michie (eds) (1999) *Innovation Policy in a Global Economy* (Cambridge: Cambridge University Press).

Barrell, R. and N. Pain (1996) 'An Econometric Analysis of US Foreign Direct Investment', *Review of Economics and Statistics*, 78, 200–7.

Barrell, R. and N. Pain (1999a) 'Domestic Institutions, Agglomerations and Foreign Direct Investment in Europe', *European Economic Review*, 43, 925–34.

Barrell, R. and N. Pain (1999b) 'Trade Restraints and Japanese Direct Investment Flows', *European Economic Review*, 43, 29–45.

Bartlett, C. and S. Ghoshal (1989) *Managing across Borders: the Transnational Solution* (London: Hutchinson).

Behrman, J.N. (1984) *Industrial Policies: Industrial Restructuring and Transnationals* (Lexington, Mass.: Lexington).

Birkinshaw, J. (1994) 'Approaching Heterarchy: a Review of the Literature on Multinational Strategy and Structure', *Advances in Comparative Management*, 9, 111–44.

Braunerhjelm, P. and R. Svensson (1996) 'Host Country Characteristics and Agglomeration in Foreign Direct Investment', *Applied Economics*, 28, 833–40.

Buckley, P., J. Clegg and A. Cross (2003) 'Foreign Direct Investment and Europe', in P.J. Buckley (ed.), *The Changing Global Context of International Business* (London: Palgrave Macmillan), 91–111.

Chakrabarti, A. (2001) 'The Determinants of Foreign Direct Investment: Sensitivity Analysis of Cross-country Regressions', *Kyklos*, 54, 89–114.

Clegg, J. and S.C. Scott-Green (1999) 'The Determinants of New Foreign Direct Investment Capital Flows into the European Community: a Statistical Comparison of the USA and Japan', *Journal of Common Market Studies*, 37 (4), 597–616.

Culem, C.G. (1988) 'The Locational Determinants of Direct Investment among Industrialised Countries', *European Economic Review*, 32, 885–904.

Cushman, D.O. (1987) 'The Effects of Real Wages and Labor Productivity on Foreign Direct Investment', *Southern Economic Journal*, 54, 174–85.

Dunning, J.H. (1977) 'Trade, Location of Economic Activity and the Multinational Enterprise: a Search for an Eclectic Approach', in B. Ohlin, P.O. Hesselborn and P.M. Wijkmon (eds), *The International Allocation of Economic Activity* (London: Macmillan), 395–418.

Dunning, J.H. (1993) *Multinational Enterprise and the Global Economy* (Wokingham: Addison-Wesley).

Dunning, J.H. (2000) 'The Eclectic Paradigm as an Envelope for Economic and Business Theories of MNE Activity', *International Business Review*, 9 (2), 163–90.

Filippaios, F., C, Kottaridi, M. Papanastassiou and R. Pearce (2004) 'Empirical Evidence on the Strategic Behavior of US MNEs within the Framework of Dynamic Differentiated Networks', in J-L. Muchielli and T. Mayer (eds), *Multinational Firms' Location and the New Economic Geography* (Cheltenham: Elgar), 178–204.

Hedlund, G. (1986) 'The Hypermodern MNC: a Heterarchy?', *Human Resource Management*, 25, 9–36.

Hedlund, G. (1993) 'Assumptions of Hierarchy and Heterarchy, with Applications to the Management of the Multinational Corporation', in S. Ghoshal and E. Westney (eds), *Organisation Theory and the Multinational Corporation* (London: Macmillan), 211–36.

Manea, J.R. and R. Pearce (2004a) *Multinationals and Transition* (London: Palgrave).

Manea, J. and R. Pearce (2004b) 'Industrial Restructuring in Economies in Transition and TNCs' Investment Motivations', *Transnational Corporations*, 13 (2), 7–27.

Narula, R. (2003) *Globalization and Technology* (Oxford: Polity).

Neven, D. and G. Siotis (1996) 'Technology Sourcing and FDI in the EC: an Empirical Evaluation', *International Journal of Industrial Organisation*, 14, 543–60.

Niosi, J. (ed.) (1999) 'The Internationalisation of Industrial R&D: Special Issue', *Research Policy*, 28, 2–3.

Papanastassiou, M. and R. Pearce (1999) *Multinationals, Technology and National Competitiveness* (Cheltenham: Elgar).

Pearce, R. (1999) 'Decentralised R&D and Strategic Competitiveness: Globalised Approaches to Generation and Use of Technology in Multinational Enterprises', *Research Policy*, 28 (2), 157–78.

Pearce, R. and M. Papanastassiou (1999) 'Overseas R&D and the Strategic Evolution of MNEs: Evidence from Laboratories in the UK', *Research Policy*, 28 (1), 23–41.

Seyf, A. (2001) 'Can Globalisation and Global Localisation Explain Foreign Direct Investment? Japanese Firms in Europe', *International Journal of the Economics of Business*, 8, 137–58.

Taggart, J.H., K. Macharzina and R. Pearce (eds) (2000) 'International Management of Technology: Theory, Evidence and Policy – Special Issue', *Management International Review*, 40 (1).

Veugelers, R. (1991) 'Locational Determinants and Ranking of Host Countries: an Empirical Assessment', *Kyklos*, 44, 363–82.

Wheeler, D. and A. Mody (1992) 'International Investment Location Decisions; the Case of US Firms', *Journal of International Economics*, 33, 57–76.

12

New Directions in International Business

Simon Collinson, Peter Buckley, John Dunning and George Yip

Introduction

Rather than focusing on a distinct piece of international business research, this chapter tries to capture the views put forward by Peter Buckley, John Dunning and George Yip, three leading figures in the field, during a panel session at the 32nd Annual Conference of the Academy of International Business (UK Chapter) held at the University of Bath. This panel session was designed to focus on continuity and change in the themes and methods of research in international business and, in particular, to look forward at the emerging issues in the field.

Issues such as innovation and knowledge management, emerging markets, socio-political uncertainty, the role of institutions, entrepreneurial networks, the regional nature of competition, international joint ventures, strategic 'fit', corporate social responsibility and the development of global services industries are increasingly prevalent in the main journals. What are the others? To what degree are they replacing more traditional themes? Do these new areas of analysis demand new methodological approaches? What are the implications for general, long-standing theories of international business? These were the questions posed for the panel session that was chaired by Simon Collinson.

Peter Buckley considered the overarching 'domain of international business' and the contested boundaries around the field. John Dunning suggested a broader, more responsible role for international business research, in terms of its evolving theoretical and empirical agenda, in line with the need for managers to address increasingly pressing human issues and environmental factors in multinational operations. George Yip looked at the changing field of global strategy, focusing firmly on the management agenda. Before each of these contributions is examined in turn, an overarching framework is put forward both to situate the reflections of these leading academics and to allow others to reflect on their own contributions. Finally, the management implications of these panel session presentations and discussion are considered.

Rigour and relevance in international business

The panel session at the University of Bath had a double agenda. One was to discuss trends in the field; which theories, methods, topics and themes would increasingly dominate our subject. In part, this was to see if there was any consensus about the relevance of various trends. Another was more reflexive; to discuss what is coherent and distinctive about our contribution and to what degree we are able to guide this contribution towards a particular, shared end goal. The term 'contribution' here refers both to our role and input as a subgroup of specialists within the overall field of management studies and to our role and influence as regards management practitioners, policy-makers and the public at large. Neither is particularly new but they are evolving and important enough to deserve revisiting periodically.

In addressing these constituencies, it is useful to adopt Pettigrew's (1997) notion of the 'double hurdle' of rigour and relevance. This describes the dual challenge faced by researchers in both meeting the standards required by academia in terms of methodological and theoretical rigour, and investigating real-world phenomena and developing findings that are relevant to non-academics. Figure 12.1 shows both hurdles against two characterizations of the expertise that forms the basis of our contribution. As specialists, we have a distinctive set of theories, approaches and methods, a 'toolbox' that meets the standards for quality research set by the broader discipline (box 1). This toolbox can add value to public debate, policy-making and corporate decision-making by identifying relevant trends or causal factors and relationships, or providing insights into future patterns of change that are relevant to these constituencies (box 2). But our expertise can also be applied in

IB EXPERTISE → ↓	Academic Rigour	Real-world Relevance
Specialization/ Differentiation	(1) Theories, methods, tools, perspectives unique to IB	(2) Adding unique and contemporary value to public debate, policy-making, corporate decision-making
Integration/ Combination	(3) Integrated and inter-disciplinary theories; complementary methods and perspectives	(4) Interdisciplinary perspectives. Contribution in combination with other approaches (regional studies, political science, etc.)

Figure 12.1   Rigour and relevance in international business

combination with other subdisciplines to add complementary value alongside other specialists (boxes 3 and 4).

These interrelated areas of contribution are perhaps more appropriately framed as questions, rather than statements. Do we have such expertise (or should we aim to develop such expertise) and does it (or should we aim to) meet the double hurdle requirements? If the answer is 'yes', then these should be seen as challenges for bringing coherence and clear goals to the international business field. The central aim would be to develop and maintain a level of specialization and distinctiveness through which the field of international business contributes on both fronts of rigour and relevance. We can add value by being different from other subdisciplines, but also make a contribution in combination with other subdisciplines. Moreover, some would say that one of our major advantages lies in our capacity to integrate different disciplines and approaches and this is explored later in the chapter.

Peter Buckley most directly addresses these kinds of issues in examining the 'domain of international business'. He asks what is our domain and how do we define and defend the boundaries that delineate our specialization? He also looks at this both across analytical levels – the individual manager, the firm, the industry and the environment – and across disciplines, such as sociology, economics, political science and regional studies.

Recent commentary seems to point to a general disappointment with our track record on both fronts. Some suggest we may as well view the international business field as best characterized by pockets of rigour, but near irrelevance, alongside pockets of relevance, which are lacking in rigour. Elements of this dissatisfaction are clear in recent calls for international business scholars to take a broader view and step back from over-focused, quantitative approaches, to embrace more qualitative and contextual approaches. This is partly to improve relevance, perhaps at the expense of what some might see as meaningless rigour. A good recent example is Gordon Redding's (2005) call for more recognition of the importance of context and a more holistic examination of firms and their development patterns. He suggests that international business studies have tended to focus on rigorously modelling the connections between a limited set of factors, such as culture or institutional and policy regimes, with investment patterns and decision-making in multinational firms. To a certain extent these approaches have been successful in empirically validating tight propositions, with a range of restrictive assumptions, but they fail to contribute much of relevance to broader debates.

Redding points to an alternative set of approaches that provide limited empirical validation but propose a more holistic view (through 'thick descriptions' of societal systems of capitalism) of how national contexts differ and suggest ways in which specific differences represent particular challenges for multinational firms in the way that they adapt to different environments (see also Collinson and Rugman, 2005). He characterizes this set of approaches as a search for 'understanding' rather than 'proof' and provides the beginnings of an over-arching framework as a more 'complete way to handle determinacy'.

Redding refers extensively to the work of Whitley and others on business systems and 'varieties of capitalism' (Whitley, 1999, 2002; Hall and Soskice, 2001). These characterize national contexts as complex, evolving and unique combi-nations of culture, societal norms and values; historic influences; government institutions and policies; interest groups; capital markets and ownership pat-terns; labour markets, skills and capabilities; inter-firm networks, and business practices. Such approaches encompass, but go well beyond, Porter's (1990) characterization of the national components that underpin competitive advantage, including factor endowments (natural and acquired), infrastructure, supporting industries and demand conditions (see also Collinson and Morgan, forth-coming). This convincingly demonstrates the integrative potential of the international business field.

Similarly, a special research forum entitled 'Building Bridges across Levels' is the subject of a recent call for papers in the *Academy of Management Journal* (with Paul Beamish, Michael Hitt, Susan Jackson and John Mathieu as guest editors; see Beamish et al., 2005). This calls for a more holistic, system-wide perspective in management studies overall. In reality, regions, nations, industries, firms, functions, divisions, communities of practice and individual decision-makers are innately connected. These different levels are far more integrated and interrelated in practice than the specialists that research them and the theories that are developed to explain them. The bridges referred to include those linking the above levels of macro-to-micro analysis, as well as disciplines, and qualitative and quantitative approaches. The call cites March (1996) who points to the continual threat that the field becomes 'not so much a new integrated semi-discipline as a set of independent, self-congratulatory cultures of comprehension'.[1]

This and other signs of reflexivity in management studies and in the inter-national business field suggest that the contributions described below are exactly what are needed. In some ways, they are attempts to fill the gap between meaningless reductionism and over-general theorizing. Before moving on to the panellists' contributions, there is a final question to ask in relation to Figure 12.1 above.

Are we relevant?

There are a variety of external interest groups and constituencies whose goals we might aim to contribute to or influence through our research and teaching. These encompass: (1) practising managers of various kinds, in different industries, countries and types of organizations; (2) policy-makers at various levels of government, responsible for intervening in markets at the global, regional and local levels; (3) students destined for roles and responsibilities as (1) and/or (2), and (4) stakeholders and the public at large for whom, arguably, there is a growing premium on an improved understanding of international business dynamics.

Identifying those issues that are most significant to the international business field is related to the questions raised by all three of our panellists and, again, has been addressed many times in the past. For Buckley, this links to the 'next big question' to be addressed by the field, which should presumably be of relevance to one or more these constituencies. Dunning proposes some big questions and begins the process of identifying relevant constituencies and a specific set of impacts that the field should target. Yip describes the growing relevance of corporate governance but the core constituency for him clearly remains practising managers upon whose decision-making dilemmas we should shed light.

In all cases, there appear to be lessons from the past in terms of our relevance and perhaps limited overall impact. Many would see a frustrating disconnect between ourselves and many of the above interest groups. Where and how we make a relevant contribution to practising managers, policy-makers and the public at large is determined to a great extent by their perception of what constitutes relevant expertise.

The obvious mechanism for informing and influencing managers is via teaching programmes, from undergraduate to executive, and one could argue that our expertise is relevant and has some impact on management strategy and decision-making via this route. Others (such as Mintzberg, 2004) have argued otherwise, but that is another debate. Our expertise and credibility are established 'automatically' in the context of university institutions. In terms of the other main constituencies, we do not have the level of impact that our expertise should warrant. But, at the same time, we have failed to adapt this expertise to the appropriate channels of influence, suitable for government agencies or the public media. In media-led debates about globalization, for example, international business experts are conspicuous by their absence. In their place, various non-experts have conveyed uninformed opinions to the various forms of popular media and propagate a range of myths and half-truths about international business.

This is not to say we are irrelevant to these other constituencies. Despite the challenging assertions above, pockets of both rigour and relevance do exist. I could describe areas of influence and impact by each of the three panellists in our conference session. John Dunning's long-term work with UNCTAD on the World Investment Report is an example of the most direct influence over policy studies and policy-making which serves as a foundation for broadening the influence of the field to fit his ambitious agenda outlined below. My broader point is that the appropriate interface and methods of communication, in addition to the right questions and relevant research themes, are required to bring our expertise to bear more effectively on the external constituencies referred to above.

Peter Buckley: the domain of international business

In his commentary about the domain of international business, Peter Buckley cites a number of recent and forthcoming publications showing that this has been a central interest of his for some time (Buckley and Lessard, forthcoming; Buckley and De Beule, 2005; Buckley, 2004). The unifying rationale and the boundaries of our subdiscipline were the focus of his presentation. In raising big questions about 'the big question', Buckley has opened up an overdue debate about the coherence and goals of the international business field. He suggests that three big questions have dominated the last 50 years of our subdiscipline, namely how to explain flows of foreign direct investment (FDI); how to explain the existence, strategy and organization of multinational enterprises, and how to understand and predict the internationalization of firms and the new developments of globalization (Buckley, 2002, p. 365). In his view, the field has now lost its way and needs to set its sights on the next set of challenges. He sees identifying the next 'big question' as the most effective unifying device. This has led to a series of discussions about whether we should have one and if so, what it is (Buckley and Ghauri, 2004; Peng, 2004; Shenkar, 2004).

Building on these foundations, Buckley's panel presentation began by mapping out the large and complex domain of international business. The field encompasses multiple levels of analysis from the micro-level of the decision-maker (the individual manager), to the firm, the industry sector, and the region or macroenvironment. Each level also covers 'vast heterogeneity' and is analysed by multiple, interrelated, often competing disciplinary approaches. Connecting these levels of analysis and disciplinary approaches is a potential strength of international business as an integrating field of enquiry. It is also a potential weakness, given that, in attempts to be all-inclusive and holistic, there is a danger of being fragmented, unfocused and diluted.

For Buckley, the key to building on our strengths and minimizing our weaknesses lies not only in reaching a consensus regarding the big question, but on us reaching a consensus regarding the 'theoretical rocks' of the international business field. These agreed theoretical principles are connected to observable patterns in the real world. The mediating constructs by which we can link theory and reality are: observation – hypotheses – hypotheses testing – generalization (and back to observation) (see Buckley and Lessard, forthcoming). Valid research questions stem from the established theory ('concept-push') but theory is revised to account for changing reality ('observation-pull'). The agenda for international business researchers and research communities can be established by addressing both these areas. There are obvious links here with the concepts of rigour and relevance in Figure 12.1.

To identify the distinctive theoretical rocks and the relevant real-world questions for the future in international business, Buckley suggests that we need to explore our relationship with other disciplines and functional areas. This leads him to ask where and how is international business research distinctive? Is the answer in our approach to culture, comparative studies or distinctive methods? Also, how do we feed back to other disciplines? Do we lead or follow? And finally, what is the area of application; is international business a testing ground for concepts generated by other subdisciplines?

John Dunning: a personal view

In answer to Peter Buckley's central proposition, John Dunning put forward a very big question in his panel presentation. In fact, this was a call to arms put in the form of a series of challenges to international business researchers to apply their efforts to a number of very relevant, real-world issues of interest to all 'involved in or affected by the internationalization process'.

For Dunning, the big question is:

How can society benefit from the advantages of cross-border interconnectivity of people and organizations, and the reconfiguration and upgrading of global institutions, while, at the same time, accepting and, where appropriate, encouraging the cultural and ideological mores and traditions which local communities, other interest groups and individuals wish to preserve?

Building on recent publications (Dunning, 2003, 2004; Dunning and Narula, 2005), he proposed a 'responsible agenda' for addressing human issues and environmental factors as opposed to a singular focus on wealth creation in international business research. This agenda encompasses five grand themes of our time, namely:

1. Poverty and development;
2. Climate change and environment;
3. Technology and services;
4. Terrorism and security, and
5. Ageing and health.

Alongside this, Dunning proposed a multidimensional framework, the 4 I's, which can be applied to each of the grand themes. The 4 I's are:

1. Institutions, including resources, capabilities, incentives and enforcement mechanisms;
2. The interface between multiple stakeholders, including national and international constituencies;

3. Interdisciplinary methods and approaches, and
4. International business itself, which can encompass macro and micro, global and local dimensions.

Within each of the five themes there is a need for a radical rethink in terms of the significance and content in each of the 4 I's.

Table 12.1 takes Dunning's first topic area, poverty and development, as an example and lists the points under each of the 4 I's. Multinational firms, for example, are central players as owners and mechanisms for resource allocation and as both exploiters and developers. At the same time, they are a major focus of international business research. Dunning's view is that the field could (and should) switch its attention from issues such as profitability and performance to explore how changes in institutions, incentive systems and governance structures could be driven by different stakeholders. Such changes might reorient the activities of multinational firms towards the development agenda and away from more exploitative behaviour.

Again, the strengths of international business as a field lie in its potential for integrating, encompassing and connecting micro and macro and local and global levels of analysis as well as bridging the contributions of relevant disciplines. Dunning sees a 'third way' between the narrow (micro) and overly broad macro-levels of analysis. Moreover, this is necessary for following an agenda that focuses on the human environment and enhancement of the quality of life.

Table 12.1 Multidimensional framework for investigating broad themes – an example

The topic content and the 4 I's	Topic (1) Poverty and development
Topic content	• Poverty alleviation. Near top of international political agenda • Economic, social and moral imperatives • New approaches to, and analysis of, content of development • Contemporary emphasis on human environment and values
International business	• Role of FDI/alliances • MNEs as owners/accessors of key resources and capabilities • Spatially related implications • The emergence of China and India as major global players
Institutions	• New incentive structures/enforcement mechanisms: bottom-up versus top-down (for example, from Millenium goals)
Interface	• Partnerships to identify and advance poverty reduction strategies and other goals (for example, of firms, governments, NGOs and supranational entities • Recommendations of UK-based African Commission, 2005
Interdisciplinary	• Need for a multifaceted approach: political economy/business strategy/sociology

For each theme or topic, the structure and the message are the same. Institutional change, readjusting the interfaces between public and private sectors for example, could bring about human welfare improvements. Dunning examines the potential contribution of international business across these dimensions. Where does the field have expertise, tools, empirical evidence or approaches to help address these kinds of issues?

In conclusion, he observes that work has already begun (including Mayer, Narula and Dunning on poverty and development; Brewer on global warming; Suder and McIntyre on terrorism; UNCTAD research on technology and services; Kay-tee Khaw on changing life expectancy and ageing). He also believes that international business researchers are taking more account of the importance of stakeholders and institutions and that more research is being done outside academia on these fronts. But he sees an overwhelming 'need for a new thrust in scholarly research to identify, understand and evaluate an interface between international business activity and quality of life indices, at both a macro and micro level'.

George Yip: the changing field of global strategy

George Yip's contribution began with a retrospective look at the evolution of international business studies of multinational structure and strategy. He noted a tendency to begin with observable patterns of change and questioned the ability of existing theory to explain change.

In the evolution of international business research, early studies emphasized the internationalization process and how to expand abroad. The next period of studies focused on issues of managing the multinational company, having already gone international. Then early studies of global strategy revolved around product standardization to gain access to key overseas markets. Structural development was aimed at concentrating key functions and activities in places where there were cost advantages. These reflected four key industry drivers: cost, market, government and competition, all of which increasingly operate at a global level. Current research on global strategy has evolved into an emphasis on network organization structures or 'meta-nationals' and the demands these structures placed on internal coordination mechanisms to reap the benefits of managing all types of business activity and corporate function internationally (see Birkinshaw et al., 2003; Yip, 2003).

Yip sees a recent and significant change among multinational firms that needs to be the focus of attention for international business researchers. This is the growing importance of corporate governance. Specifically he talked about two levels of governance, one within the firm encompassing employees, top management teams and boards of directors, and a second relating to the regional and national contexts in which the firm operates. Shareholders, linked to local capital markets and financial institutions, and stakeholders, including employee groups and local communities, differ globally. They are situated within the broader economic, political and social contexts that emphasize and influence different governance priorities and governance structures.

Work by Yip and Aguilera (Aguilera and Yip, 2004) examines how national corporate governance systems affect internationalization strategies and organizational structures of multinational firms. Differences in patterns of internationalization are partly influenced by these contextual, national and regional level differences and the nature of these influences is a key gap in theory, despite its importance in practice. Country-level institutional constraints and enablers of international expansion need to be examined as combined systems, bridging the analytical divide between internal corporate governance mechanisms and the external environment.

Yip defines corporate governance as 'the rights and capabilities that corporate stakeholders have to allocate corporate resources and returns among different stakeholders'. There is evidence to suggest that Japanese, European and American firms have adopted different strategies and structures for internationalization as a result of local, regional and country-level differences. The timing and order of their expansion into overseas markets vary and the central proposition here is that specific differences in national corporate governance systems constrain multinational firms from 'converging on the optimal mode of globalization'.

There are clear connections between Yip's perspective on corporate governance effects and the above discussion on context, contingencies and varieties of capitalism. National institutions and actors, their interests and mechanisms influence the forms of global strategy adopted, including where and how market participation takes place, product and service adaptation, the location of various activities, appropriate forms of marketing and competitive moves. They also influence what forms of global organization are adopted by internationalizing firms, including management processes, human resources and corporate culture.

Yip's presentation featured a specific example, drawing on work with Thomas Hult, looking at variations in the customer–supplier management interface in multinational firms. Each customizes its global account management practices and systems to make them suitable for different national environments. Corporate governance institutions and practices in the home and host countries both have a combined influence on this adaptation process and lead to the heterogeneity of account management practices observed. What has been termed the 'liability of foreignness' (since Hymer, 1960) is determined by the specific similarities and differences between home and host country contexts.

Conclusions

This conference panel brought together three leading international business scholars. With distinguished track records and long-term experience of the double hurdle of rigour and relevance, they were ideally suited to comment on what it is we do and what we should be doing in the coming years.

Buckley emphasized the importance of the next big question for our field of enquiry and outlined what he saw as some of the distinctive strengths of international business, positioning us against alternative groups of specialists. Dunning was clear about the relevant questions for the field to address and pushed for us take on a 'responsible agenda', focusing on human and environmental issues rather than looking exclusively at wealth creation and narrowly defined business studies topics. Yip kept the focus firmly on the management agenda. He tracked the progress of research on the strategies and structures of multinational firms and emphasized corporate governance and the importance of the influence of country contexts for current and future research.

Among discussions about the big questions, there was some consensus among the panel about a number of the core strengths of our field. We have a clear capacity to add value by integrating approaches and insights from other disciplines and by bridging micro and macro-levels of analysis. This fits with recent calls to take firm context and contingency relationships more seriously in integrative studies of corporate behaviour. Perhaps our capability to cope with spatial contexts and bridge levels of analysis does provide a key advantage, giving us the potential to take the lead in addressing the kinds of themes presented by Dunning.

Some newer research in the international business field is increasingly taking account of context and is doing so by integrating insights from other disciplines to complement management and business studies approaches. In this book, Chapter 5 by Ferreira, Hesterly and Tavares ('A New Perspective on Parenting Spin-offs for Cluster Formation') and Chapter 6 by Pandit, Cook and Ghauri ('Towards an Explanation of MNE FDI in the City of London Financial Services Cluster') draw explicitly and implicitly on insights from economic geography to understand the spatial context within which firms operate better. These usefully integrate a business studies perspective on firms, value chains, industry groups and markets (business 'spaces') with concepts from economic geography (geographic space) that help our understanding of agglomeration economies, proximity and clustering effects. Harris and Carr (Chapter 4, 'Managerial Perspectives on Business Purpose: Values, National Values and Institutions') use previous research on national values to assess the influence of cultural context on business perceptions of their stakeholders, aims and time horizons. Context is also considered by Solberg and Askeland (Chapter 2, 'The Relevance of Internationalization Theories: a

Contingency Framework') and Duanmu (Chapter 10, 'Country of Origin Effects on Knowledge Transfers from MNEs to their Chinese Suppliers: an Exploratory Investigation').

Finally, it is one thing to map out a future direction for an organization or a subdiscipline and another to effectively direct its development along an envisaged route. There are major questions regarding the degree to which anyone can guide or influence the future of the field in any coherent way. One threat comes from the fragility of that coherence. As suggested above, a key strength of international business lies in its capacity to integrate both across disciplines and across levels of analysis, as currently appears to be in vogue more generally. This could also represent a weakness in that it fragments our 'community of practice' and dilutes our coherence as a distinctive field of enquiry. Becoming a broad, all-encompassing church means losing the distinctiveness that defines the field.

Added to this, there is the constant pull from various trends, themes and bandwagons that threaten to further fragment our efforts. The overlaps with other subdisciplines are growing and other specialists may begin to suggest that as all business is increasingly global, there is little distinctive about an international perspective.

Other limitations to proactive change, such as simple path dependency and inertia, come from inside and are generic to any such coalition of interests. Kuhnian paradigm shifts tend to be revolutionary, requiring wholesale changes to institutional structures, including organizational hierarchies and incentives. Effective change in our field is more likely to be evolutionary, led by those who influence the key journals. Journal publications represent both our main incentive system and the most explicit signal of our interests, the big questions that dominate the focus of our research. As they define the standards of academic rigour and determine what research is relevant, the alignment of journal editorial boards and referees to a coherent agenda is the key to any change in the field. Younger researchers typically cannot afford to take the risk of being alternative and so will look to the leaders in the field to signal a new agenda clearly and drive one or more new directions in international business.

Note

1. John Daniels (1991) as outgoing President of AIB made similar calls to improve the relevance of international business research through improved linkages. He referred extensively to articles by John Dunning in *JIBS* and elsewhere, calling for interdisciplinary approaches in our field in the late 1980s. While this again shows how our reflexivity may be rather cyclical, that does not diminish the importance of revisiting such issues.

References

Aguilera, R.V. and G. Yip (2004) 'Corporate Governance and Globalization: toward an Actor-centred Institutional Analysis', in A. Arino, P. Ghemawat and J.E. Ricart (eds), *Creating Value from Global Strategy* (London: Palgrave).

Beamish, P., M. Hitt, S. Jackson and J. Mathieu (2005) 'Call for Papers: Special Research Forum – Building Bridges across Levels', *Academy of Management Journal*, 48 (2), 364–6.

Birkinshaw, J., S. Ghoshal, C. Markides and G. Yip (eds) (2003) *The Future of the Multinational Company* (Chichester: John Wiley).

Buckley, P.J. (2002) 'Is the International Business Research Agenda Running out of Steam?' *Journal of International Business Studies*, 33, 365–73.

Buckley, P.J. (ed.) (2004) *What is International Business?* (Basingstoke: Palgrave).

Buckley, P.J. and F. De Beule (2005) 'The Research Agenda in International Business: Past, Present and Future,' in L. Cuyvers and F. De Beule (eds), *Transnational Corporations and Economic Development: from Internationalisation to Globalisation* (Basingstoke: Palgrave).

Buckley, P.J. and P. Ghauri (2004) 'Globalization, Economic Geography, and the Strategy of Multinational Enterprises', *Journal of International Business Studies*, 35, 81–98.

Buckley, P.J. and D.R. Lessard (forthcoming) 'The Domain of International Business', *Journal of International Business Studies*.

Collinson, S. and G. Morgan (eds) (forthcoming) *Images of the Multinational Firm* (Oxford: Blackwell).

Collinson, S. and A.M. Rugman (2005) 'Asian Business is Regional, Not Global', Academy of International Business (AIB) annual conference, Quebec, July, 2005.

Daniels, J.D. (1991) 'Relevance in International Business Research: a Need for More Linkages', *Journal of International Business Studies*, 22 (2), 177–86.

Dunning, J.H. (ed.) (2003) *Making Globalization Good: the Moral Challenges of Global Capitalism* (Oxford: Oxford University Press).

Dunning, J.H. (2004) 'Globalization Reviewed', *Transnational Corporations*, 13 (2), 95–103.

Dunning, J.H. and R. Narula (2005) *Multinationals and Industrial Competitiveness: a New Agenda*, New Horizons in International Business Series (Cheltenham: Edward Elgar).

Hall, P.A. and D. Soskice (2001) *Varieties of Capitalism* (Oxford: Oxford University Press).

Hymer, S.H. (1960; published in 1976) *The International Operations of National Firms: a Study of Direct Foreign Investment* (Cambridge, Mass.: MIT Press).

March, J.G. (1996) 'Continuity and Change in Theories of Organizational Action', *Administrative Science Quarterly*, 41, 278–87.

Mintzberg, H. (2004) *Managers Not MBAs: a Hard Look at the Soft Practice of Managing and Management Development* (San Francisco, Calif.: Berrett-Koehler Publishers Inc.).

Peng, M.W. (2004) 'Identifying the Big Question in International Business Research', *Journal of International Business Studies*, 35, 99–108.

Pettigrew, A.M. (1997) *The Double Hurdles for Management Research, Advancement in Organizational Behaviour* (Aldershot: Ashgate).

Porter, M.E. (1990) *The Competitive Advantage of Nations* (New York: Macmillan).

Redding, G. (2005) 'The Thick Description and Comparison of Societal Systems of Capitalism', *Journal of International Business Studies*, 36, 123–55.

Shenkar, O. (2004) 'One More Time: International Business in a Global Economy', *Journal of International Business Studies*, 35 (2), 161–71.

Whitley, R. (1999) *Divergent Capitalisms* (Oxford: Oxford University Press).

Whitley, R. (ed.) (2002) *Competing Capitalisms* (Cheltenham: Edward Elgar).

Yip, G. (2003) *Total Global Strategy II* (London: Prentice Hall).

Index